Locating Guyane

Contemporary French and Francophone Cultures, 53

Contemporary French and Francophone Cultures

This series aims to provide a forum for new research on modern and contemporary French and francophone cultures and writing. The books published in *Contemporary French and Francophone Cultures* reflect a wide variety of critical practices and theoretical approaches, in harmony with the intellectual, cultural and social developments which have taken place over the past few decades. All manifestations of contemporary French and francophone culture and expression are considered, including literature, cinema, popular culture, theory. The volumes in the series will participate in the wider debate on key aspects of contemporary culture.

Recent titles in the series:

38 Nicki Hitchcott, *Rwanda Genocide Stories: Fiction After 1994*

39 Sara Kippur and Lia Brozgal, *Being Contemporary: French Literature, Culture and Politics Today*

40 Lucille Cairns, *Francophone Jewish Writers: Imagining Israel*

41 Leslie Kealhofer-Kemp, *Muslim Women in French Cinema: Voices of Maghrebi Migrants in France*

42 Katelyn E. Knox, *Race on Display in 20th- and 21st Century France*

43 Bruno Chaouat, *Is Theory Good for the Jews?: French Thought and the Challenge of the New Antisemitism*

44 Denis M. Provencher, *Queer Maghrebi French: Language, Temporalities, Transfiliations*

45 Nicholas Hewitt, *Montmartre: A Cultural History*

46 Oana Panaïté, *The Colonial Fortune in Contemporary Fiction in French*

47 Jason Herbeck, *Architextual Authenticity: Constructing Literature and Literary Identity in the French Caribbean*

48 Yasser Elhariry, *Pacifist Invasions: Arabic, Translation and the Postfrancophone Lyric*

49 Colin Davis, *Traces of War: Interpreting Ethics and Trauma in Twentieth-Century French Writing*

50 Alison J. Murray Levine, *Vivre Ici: Space, Place and Experience in Contemporary French Documentary*

51 Louise Hardwick, *Joseph Zobel: Négritude and the Novel*

52 Jennifer Solheim, *The Performance of Listening in Postcolonial Francophone Culture*

SARAH WOOD
and
CATRIONA MACLEOD

Locating Guyane

LIVERPOOL UNIVERSITY PRESS

First published 2018 by
Liverpool University Press
4 Cambridge Street
Liverpool
L69 7ZU

British Library Cataloguing-in-Publication data
A British Library CIP record is available

ISBN 978-1-78694-111-4 cased

Typeset by Carnegie Book Production, Lancaster
Printed and bound in Poland by BooksFactory.co.uk

Contents

Illustrations

Introduction

Sarah Wood, University of Connecticut and
Catriona MacLeod, University of London Institute in Paris

Remedying dislocation?

On official maps of France, it is common practice to superimpose an outline of Guyane next to an image of the 'Hexagon'. This mapping of France obscures certain facts—and implies some falsehoods—about the location of 'its' Overseas Departments. Firstly, it shows all five *départements d'Outre-mer* (DOM) as abstracted from their geographical contexts. In accordance with its administrative function, the map makes a clear statement about the DOMs' political relationship to France: they are first and foremost satellites, adjuncts to the 'mainland', their geographical identities secondary to this primary relationship. When it comes to Guyane, however, such cartographic dislocation has particular implications for what—and where—readers of this map can assume it to be, in the absence of prior knowledge. Seen alongside the other DOMs, there is no indication that Guyane is not, as they are, an island. There is no indication of where in the world it is situated. The size of the place, moreover, is misrepresented: from this depiction, one might conclude that it had a similar surface area to that of Martinique or Mayotte. In fact, Guyane is of a similar size to Portugal (around 90,000 square km), and is situated in the north-east of the South American continent between Brazil and Suriname. When seen as part of the broader geographical system of 'the Guiana shield', it suddenly looks very different. Guyane might well appear to be 'small'—relative to the rest of South America. Compared to other departments of France, it is vast.

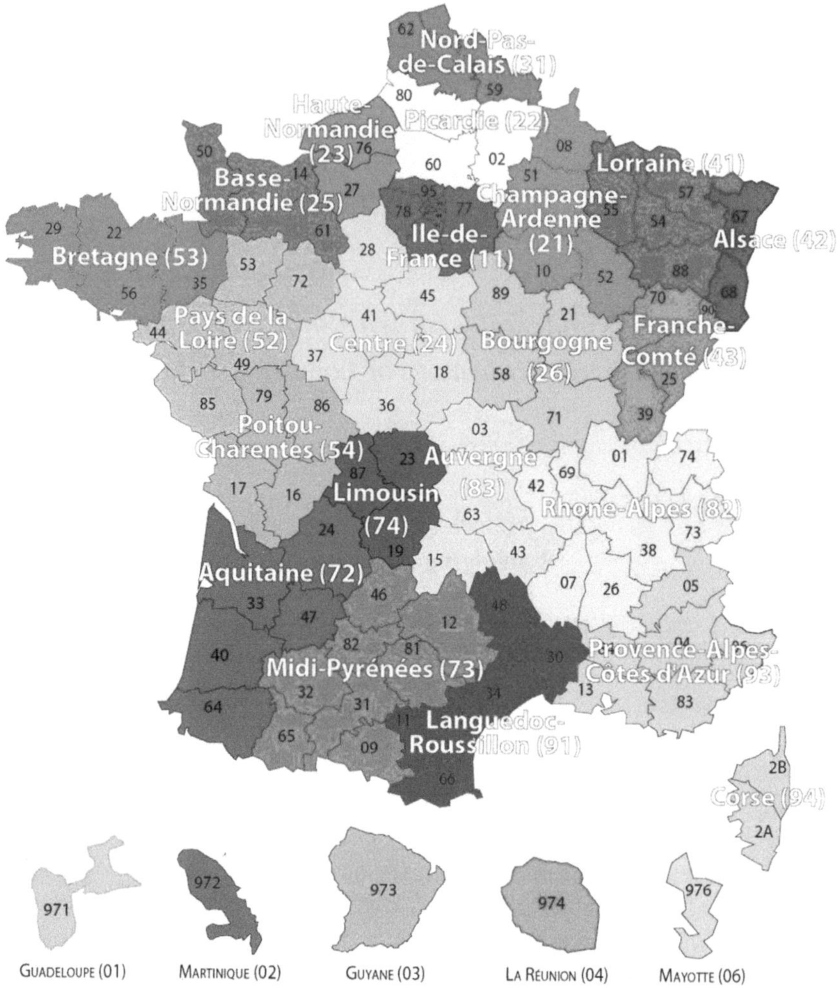

Figure 1: Map of France as envisaged by the INSEE and publicized by the Ministry of Culture and Communication.

Maps such as that produced by the INSEE may serve a seemingly banal, instrumental function—in this case to enumerate the departments of France—but they are nevertheless part of a systematic, administrative production of ignorance about geographical realities. The dislocation of Guyane gives a false idea of an unproblematic, ready-defined entity; it is a 'state simplification' (Scott, 1999). The map sketches an imagined template of geographical wholeness when in fact Guyane remains a part of the world where political borders are not only regularly ignored in practice but also actively contested by governments. Indeed, this territory was not mapped to any great degree of accuracy by cartographers until after the Second World War. Our aim in this volume is not to pinpoint Guyane once and for all: to try to 'fix' bounded places, definitions and categories as state-builders in Europe, the Americas and elsewhere have long sought to do (see Craib, 2004). Rather, the aim of this book is to explore possible conceptual locations of a territory which in geographical terms is at the juncture of the Caribbean and Amazonia but, in political and administrative terms, is French and, indeed, European.

Guyane is a unique legacy in continental South America of France's formerly vast American empire, much of which it lost in 1763 following the Seven Years War between France and Britain (Baugh, 2011). The majority of Guyane's current inhabitants find their stories excluded from conventional narratives (that is, those told from a French perspective) of Guyane's history since most were born outside the department (INSEE, 2012). With the exception of rare, pre-Columbian histories and archaeologies, such as those of Whitehead (1999) and Migeon (2008), these narratives begin with Guyane's visitation by Europeans from the late fifteenth or early sixteenth century and then proceed to cover the small settlements based on African slavery which were created in coastal regions throughout the seventeenth century. They address the disastrous 1763 mission to install thousands of families from across Europe and the former French American empire on the banks of the Kourou River: an idealistic plan to develop an agricultural colony with no African slaves (but, rather, with migrants, many of whom had little choice but to be transported), it ended in the death or evacuation of almost all the migrants—between 15,000 and 20,000 in all (Rothschild, 2006; Godfroy, 2011: 2012; Hodson, 2007). Guyane was subsequently used as a site of exile for refractory priests after the 1789 Revolution, and during the nineteenth century, plantation cultures and other settlement projects were formulated for the territory, including doomed plans for resettlement of free Black and Irish migrants and a more successful, utopian colony for freed slaves run by the Catholic Sister of Saint-Joseph-de-Cluny Anne-Marie Javouhey. These projects developed in fits and starts with much depending on the 1794 abolition of slavery, its reinstatement then final abolition in 1848 (Boromé, 1967, 44; Curtis, 2010). In 1854, a penal colony—otherwise known as the *bagne*—was established, helping to put the brakes on other kinds of *mise en valeur* of the territory, as the Guyanais poet Léon-Gontran

Damas complained in his 1938 tract, *Retour de Guyane*. The *bagne* was officially closed in 1946, coinciding with the official end of Guyane's status as a colony. With the notable exception of the 'Territoire de l'Inini', a vast chunk of the relatively sparsely inhabited interior—which was run under an ambiguous, 'special' administrative regime until 1969 (see Maurice's chapter in this volume)—Guyane has since 1946 been considered to be politically fully integrated into the French Republic as an 'overseas department'. In 1964, construction began on the Centre Spatial Guyanais, which has since sent the famous Ariane rockets into outer space and provided a locus of international exchange for scientists and migrant labourers alike. A hydroelectric dam built to power it, completed in 1995, brought further environmental and infrastructural transformations, both localized and department-wide. More recently, Guyane's national and European status has been adjusted again as it has been given the additional categorizations of 'overseas region' (ROM) of France and 'ultraperipheral region' of the European Union. From colonization to the EU, this timeline provides a starting point, but its European focus, as Glissant (1997) reminds us, obscures other chronologies. Nevertheless, it does begin to allow us to understand something of the production of French imperial space over the course of several centuries, and its mutations in the supposedly postcolonial era inaugurated by 'departmentalization' in 1946.

In this book, we use the term 'Guyane' to refer to the territory known in French as la Guyane française, in English as French Guiana, and in Créole (Kreyol Lagwiyann) as Lagwiyann. Guyane is distinct from the predominantly anglophone Republic of Guyana (formerly British Guiana). Inhabitants of Guyane are referred to here as Guyanais. We choose to avoid reference to 'French Guianese' as to 'French Guiana' since these terms imply a French nationality or identity that—although in many ways, not least politically, does define the place—may not always be assumed to exist. Indeed, the common confusion of toponyms in the Guianas is a legacy of the shared history of these lands. The rivers between Guyane and its neighbouring territories (Suriname to the west and Brazil to the east) do more to connect than to divide the political entities, as do the hills in the south of the territory, where the Parc Amazonien de Guyane—France's largest national park—now borders with Brazil's similarly vast Tumucumaque Mountains National Park. Repeated clashes between French, 'Amerindian', Portuguese, Dutch and British forces in the seventeenth century gave way to more diplomatic border disputes, and at the turn of the twentieth century, the frontier between French Guyane and Brazil was fixed by Swiss arbitration (Vidal de la Blache, 1901). The fixing of the Franco-Surinamese border is as yet unfinished, however, as the two countries continue to disagree on which tributary of the Maroni River the boundary ought to be attributed to (Donovan, 2004).

Guyane is a much misunderstood place. It ought to be at the forefront of Caribbean and Latin American studies, since its non-decolonization differentiates it from other territories of the circum-Caribbean and hence provides a powerful point of comparison. It ought, also, to be a key focus of French studies, since it is surely the locality where the republican model meets its staunchest challenges. Yet it is rarely mentioned as more than an addendum to the Antilles. As Richard Price indicates in the first chapter of this volume, Guyane has the highest birth rates in France, but also the highest rates of educational failure and crime. It is a place of remarkable cultural diversity and is part of Amazonian political ecologies. In addition, a number of the most remarkable political actors of recent times, as Sarah Wood relates in her chapter, have grown up in the department. And yet, scholars of France and the francophone world have most often ignored Guyane or assumed it to be relevant only because of the penal colony whose hellish conditions—famously depicted in the Hollywood film *Papillon* (Schaffner, 1973) and in the book by former convict Henri Charrière (1969) on which the film is based, as well as by Damas (1938) and reporters such as Albert Londres—have, as Kari Evanson explores, shaped perceptions of the place as a whole. Clichés, misinformation and negative stereotypes have endured, and this book subjects them to critical examination. It addresses how and why discourse on Guyane has come to be characterized by paradoxes and lacunae, and suggests ways in which this can be redressed. As they explore literary, historical and cultural 'locations' of Guyane, chapters acknowledge and trace the production of its marginal status, but challenge its relegation to the 'periphery'.

It is not our intention to argue for the uniqueness or exceptionality of a particular place amid histories of European empires and the Atlantic world. As Partha Chatterjee (2005, 495) reminds us, those who set out to define the terms, the norms and thus the exceptional may exercise an 'imperial prerogative' by staking a claim on the 'power to declare the colonial exception'. We aim to historicize, rather than to reproduce, this process. Contributors to the volume explore ways in which past actors have attempted to 'locate' Guyane, but they also propose new ways in which we might think about this locality and about those who inhabit and imagine it. Certainly, the volume aims to remedy the 'dislocation' of Guyane as it is envisioned on the map of France. But rather than merely replacing a faulty model with new certainties, it aims to open up emerging spaces of possibility. How might we site Guyane—and its constituent parts and people—amid malleable and changing sets of wider political, geographical, historical and cultural formations?

Bridging boundaries, crossing borders: Guyane in academic discourse

More often than not, the most illuminating and powerful studies of Guyane have in common the crossing of boundaries. Some head for the borderlands, widening their scope beyond the political limits of Guyane, and recent work in the fields of geography, anthropology and international relations by Marjo de Theije and Marieke Heemskerk (2009), Frédéric Piantoni (2009), Clémence Léobal (2013) and Bishop et al. (2016) offers examples of this. Other studies transgress, reflect on or deconstruct the methodological constraints of academic disciplines: Richard and Sally Price have challenged convention in their novel *Enigma Variations* (1997) and Richard Price's pioneering ethnohistory in works such as *Travels with Tooy* (2008) has brought the voices and historical consciousness of Saamaka Maroons into wider academic and public—even legal—discourse. Peter Redfield (2000; 2005) connected the colonial past of Guyane—its use as a *bagne* for the ejecta of metropolitan France—to its transformation into a high-tech space of the future via the construction of the rocket-launching base at Kourou, exploring themes of confinement, power and modernity.

Work sited 'within' particular academic disciplines has also helped to build useful foundations for students of Guyane. The first port of call for many a historian looking to engage with a situated history of Guyane remains the work of Serge Mam Lam Fouck (2002). In the Anglosphere, the work of Stephen Toth (2006) has explicated the roots and function of the penal colony in Guyane in tandem with that in New Caledonia, and their role in the Third French Republic, while Miranda Spieler's 2012 historical study broke new ground both in its use of historical sources and in its interpretation of Guyane as the 'underworld' of post-Revolutionary France with its new supposed rights and norms. Patrick Chamoiseau's poetic ruminations on the ruins of the *bagne*, their meaning and their possible futures also touch upon the theme of utopia/dystopia, and have inspired analytical reflections on ruination and memory after empire by Silverman (2010; 2013) and Stafford (2008). Similarly grounded in cultural studies, Bill Marshall (2009) has synthesized literary analysis and cultural history in his study of Cayenne's place in French Atlantic networks. Ethnographers such as Jean Hurault, Françoise Grenand, Pierre Grenand and Gérard Collomb have offered invaluable interpretations of Maroon and 'Amerindian' cultures and their relationships with French state structures, while Isabelle Hidair (2008) has also tackled questions concerning diversity and the Republic, as well as exploring gender roles and the position of women in Guyane.

The academic work on Guyane is rich but can appear diffuse, in part because the place is a crossing point for so many and diverse histories and people, intersecting local, national, global and imperial foci of research. Dialogue between disciplines is needed, as it is between scholars working in and across different national and linguistic frameworks. Developing on the valuable works above, our volume—the first multi-authored study of Guyane written in English—presents a plurality of approaches from scholars working across different disciplines. This diversification allows the contradictions and ambiguities which present themselves when trying to 'locate' this multipositional region to be explored. The contributors to this volume tackle three related sets of questions. First of all, how has Guyane been located textually; that is to say, how has it been conceived of and represented in written texts destined for certain audiences—whether in Europe or elsewhere—and how has this changed over time? Secondly, how has the ideological construction of Guyane's place and use within the French empire been (re)conceived since its colonization? How might the historiography concerning this relationship be challenged? Finally, how is/are Guyanais identity/identities being reimagined and relocated in the midst of 'global flows'? How are the physical borders of Guyane challenged by the cultural practices and processes of identification of those living within it?

The volume is comprised of three sections, each bringing together a range of academic foci—historical, linguistic, sociological—in answer to the questions posed above. The first section, entitled 'Imagining the Tropics: Writing on and from Guyane', addresses the prevalence of certain tropes in writers' accounts of Guyane. These tropes—of decay, destitution, vegetation, and chaotic growth—are variously used over time, from nineteenth-century examples to reflections on the present day, to define, defend and condemn Guyane to uninitiated, mostly

European audiences. In his opening chapter, 'The Oldest Daughter of Overseas France', Richard Price tours Guyane, from Cayenne to (briefly) Kourou and then Saint-Laurent-du-Maroni and Maripasoula, comparing writers' historical perspectives with his own subjective observations borne of extensive fieldwork, which at times confirm and at others revise long-held points of view concerning the region. This is followed by Kari Evanson's 'Grand Reporters in Guyane: Bringing the Exotic Back Home', a chapter which considers the establishment of certain of these long-held views in the metropolitan French imaginary via the early twentieth-century trend for *grands reportages*. Examining texts written by Albert Londres, Louis Roubaud and Marius Larique, Evanson analyses both complementary and competing notions regarding Guyane emanating from their reports—from the wretchedness of the *bagne* and the impression of moral decay amidst pervasive criminality and corruption to critiques of inhuman suffering and stifling conditions. The first section is concluded by Kathleen Gyssels's 'Kor and Karnival, the Carnal Road of Léon-Gontran Damas: "Evidence of Things Not Seen"'. Where Price's and Evanson's chapters study tropes presented by writers external to Guyane, Gyssels's contribution analyses the work of Cayenne-born Damas and examines how this work—and its author—has been perceived (and indeed ignored) by other commentators. Writer, poet and co-founder of the Négritude movement, Damas's *Retour de Guyane* (1938) addressed some of the same themes found in work by Londres, Roubaud or Larique—the poor social and physical conditions endured in the then-colony, the prevalence of the *bagne* in the identity of the region—adding to his account a biting political critique and a challenge to the French government: 'either improve [Guyane] or leave it' (qtd. in Wilder 2005, 218). Gyssels's chapter looks beyond *Retour de Guyane* and to Damas's poetic work, studying his critiques of the conditions and consequences of slavery and colonialism in Guyane and other colonies of the French empire. Focusing particularly on his questioning of established notions regarding gender and sexuality in the African diaspora, Gyssels closes this section by analysing the concerns of a writer speaking from a Guyanais perspective, underlining the sometimes similar but often contrasting concerns to those writing about Guyane from the outside.

The second section, 'Colonial Locations: Imperialism and the Production of Place', examines Guyane's evolving place within and beyond colonial history, underlining its existence as a site of (inter)national and ideological conflict from the seventeenth to the twenty-first century.

In the first section, Richard Price describes modern-day Guyane in colonial terms—but how have the colonial relationships imposed upon, and fought over in, Guyane changed over time? What specific challenges has Guyane posed to European imperial powers throughout its colonial history and what do they reveal about the territory? Finally, how and by whom have these conflicts and challenges been recorded, and to what extent may this historiography be challenged?

In response to these questions, contributors in this second section examine, and propose new analyses of, historical instances of contact, conjunction and transition. They examine changing relationships between different agents within the French imperial system—both the governors and the governed of empire—and in doing so disrupt assumptions about the relationship between 'colonial pasts and postcolonial presents' which, as Ann Laura Stoler warns, cannot be taken to be 'self-evident' (2013, 7). This is a section about physically and conceptually contested space, which both critically examines the perceived place of Guyane within, and at the margins of, the French empire and studies how people have enacted and lived through processes of change within the region.

Sílvia Espelt Bombín's chapter, 'Frontier Politics: French, Portuguese and Amerindian Alliances between the Amazon and Cayenne, 1680–1697', opens the response to the questions posed above. It queries existing historiography concerning seventeenth-century territory disputes between French and Portuguese forces which sidesteps Amerindian agency in favour of a fully European narrative. Seeking to redress the inaccuracies resulting from this focus, Espelt Bombín highlights in two case studies examples of key Amerindian interventions which significantly impacted the conflict between these competing European hierarchies. Thus she reconceptualizes seventeenth-century Guyane not only as a frontier space and battleground between European colonizers, but also as a space peopled and shaped by independently acting Amerindian groups.

This is followed by 'Producing the Periphery' by Jonna M. Yarrington, a chapter which examines the changing colonial 'use-value' of Guyane during the nineteenth century as the need for Antillean cane sugar declined and the desire for an offshore penal colony grew. Studying the region as a place of ideological, rather than international change and conflict (as Espelt Bombín does), Yarrington asserts that the change from plantation to prison during the period 1800–1860 contributed greatly to the conceptual establishment of Guyane as 'peripheral or marginal'—a consideration which, she suggests, is not naturally tied to Guyane's location but colonially produced, based on the use-value of the territory.

Edenz Maurice's chapter 'A School in Boniville? Political Skills and "Primitives" in Guyane (1930–1969)' then studies questions of colonialism, territorial tension and republican integration in the mid-twentieth century. Focusing on the endeavours to open a school in Boni Maroon country from the 1930s onwards, Maurice examines the various motivations behind this process—notably, the French desire to secure the Bonis' allegiance to France rather than to the Netherlands, the rival colonial power in the border region of the Maroni. Like Espelt Bombín, Maurice questions the accuracy of existing accounts of this process and, in so doing, underlines the international and local political dynamics at play in Guyane during the mid-twentieth century.

Finally, in her chapter 'Reclaiming Félix Éboué', Sarah Wood hones in on two important moments of transition in the history of French empire—the end of the Second World War and birth of the Fourth Republic, and the launch of the Fifth Republic—looking at examples of their material manifestation *in situ*. She traces the commemorative afterlife of Félix Éboué, the colonial governor and Second World War hero born in Guyane, asking what became of imperial and nationalist hubris attached posthumously to this figure in his native land, as well as tracing its manifestations in Paris and in other territories of the short-lived 'French Union'.

The final section of the volume, 'Relocating Culture: Language, Art and Identity', considers shifting dynamics of identity and memory in modern-day Guyane. Where the previous sections most often study Guyane as a physical and conceptual borderland, taking a critical approach to the ideological production of the region as a 'peripheral' space, this section considers the multipositional and evolving identities of those living within this space. It broaches the topic of Guyane's traditions and practices amid cultural 'flows' associated with globalization and asks what happens as the French nation state meets transnational realities in South American borderlands. Are 'global flows' (Hardt and Negri, 2001) overtaking national governmental frameworks in significance, and what becomes of 'identity' in all this? Examining such questions from linguistic, sociological and literary perspectives, the chapters in this section finally ask: as certain practices are reinstated and other traditions questioned and reinvented, how does Guyanais identity locate itself today?

Antonia Cristinoi and François Nemo begin the response to these questions. In 'Palikur, a Language between Two Worlds', the two sociolinguists analyse the revival of the Palikur language after the turn of the millennium. Examining the increasing use of the language among the modern-day Palikur people, and the effects of this on their practices and self-identification, Cristinoi and Nemo note, among other factors, the importance of contacts and movement between Palikur speakers living in Guyane and Brazil, asserting the salient truth that 'the linguistic and symbolic borders of Guyane go far beyond the current political borders'.

Sally Price's chapter 'Maroon Art in Guyane: New Forms, New Discourses, then considers an interesting effect of the continued *francisation* of Guyane on traditional Maroon woodcarving art. Examining the recent 'reinvention' of the historical roots of this art to include references to slavery, Price also locates this changing discourse among similar shifts in explanations of 'ex-Primitive' art worldwide, as artists try to gain a commercial foothold in a market economy often oriented towards the expectations of tourists and other outsiders. Both influences on this retrospective reimagining of Maroon art history evidence a fluidity of identity and memory encouraged by the changing (trans)national positioning of the region from the late twentieth century onwards.

In 'Performing and Parading Gender in Guyane's Carnival', Catriona MacLeod considers the changing traditions of carnival in the modern-day DOM and what they reveal about the presence of two characters, the *travesti* and the *touloulou*. MacLeod studies these figures, ostensibly transgressive of traditional sexual roles, in order to unpack what they fully symbolize regarding gender in today's Guyane. This chapter reflects on carnival as a means of performing identity, asking how evolving practices are indicative of changing (or static) social and international dynamics at play within the territory.

Finally, Bill Marshall's chapter 'Equality and Difference: Queering Guyane' recalls how the Guyanaise former Minister of Justice Christiane Taubira deployed the words of Guyanais poet Damas during National Assembly debates over *le mariage pour tous* (equal marriage). Marshall does so in order to explore the potential of a theoretical 'queering' of Guyane to help us rethink how distinctions are drawn and categories of identity constructed. In this closing chapter, Marshall locates same-sex desire and the Republic amid Guyane's 'cocktail of indigenous peoples, slavery, colonialism and racism, uneven Creole assimilation, penal colony and abjection, space programme and exaltation, immigration, and a nationalism that can neither attain plenitude nor cease to exist'. The complex interactions of histories, ideologies and identities emanating from and reflective of Guyane are visible in the wide range of subject matter studied across these chapters. This volume brings together these different concerns and foci, highlighting the plurality of approaches possible when considering how to 'locate' a territory that is both ultra-peripheral and of central importance in South America and in France.

Works cited

Baugh, Daniel. 2011. *The Global Seven Years War 1754–1763*. London: Routledge.

Bishop, Matthew, Petter Clegg and Rosemarijn Hoefte. 2016. 'Hemispheric reconfigurations in Northern Amazonia: The "Three Guianas" amid regional change and Brazilian hegemony', *Third World Quarterly* 38.2: 1–23.

Charrière, Henri. 1969. *Papillon*. Paris: R. Laffont.

Chatterjee, Partha. 2005. 'Empire and nation revisited: 50 years after Bandung', *Inter-Asia Cultural Studies* 6.4: 487–496.

Craib, Raymond B. 2004. *Cartographic Mexico: A History of State Fixations and Fugitive Landscapes*. London: Duke University Press.

Damas, Léon-Gontran. 2003 [1938]. *Retour de Guyane. Suivi de 'Misère noire' et autres écrits journalistiques*. Paris: Editions Jean-Michel Place.

de Theije, Marjo and Marieke Heemskerk. 2009. 'Moving frontiers in the Amazon: Brazilian small-scale goldminers in Suriname', *European Review of Latin American and Caribbean Studies* 87: 5–25.

Donovan, Thomas W. 2004. 'The French Guiana-Suriname boundary dispute at the Itany-Marouini Triangle', *The Journal of Caribbean History* 38.2: 213–243.

Godfroy, Marion. 2011. *Kourou, 1763: le dernier rêve de l'Amérique française*. Paris: Vendémiaire.

Godfroy, Marion. 2012. '*Passengers to the West.* De Coblenz à Kourou: recrutement et stratégies d'une migration transcontinentale et transatlantique en 1763', *Annales de démographie historique* 124.2: 89–104.

Hardt, Michael and Antonio Negri. 2001. *Empire*. London: Harvard University Press.

Hidair, Isabelle. 2008. 'Voyage aux origines du mythe constructeur de l'identité des femmes créoles guyanaises', *Nouvelles Études Francophones* 23.2: 129–143.

Hodson, Christopher. 2007. '"A Bondage so Harsh": Acadian labor in the French Caribbean, 1763–1766', *Early American Studies* 5.1: 95–131.

INSEE. 2012. 'Migrations, famille et vieillissement: défis et enjeux pour la Guyane', *Antianéchos*. http://www.insee.fr/fr/themes/document.asp?reg_id=25&ref_id=19085 (accessed 31 October 2016).

Léobal, Clémence. 2013. *Saint-Laurent-du-Maroni. Une porte sur le fleuve.* Matoury: Ibis Rouge.

Mam Lam Fouck, Serge. 2002. *Histoire générale de la Guyane française.* Matoury: Ibis Rouge.

Marshall, Bill. 2009. *The French Atlantic: Travels in Culture and History.* Liverpool: Liverpool University Press.

Migeon, Gérald. 2008. 'Le Rôle de la Guyane précolombienne dans la zone d'interaction caribéo-Amazonienne', *EchoGéo* 6. http://plc.revues.org/528.

Ministère de la Culture et de la Communication. 2014. *Carte des codes INSEE (régions et départements).* http://www.culture.gouv.fr/Thematiques/Innovation-numerique/Numerisation/Recommandations-techniques/Identifiants-des-images-numerisees-codes-pour-les-producteurs/Carte-des-codes-INSEE-regions-et-departements (accessed 1 April 2015).

Piantoni, Frédéric. 2009. *L'Enjeu migratoire en Guyane française.* Matoury: Ibis Rouge.

Price, Richard. 2008. *Travels with Tooy: History, Memory and the African American Imagination.* London: University of Chicago Press.

Price, Richard and Sally Price. 1994. *Equatoria.* London: Routledge.

Price, Richard and Sally Price. 1997. *The Enigma Variations: A Novel.* London: Harvard University Press.

Redfield, Peter. 2000. *Space in the Tropics: From Convicts to Rockets in French Guiana.* London: University of California Press.

Redfield, Peter. 2005. 'Foucault in the tropics: Displacing the Panopticon', in *Anthropologies of Modernity: Foucault, Governmentality, and Life Politics*, ed. Jonathan Xavier Inda. Oxford: Blackwell, 50–79.

Rothschild, Emma. 2006. 'A horrible tragedy in the French Atlantic', *Past and Present* 192: 67–108.

Schaffner, Franklin J., dir. 1973. *Papillon.* United States: Columbia Pictures.

Scott, James C. 1999. *Seeing Like a State: How Certain Schemes to Improve the Human Condition Have Failed.* London: Yale University Press.

Silverman, Max. 2010. 'Memory traces: Patrick Chamoiseau and Rodolphe Hammadi's *Guyane: traces-mémoires du bagne*', *Yale French Studies* 118–119: 225–238.

Silverman, Max. 2013. *Palimpsestic Memory: The Holocaust and Colonialism in French and Francophone Fiction and Film.* Oxford: Berghahn.

Spieler, Miranda. 2012. *Empire and Underworld: Captivity in French Guiana.* London: Harvard University Press.

Stafford, Andy. 2008. 'Patrick Chamoiseau and Rodolphe Hammadi in the penal colony. Photo-text and memory-traces', *Postcolonial Studies* 11.1: 27–38.

Stoler, Ann Laura. 2013. 'Introduction: "The Rot Remains": From ruins to ruination', in *Imperial Debris: On Ruins and Ruination*, ed. Ann Laura Stoler. London: Duke University Press, 1–35.

Toth, Stephen A. 2006. *Beyond Papillon: The French Overseas Penal Colonies, 1854–1952*. London: University of Nebraska Press.

Whitehead, Neil. 1999. 'Native peoples confront colonial regimes in Northeastern South America', in *The Cambridge History of the Native Peoples of the Americas Volume III: South America: Part 2*, ed. Frank Salomon and Stuart B. Schwartz. Cambridge: Cambridge University Press, 382–442.

Wilder, Gary. 2005. *The French Imperial Nation-state: Negritude and Colonial Humanism between the Two World Wars*. Chicago: The University of Chicago Press.

PART I

Imagining the Tropics: Writing on and from Guyane

CHAPTER ONE

The Oldest Daughter of Overseas France[1]

Richard Price, www.richandsally.net

Guyane, today, is a remarkably vibrant society, undergoing tremendous expansion and change. While its sister neo-colonies Martinique and Guadeloupe are slowly losing population, Guyane is burgeoning, with the highest rate of population increase of any region of France—fully six times higher than the national average with roughly half of its population under 20 years old and with very few people over 70 (INSEE, 2013). Three-quarters of Guyane's adult population was born outside Guyane and nearly 70% of those born in Guyane have parents born elsewhere (Yahou-Dauvier, 2013). Maroons, the people I mainly work with, are leading this population explosion and now constitute at least 26% of residents, second only to Creoles (see Price, 2013).

With a society and economy controlled by far-away France (and with the European Space Centre—le Centre Spatial Guyanais—constituting roughly half of its economy), administered locally by Creoles who constitute only a minority of the population, Guyane presents numerous contradictions. From the perspective of the Creoles, whose identity is at once French, European and Guyanais, they live in a *pays dominé*, a largely unproductive postcolony that is nonetheless an enormous

1 This essay is presented here as delivered at the Locating Guyane colloquium (University of London Institute in Paris, 2014) in order to retain the informal tone of that gathering (though necessarily without accompanying images and with the addition of a bibliography).

beneficiary of French government largesse and well up the scale of world leaders in consumption. Sparkling new shopping and leisure centres encircle Cayenne and BMWs are rampant—as, at the other end of the economic scale, are bicycles and good old walking for transport. From the perspective of Guyane's non-Creole populations, who make up the majority of its residents, the country is doubly colonized, by the French and by the Creoles who look on them with a steeply downward gaze. Yet the benefits of decent schools, a superior system of public health, opportunities for menial jobs and generous social security benefits make this distant corner of Europe a beacon of hope for the immigrant Surinamers, Haitians, Brazilians, Chinese, Hmong and others, who now (along with their Guyane-born children) make up well over half the population.[2] These immigrants also make up some 80% of the population of the Centre Pénitentiaire (Price, 2008, 204.).

The INSEE says that 10–15% of the population is metropolitan French, including a substantial number of *gendarmes*, *légionnaires* and other *fonctionnaires* who preside over a second tier of *fonctionnaires*, many of whom are originally from Martinique and Guadeloupe. Unlike those in Martinique and Guadeloupe, Guyane's administrative offices, even in small *communes*, tend to be run by metropolitans or Antilleans, that is, by people not born in Guyane. This colonial-style situation was the norm in the French Antilles until 40 or 50 years ago but it persists in Guyane, contributing to the territory's strongly colonial aura. Guyane's greatest writer, Léon-Gontran Damas, put it this way:

> *Fonctionnaires*: Their number is incredible ... In place of action or accepting responsibility, they prefer 'the rules'. So it makes no sense to ask them to exercise their own judgement or will. They do not like to make decisions. They refuse to take any initiative. Something essential is missing: the human touch. They recoil from any problem that requires a quick resolution, since it means they would have to take some initiative ... Guyanais public opinion, I would add, has to date ignored this state of affairs ... Yet nowhere has this epidemic of bureaucrats spread with such virulence and destruction as in this land of Guyane. (1938, 113)

Sociologist Marie-José Jolivet adds the trenchant observation that 'The internalization of the Metropolitan Ideal is the final product of this long relationship of domination, at the same time as the privileged means of its continuance' (1982, 441).

2 My estimates of population distribution include more *sans papiers* than do official ones. On immigration to Guyane more generally, see Piantoni (2011).

Guyane's ethnically mixed population, dominated by immigrants, gives its society an edgy feel that is absent in the more French-style (bourgeois) islands of Martinique and Guadeloupe. Much greater inequality of wealth, many more non-French speakers, more crime and tremendous unemployment make Guyane feel Third World, which tends to horrify Creoles but makes many immigrants feel right at home. The extreme may be found in certain Brazilian neighbourhoods of Cayenne, where hijacked electricity lines feed giant satellite dishes that bring Globo into *favela*-like jerry-built homes without running water or sanitation but where there is a strong sense of (foreign) community, with its own churches, language and recreations. And Guyane still has the highest unemployment rate in all of France—at last count, nearly 60% for those aged under 30 without a *diplôme* (Mekkaoui, 2012)—which means the very great majority of Maroon and other immigrant youths.

For Sally and me, living in this world (even temporarily) is an ongoing adventure, the way living in Martinique quickly becomes routine. At our friend Léon's dinner table in Saint-Georges-de-l'Oyapock, across the river from Brazil, where we eat a fish that this son of a Saamaka man and a mother whose parents immigrated from Saint Lucia caught that morning, conversation passes fluidly from Saamakatongo to Guyanais Creole (the mother tongue of his wife Julie), to Portuguese (a son-in-law's language), to French (for the benefit of a visitor).[3] And at our Saamaka friend Tooy's home in a Brazilian neighbourhood on the outskirts of Cayenne, in the course of the day, we hear conversations in Saamaka, Ndyuka, Aluku, Guyanais Creole, Haitian Creole, Sranantongo, Portuguese and French. Meanwhile, young Saamaka adolescents, whether in Tooy's rudimentary house or in social housing blocks in Kourou or shacks in Saint-Laurent, gather round laptop computers to sing along to Black music videos from the States, in very good English. Though Saamaka women in Kourou no longer go bare-breasted, what Sally and I witnessed 25 years ago could have happened today:

> Not long ago, we had the occasion to visit some old friends in the so-called 'Village Saramaka' at Kourou. Living in mean little shacks almost in the shadow of the Ariane rocket, these immigrant workers continue to supply much of the manual labor at the missile base. We accompanied a woman (who had been our neighbour twenty years earlier in Dangogo

3 The Saamakas are descendants of self-liberated enslaved Africans from Suriname. Today they number nearly 100,000, and one third of them live in Guyane.

> [Suriname]) on what she called 'a little trip to her provision-ground'; entering the small supermarket nearby, barefoot and bare-breasted, she selected her groceries—a frozen chicken from Brittany (with labels in French and Arabic), a tin of sardines from Nantes, some Parisian candies for the kids. The next day, back in Cayenne, we were invited by colleagues from ORSTOM [now IRD, the major French scientific research organization in Guyane] to a posh restaurant where, under a set-piece 'tropical' thatch roof, we drank fine wines from the metropole and ate delicious stews of monkey, armadillo, and tapir—all everyday foods of Saramakas back home in Suriname. (Price and Price, 1989, 199)

In short, what a place!

(Con)textualizing Cayenne

Sally and I have always felt Guyane to be a space of palimpsests, where layers of history weigh heavily. Wherever we've gone, we've felt this weight and, in a couple of our books (*Equatoria* and *Enigma Variations*) we trotted out some of the citations of others who had preceded us on the journey. Those travellers' accounts still resonate for us. Here's Lafcadio Hearn anticipating his arrival in 1890:

> It is the morning of the third day since we left Barbadoes, and for the first time since entering tropic waters all things seem changed. The atmosphere is heavy with strange mists; and the light of an orange-colored sun, immensely magnified by vapors, illuminates a greenish-yellow sea,—foul and opaque, as if stagnant … A fellow-traveler tells me, as we lean over the rail, that this same viscous, glaucous sea washes the great penal colony of Cayenne—which he visited. When a convict dies there, the corpse, sewn up in a sack, is borne to the water, and a great bell tolled. Then the still surface is suddenly broken by fins innumerable,—black fins of sharks rushing to the hideous funeral: they know the Bell! (1923, 64–65)

Or French physician-explorer J. Tripot, in 1910:

> Cayenne: the town where the buzzards, those predators with metallic, funereal feathers, half-crow, half-vulture, have appointed themselves as reprocessing agents for the garbage system …
>
> Cayenne: it's an incoherence of races, a confusion of colors, a Tower of Babel of languages, a Babylon of imported vices, a Capernaitical shambles of family, an imbroglio of kinship, as well as a den of gold

> miners and convicts, a place of force and degradation, dazzle and gloom, gold and garbage! (277–278)

Or our anthropological predecessor, Alfred Métraux, who arrived in 1947:

> The passengers in the van confirm everything I've heard about the destitution and decadence of Cayenne. The descriptions of the city that have been told to me were so unfavorable that I expected the worst, but in fact, Cayenne is even more down-and-out than it was possible for me to foresee. The Place des Palmistes is a wasteland … The houses, mostly of a yellowish or brown tone, are terribly dilapidated. Vultures roam the streets … Talked with a blind convict. A beggar with twisted limbs cries out 'God is crazy!' (1978, 191–192: see diary entries for 28–30 May 1947)

Or, finally, a travel writer who just 'loves' the tropics, in 1952:

> We knew that this darkness was Cayenne, because the car had stopped … The room, the swaying, punctured ghost of mosquito-netting, the moon through a latticed window, the chamber-pot, the mildew, the frowsty candle, the twitter of bats echoing beneath the roof of corrugated iron, the sweat in the eyes smarting, and the taste of it, were curiously good again. The colonies I had lived in were blended of these. I was home again, in the dank discomfort which I loved. (Davis, 11)

Alfred Parépou, who wrote the first novel published in Guianese Creole, published a response to these outsider gazes as early as 1885:

> 'There's lots of whites', began Atipa, 'who don't know anything about us or Cayenne. But they think they can talk about us, and they think they know more about our lives than us folks whose navel-strings are buried here … There was one white man who came here; he stayed two weeks. If you heard what he said in France, about how snakes here swallow little kids alive, if you had someone read you what he wrote, Compère, you'd even be afraid to go out in the streets of Cayenne!' (175–179)

On the other hand, Sally and I have twice seen anacondas emerging from the water onto the streets of Cayenne (I describe one such incident in Price, 2008, 208–209). The truth is that anacondas, like the infamous piranhas that evoke similar fears, are more threatening to humans in their imagined exoticism than they are, so to speak, in the flesh. And in any case, an *Air France* in-flight magazine we read around 1990 on one of our flights to Guyane may serve to reassure all of us: 'In the streets of Cayenne', it states, 'a diversity of people rubs shoulders … Indeed, the whole world seems to have arranged to meet here. Amerindians, Chinese,

Lebanese, Hindus, Laotians, Europeans, Brazilians, and Creoles mingle in total harmony'.[4]

Despite that commercial rhetoric—which, by the way, matches Suriname's national rhetoric about being the world's most peaceful and happy ethnically diverse country—we have always found Guyane, particularly Cayenne and Kourou, to be a highly stratified as well as a segregated place. Of course, people rub shoulders if they go to the market (but much of the upper strata have domestics who do that for them). 'Profoundly colonial' was the way we once described Cayenne (Price and Price, 1995, 1). As Peter Redfield reminds us: 'To be remembered as a penal colony is to be remembered not only as a prison and exotic place of horror, but also as a colony, the object and product of another' (2000, 108).

Our perception that Guyane is one of the most colonial-feeling places in the world is renewed by each visit. Last year, for example, we attended a dinner party in which we felt thrust backwards to the late nineteenth century and across the waters to, say, French West Africa. At a table laden with fine wine and French food, surrounded by white French couples who'd all arrived from the metropole during the past one to four years (and would soon be departing), each of whom had at least one member who was a high official (there was a *sous-préfet*, a representative of France's Ministry of Culture, another from the Ministry of Education and one from the Ministry of Justice), we listened to conversations about the locals that, at best, reeked of the *mission civilisatrice*. Alarm, consternation and disbelief were expressed when we answered the inevitable question of what hotel we were staying in by saying we were living with our Saamaka friend Tooy in the Brazilian ghetto of Les Paletuviers: 'But we've been told that white people can't go there at night!' We would expect much the same rhetoric from the highest *couche* of Creole society which, while excluded from colonial white society, does a lot of downward gazing of its own. The shrinking Creole elite, with its low, bourgeois birth rate, feels increasingly overwhelmed by the rising tide of migrants and their many babies, and embattled, despite their control of local political institutions. And of course the immigrant communities themselves have strong (often negative) prejudices about one another—interethnic *méfiance* rather than Air France's harmonious mingling, continues to be the order of the day.

Not that the occasional metropolitan woman doesn't seek out a Saamaka lover or that other kinds of interchange across ethnic lines

4 We made a note of the quotation but not the date of this magazine.

don't occur. But Guyanais society is deeply divided and stratified into distinct ethnic communities, all of whom live in the shadow of the representatives of the French state and the local Creole politicians and civil servants. The half of Guyane's residents who are not French daily confront one or another of the institutions of the state: the Prefecture, which controls residence papers and much else, the system of police and *gendarmes* and the whole system of justice, the hospitals, the schools, the social security system (*allocations familiales*, unemployment benefits, old-age pensions and so forth). Whatever the laws and their application in France, Guyane functions as a world apart—in terms of granting *cartes de séjour*, in terms of penal sentencing, in terms of identity checks on the roads and expulsions from the territory (see for example Benoît, 2016). And the proportion of illegal (off the books) work in the local economy, which the state estimates at 10%, is in fact much higher (see INSEE, 2003). Cheap and willing immigrant labour is everywhere in Guyane. A few years ago, I described how our Saamaka friend Kaluse became implicated in the ongoing system:

> Kaluse's strong physique, quick mind, and 10-year carte de séjour made him a popular construction worker with both Creole and metropolitan bosses and he was often asked to bring along a dozen other Saramakas without papers who were grateful for day-work at half the minimum wage. In the mid-1990s, he was excited to be working on the construction of the enormous new penitentiary going up just outside Cayenne. 'It's got two restaurants, a basketball court, and a swimming pool—just like a hotel in the movies', he told us. (2008, 57)

Like so much in Guyane, official rules and laws are flouted by nearly everyone (*pace* Damas's observation, now 80 years old, cited above)—employers, employees and the representatives of the state. It's the Wild West of France, barely in the state's control despite the enormous presence of *les forces de l'ordre*—police, *gendarmes*, *légionnaires*.

The experience of living as an undocumented alien, a 'sans-papiers', is awful anywhere in the world. The Haitian novelist Évelyne Trouillot (2013) recently evoked the incessant, cold fear in the guts of a Haitian man living illegally in Brooklyn for a decade and a half, his constant efforts not to be noticed, his little tricks to get from home to work or to the grocery store, the horror of it all. Our many Saamaka friends in Guyane *sans papiers* experience a similar plight. The lucky ones are told, for example, that the sub-minimum wage without benefits they're being paid for working at a tyre shop will become the minimum wage with benefits if they get a *carte de séjour*, and in one recent case that actually happened. But in our experience, it's the exception. Many of these immigrants languish for years without residence permits, scraping by on occasional *djobs*, and ever vigilant to the possibility of a policeman or *gendarme* appearing down the street. Newcomers are especially vulnerable. I described a relevant incident in *Travels with Tooy*:

> Two of Tooy's 'grandsons' visit—they've just come over from Paramaribo to see their mothers, who live nearby. One sports a white, furry, oversized pimp cap, a gold necklace, red shades, baggy jeans, and Nikes, the other has Rasta-inspired tresses and dark shades. Tooy gives them an affectionate dressing down about how they're stashed, telling them he knows this country and they don't. Unless they change their looks, he says, the police will pick them up for sure, thinking they're from Georgetown. They do have that cultivated hard, urban Kingston rude-boy look. But they're sweet kids. They smile and say 'Yes, opa' ['grandpa' in Dutch]. Two teenage girls from the house across the street join us. Tooy goes on about how if the boys are standing on the street with the two girls (who are dressed in the proper style for Saramaka girls in Cayenne), the police will only be interested in them, not the girls—especially since they don't have papers of any kind. (209)

Some Saamaka boys only a few years older expressed incredulity when we pleaded with them to testify at Tooy's upcoming rape trial in order to keep him out of jail—they had told us they'd slept with the (non-Saamaka) girl in question when she was a minor and that they were hardly alone. If that had been entered into the trial, the girl's claim of virginity would have been thrown out of court. But the idea of going anywhere near the courthouse with its *gendarmes* and other officials, no matter whom it would save from jail, was not something these young men could even contemplate (Price, 2008, 193). Their lives, like those of other undocumented immigrants in Guyane, revolved around keeping their heads down and remaining ever vigilant.

Northwards and inland

Let's drive west from the capital, through the savannahs, arriving an hour later in Kourou, with its space-based economy. The outlines of the town's history are by now well known, from Howard French's observation in the *New York Times* that, 'As recently as the early 1970s, Kourou slumbered in oblivion as a quiet fishing village whose main distinction [serving as port of embarkation for Devil's Island] was a feature that many of its several hundred residents would have just as soon forgotten', through to the excellent description of its starkly segregated urban planning design by sociologist Marie-José Jolivet (1981, 446–447), which Sally and I quoted at length in *Equatoria* (1992, 42–44). As we described one of our scores of visits, 'we pass a sign touting "Lingerie Féminine Fantaisie", and drive by the high-rise apartment blocks for lower-level employees of the space center, the large French Foreign Legion encampment, and the manicured lawns of whitefolks' villas, before turning into the dirt road that leads to the "Village Saramaka"' (Price and Price, 1992, 41–43). That insalubrious 'village' has now, for the most part, been demolished and its residents resettled in concrete housing nearby. Yet, we're told by police that it's still one of Guyane's hotspots for drug dealing, thanks to Maroon connections (by a combination of motorcycle and canoe) to eastern Suriname, where the local trade originates. Kourou, with its segregated housing and vast inequalities of wealth and power compressed into a relatively small geography, remains for us halfway between the urbanity of Cayenne and the truly Wild West feeling of our next destination, a couple of hours to the west, past Sinnamary and Iracoubo: the border town of Saint-Laurent-du-Maroni.

Léon-Gontran Damas dismissed this ancient capital of the *bagne* as 'a veritable Sodom' (1938, 45), and a half-century later the journalist Alex Miles enlarged upon that perspective:

> St. Laurent is not much of a place. It never was to begin with. Four or five rat-infested streets of decaying wooden houses in the old colonial style—some occupied, some deserted. You can see it all in ten minutes. The whole place reeks of decay. Old Creole women peer out through the windows of their crumbling structures at any stranger who walks the streets. The open sewers are clogged with filth and drowned rats. Stray dogs paw hungrily at the rodent carcasses. The stench is sickening. (1988, 2)

But the good news is that today's Saint-Laurent is none of these things. One of the fastest-growing cities in the world, it would seem to represent the future of Guyane. Clémence Léobal's recent *Saint-Laurent-du-Maroni: une porte sur le fleuve* (2013) tells the story nicely and predicts that by the end of the decade, the *commune* of Saint-Laurent will have a larger population than Cayenne. Right now, she estimates, the town's population stands at some 45,000 and at least 30,000 of these residents are Maroons, making it at once the largest Aluku-, Ndyuka-, Pamaka- and Saamaka-speaking city in the world. As in the schools spread out along the Maroni, the rapidly growing number of schools in Saint-Laurent feature white teachers, many recently arrived from France, and Maroon students who speak French only as a second language. The 'civilizing mission' is tested to it limits here and, surprisingly, it works to some extent, though school failure and drop-out rates remain high. Saint-Laurent, this majority-Maroon city, looks increasingly modern, with enough hotels and restaurants to have comfortably hosted an international academic conference with more than 50 speakers in 2013. A decent bookstore, a cinema and an attractive tourist office, but all around the edges considerable poverty. And children (and new schools) everywhere. Saint-Laurent is the baby capital of Guyane, with a birth rate something like eight times that of France.[5]

Let's transport ourselves up the Maroni from Saint-Laurent for a final stop on the tour, as the story of what France did to that part of Guyane upriver from the *bagne* deserves a special place in the saga of French colonialism. Guyane's Inini Territory—until 1969 a vast, separate and largely unspoiled and unadministered forest world, with a couple of thousand Amerindians and Aluku Maroon residents—began to be cut up by the French state into *communes*, *arrondissements*, and *cantons* (with all their attendant institutions: *mairies*, *gendarmeries*, *écoles*, *cadastre*) only during the 1970s. Ken Bilby, eyewitness to the first two decades of change, described the situation:

> In 1969, Maripasoula was transformed overnight, as was the rest of the interior, by the policy of *francisation*. As the *chef-lieu* of a new commune, it became the site of a town hall, a new school, and an expanded clinic ... It was chosen as the main administrative centre for the entire region encompassed by the Lawa and its tributaries ...
> By the mid-1970s, Maripasoula had metamorphosed into the largest settlement in the Lawa River area ... [and] had the distinction of simultaneously being the largest and one of the least populated communes in the entire republic of France ... In 1974 the commune included: 248 Wayana and Emerillon Indians, 387 Maroons, almost all Aluku, and 168 Creoles ... [total population of the *commune*: 803 people].
>
> The Aluku were living in a dizzying world that had been abruptly and radically remade by forces beyond their control or comprehension ... By the mid-1980s, roughly one-half of all Alukus from the Lawa River region were living in one of the two new communities built

5 This is attested to on various INSEE websites. Because many Surinamese women come over to the Saint-Laurent hospital at the last minute to give birth on French soil, these figures are difficult to pin down exactly.

> in the interior with [French] government funds (Maripasoula and Pompidouville [Papaïchton]), while nearly a third resided in coastal towns; the rest of the population, less than a fifth, remained thinly scattered in the interior, divided between the old villages and the few horticultural camps still in use. The amenities offered by ... the coastal way of life—wage-earning opportunities, Western medicine, running water, electricity, and consumer goods, to name a few—had made their way to the [new towns in the] interior and drawn most Aluku away from their ancestral villages.
>
> ... thanks to *francisation*, [the Aluku] are a 'subsidized' people ... In 1983, 1,800,000 francs (a little less than U.S. $250,000 at the time), which had originated in metropolitan France, passed through various intermediaries in Cayenne and made its way to the commune of Grand-Santi-Papaïchton ... Since that time, yearly budgets have increased ... In 1986, the standard monthly amount paid out for old-age pensions was 1,500 francs [=$300] per person. In contrast, agricultural allowances varied to some extent. One woman received 7,500 francs in such payments over a period of three months ...
>
> The influx of 'free' (or 'cheap') money has helped create an enormous appetite for gain, and has sparked what at times seems like a frenzy of buying and selling ... There remains almost nothing that cannot be sold. (Bilby 1990, 268–269, 139, 623, 195, 151–152, 173–174, 178–180; see also Sausse, 1951, 42–43)

For the Aluku Maroons, descendants of self-liberated slaves who had been living along the Lawa for two centuries organized in matrilineal clans that controlled the land, each presided by a political/religious chief who answered to the *gaanman* (paramount chief), the imposed change came as a tsunami. Where before they had practised hunting, fishing, gathering and shifting cultivation, with wealth distributed relatively evenly and exchange among villagers and kinsfolk the rule, suddenly money became king. The effect is that traditional villages have largely emptied out in favour of migration to the coast or to the new administrative centres, where large numbers of outsiders now live as well. Subsequent *francisation* has eroded transmission of what were widely shared artistic skills—woodcarving for men, sewing and calabash decoration for women, as well as song and dance—and oral traditions, whether folktales or historical or ritual knowledge, are fast being lost (or carried on only by specialists, directing their products to tourists). Suriname's civil war of the 1980s and '90s, and the more recent gold rush in what was once Aluku territory, brought tremendous disorder as well as a new influx of wealth to the villages which, today, bear little resemblance to those of 40 years ago or of centuries past. The population of Maripasoula has quadrupled since the start of the millennium. Mercury from artisanal gold mining now pollutes water and air, posing serious health threats to future generations. And Alukus now form a minority within their own traditional territory, which is today thoroughly multiethnic.[6] In his *Discours sur le colonialisme* (1955), Aimé Césaire wrote of 'sociétés vidées d'elles-mêmes, terres confisquées, religions assassinées, magnificences artistiques anéantis, d'extraordinaires *possibilités* supprimées' (19–20).[7] That begins to sum it up, doesn't it?

But, in fact, recent reports from the Lawa paint a yet more dire situation of environmental degradation and rampant change. In late 2009, Ken Bilby wrote to me about a recent visit to Maripasoula, noting his impression of Benzdorp, almost across the river: 'I briefly passed Benzdorp on this trip, and the amount of activity (constant air traffic) and the explosion of ramshackle "development" there is truly incredible—but it's all over the Suriname side of the Lawa and farther upriver'. Aluku Gaanman Adochini 'complained fervently' to Bilby about the wholesale granting of logging and mining concessions in this region by the Paramaribo government, with complete disregard for pre-existing Aluku claims. He also complained about the large frontier settlement that has mushroomed directly across the river from Maripasoula, on the Suriname side (replete with restaurants, nightclubs and brothels), populated mostly by Brazilians, Ndyukas and people from Paramaribo—outsiders living as they wish on Aluku territory, with no respect for Aluku law. Bilby asks, rhetorically, 'But what can the Aluku do against this influx, which continues to grow and threatens to outnumber the Aluku and Wayana populations combined?'

For nearly a decade now, anthropologist Marjo de Theije has been carrying out fieldwork along precisely this French-Suriname gold rush borderland. What she reports makes other recent developments in Guyane sound sluggish and tame. I'd like to summarize and paraphrase one of her most recent studies, from 2014. The people living in this Guyane-Suriname border region now include the original Maroon and Amerindian inhabitants as well as French, Surinamese and Brazilian gold miners, sex workers from different backgrounds and a large

6 I draw this conclusion from the most recent INSEE figures on the *communes* of Apatou, Papaïchston and Maripasoula.

7 'Of societies emptied of themselves, of lands stolen, of religions assassinated, of artistic glories annihilated, of extraordinary *possibilities* suppressed'.

number of merchants and hawkers of diverse origins plus an increasing number of Chinese. The amount of petroleum products needed to keep the machines running for transportation and gold extraction defies belief: about 15 million litres of diesel and 50,000 litres of oil and grease are used in small-scale mining each year (Fritz-Krockow et al., 2009, 83, cited in de Theije, 2014). And fuel transport brings big profits. A 200-litre barrel of fuel costs five grams of gold in Paramaribo but 50 or more in the illegal mines along the Lawa in Guyane. Almost all food and drink for the many thousands of residents is also imported from the coast, mainly by canoe from Albina. There is no longer any other serious economic activity in the region—90% of households in the villages along the Tapanahoni, Marowijne and Lawa are financially dependent on small-scale gold mining (Heemskerk, 2009, 35 cited in de Theije, 2014).

Because the French have been more aggressive than the Surinamese in closing down illegal small-scale mining (destroying machinery, expelling illegals), first through Operation Anaconda (2002–2008) and later Operation Harpie (since 2008), miners and their supporting populations find a more comfortable existence on the Suriname side of the Lawa.[8] Indeed, what Bilby saw as he passed by Benzdorp in 2009 had been building for a decade. Dona Maria, a Brazilian immigrant, had been a cook in a mining camp but, with the World Cup of 1998 fast approaching, bought a satellite dish and began selling drinks and snacks in Benzdorp. This soon turned into a restaurant, later adding on a brothel. Benzdorp was born, becoming the commercial and recreational centre for the whole region. Today's vast lineup of bars, brothels and supermarkets all stems from these beginnings. But the past several years have seen a sudden change—the Chinese have taken over most commerce. De Theije writes that:

> In the space of three years, between 2007 and 2010, Chinese entrepreneurs took over the entire commerce in the gold fields on the Lawa River. In Benzdorp alone, I counted fourteen Chinese supermarkets in 2012, all selling basically the same products. Only some Brazilian clothing stores and beauty salons have survived the competition with these newcomers. (2014, 68)

8 Suriname's hands-off attitude toward artisanal mining stems, in large part, from the tremendous profits which politicians—including the president and his friends and family—make from it. A recent book describes how the system works and includes further materials on the Lawa region (Trommelen, 2013).

And there are also women travellers who buy luxury goods such as perfumes, clothes and cigarettes in Brazil or Suriname and sell them in distant places up the Lawa that are only accessible by canoe. In general, the operators of small-scale mines, in Guyane as well as Suriname, now find it cheaper to buy from Chinese supermarkets along the Lawa than to import their goods directly from Albina.

De Theije reports that substantial new settlements are continuing to spring up along the Lawa. Kabana-vo on the Suriname side, for example, has morphed from an Aluku garden camp in 2008 to a settlement of several hundred Brazilian and Surinamese today. While it slumbers during the day, she writes:

> At night or during the early morning, however, Kabana-vo bursts with activity as it is the departure point for smuggling people and goods into the Waki Creek and other *garimpos* on the French side of the river. Boats are filled with merchandise and mining gear, and leave before dawn to cross the part of the river that is controlled by the French police when it is still dark. Jaw Pasi is a similar place, further up the Lawa River, in the customary territory of the Wayana Amerindians. ... In the last eighteen months, several Chinese entrepreneurs have set up supermarkets there, and they have now forced the Brazilian shop owners out of the market, just as happened a few years ago in Benzdorp and other places. (73–74)

The most recent news is that, directly across from Maripasoula, on the Suriname bank of the river, there is a virtual Chinese shopping mall—18 Chinese supermarkets lined up in a row. This place, called Antonio do Brinco, not only caters to miners but to the inhabitants of Maripasoula and other Guyanais towns. And the latest innovation: the supermarkets furnish shoppers easy transport by canoe from Maripasoula to the mall and back, free of charge.

We end this little tour of Guyane here, far upstream. Space constraints don't permit even a brief venture towards the eastern border, where the Saint-Georges to Oiapoque bridge across the River Oyapock has in early 2017 still not been officially opened and promises to bring all sorts of further changes. But these brief remarks should still communicate our continuing sense of wonder at the place—Guyane remains for Sally and me quintessential Equatoria, a contradictory space, at once enigmatic, opaque, colonial, ever-changing and forever challenging.

Works cited

Benoît, Catherine. 2016. 'Etre de quelque part mais être né nulle part … Frontières et état civil en Guyane', in *Mobilités, ethnicités, diversité culturelle: La Guyane entre Surinam et Brésil*, ed. Gérard Collomb and Serge Mam Lam Fouck. Matoury, Guyane: Ibis Rouge, 161–170.

Bilby, Kenneth M. 1990. *The Remaking of the Aluku: Culture, Politics, and Maroon Ethnicity in French South America*. PhD diss., Johns Hopkins University.

Césaire, Aimé. 1955. *Discours sur le colonialisme*. Paris: Présence Africaine.

Damas, Léon-Gontran. 1938. *Retour de Guyane*. Paris: José Corti.

Davis, Hassoldt. 1952. *The Jungle and the Damned*. London: The Travel Book Club.

de Theije, Marjo. 2014. 'Small-scale gold mining and trans-frontier commerce on the Lawa River', in *In and Out of Suriname: Language, Mobility and Identity*, ed. Eithne Carlin, Isabelle Léglise, Bettina Migge and Paul Tjon Sie Fat. Leiden: Brill, 58–75.

French, Howard W. 1991. 'A space center or not, some say it's a jungle', *New York Times*, 26 April.

Fritz-Krockow, Bernhard, Gamal El-Masry, Masahiro Nozaki, Tobias Roy, Rafael Portillo, Mariana Torres and Pawel Dyczewski. 2009. *Suriname: Toward Stability and Growth*. Washington, DC: International Monetary Fund.

Hearn, Lafcadio. 1923 [1890]. *Two Years in the French West Indies*. New York: Harper and Brothers.

Heemskerk, Marieke. 2009. *Kleinschalige goudwinning in Suriname. Een overzicht van sociaaleconomische, politieke, em milieu aspecten*. Amsterdam: CEDLA.

INSEE. 2003. '"Contrat de Projet Etat-Région", en cours d'élaboration par les pôles régionaux de l'Etat (2006)', *Antiane Eco* 56, June.

INSEE. 2013. 'La Guyane poursuit sa transition démographique – légère inflexion de la natalité', *Antiane Eco* 26, June: 29–30.

Jolivet, Marie-José. 1982. *La Question créole: essai de sociologie sur la Guyane française*. Paris: ORSTOM.

Léobal, Clémence. 2013. *Saint-Laurent-du-Maroni: une porte sur le fleuve*. Matoury: Ibis Rouge.

Mekkaoui, Jamel. 2012. 'INSEE: l'enquête emploi en Guyane deuxième trimestre 2012'. https://www.insee.fr/fr/statistiques/fichier/1291015/pr_ee2012_gy.pdf (accessed 14 March 2018).

Métraux, Alfred. 1978. *Itinéraires 1 (1935–1953): carnets de notes et journaux de voyage*. Paris: Payot.

Parépou, Alfred. 1885. *Atipa (roman guyanais)*. Paris: A. Ghio.

Piantoni, Fréderic. 2011. *Migrants en Guyane*. Arles: Actes Sud.

Price, Richard. 2008. *Travels with Tooy: History, Memory, and the African American Imagination*. Chicago: University of Chicago Press.

Price, Richard. 2013. 'The maroon population explosion: Suriname and Guyane', *New West Indian Guide* 87: 323–327.

Price, Richard and Sally Price. 1989. 'Working for the Man: A Saramaka outlook on Kourou', *New West Indian Guide* 63: 199–207.

Price, Richard and Sally Price. 1992. *Equatoria*. New York: Routledge.

Price, Richard and Sally Price. 1995. *Enigma Variations: A Novel*. Cambridge, MA: Harvard University Press.

Redfield, Peter. 2000. *Space in the Tropics: From Convicts to Rockets in French Guiana*. Berkeley: University of California Press.

Sausse, André, 1951. *Populations primitives du Maroni (Guyane française)*. Paris: Institut Géographique National.

Tripot, J. 1910. *La Guyane: au pays de l'or, des forçats et des peaux-rouges*. Paris: Plon.

Trommelen, Jeroen. 2013. *Gowtu: Klopjacht op het Surinaamse goud*. Schoorl: Conserve.

Trouillot, Évelyne. 2013. *Absences sans frontières*. Montpellier: Éditions Chèvre-feuille.

Yahou-Dauvier, N'ouara. 2013. *La Situation socio-économique de la Guyane. De sa démographique à son économie*. http://www.iedom.fr/IMG/pdf/presentation_insee_etudiant_master_aout_2013_cr.pdf (accessed 14 March 2018).

CHAPTER TWO

Grand Reporters in Guyane

Bringing the Exotic Back Home

Kari Evanson, Fordham University

Albert Londres's first article on the *bagne* in Guyane appeared in *Le Petit Parisien* on 8 August 1923 and the series continued weekly until 5 September. Published by Albin Michel later that same year, *Au bagne* signalled a watershed moment in the history of *grand reportage*.[1] Though two reporters, Jacques Dhur in 1905 and Henri Béraud in 1922, had already touched on the subject of the overseas penal colony, these two investigations passed almost without notice.[2] Following Londres's investigation, numerous French newspaper and magazine editors wanted their own investigation of the overseas penal colony—though several publications simply reprinted Londres's findings in their pages—and the résumé of all aspiring and established *grands reporters* was not complete without a voyage to Guyane.

Albert Londres's reputation is such that his visit to the *bagne* often overshadows the numerous other reporters who followed him. Indeed, no other investigation of the *bagne* enjoyed such success. The quality of the writing and the subject itself played a large role, but it was certainly the mode of diffusion that set this investigation apart from those that

1 For a history of *grand reportage*, see Boucharenc (2004).

2 Jacques Dhur's investigation, *Visions de bagne* (1925), primarily of the penal colony in New Caledonia was re-edited following the success of Albert Londres. Henri Béraud's article for *Le Journal* was later published in *Le Flâneur salarié* (1927).

had come before. In the 1920s, *Le Petit Parisien* boasted a circulation of over a million copies that were sold directly on the street to the 'common man who found over the course of the articles the exoticism, adventure, and "parade of notoriety and shame" (Foucault) offered by the portrait gallery of famous *forçats*' (Donat-Vincent, 1992, 40, citing Foucault, 1975). With the publication of these investigations in book form, the subject of the *bagne* found an additional, highbrow audience. Indeed, editors soon found that *reportage* was a profitable niche (Boucharenc, 2004, 31). Albin Michel, for example, launched its collection 'Les Grands Reportages' with the publication of *Au bagne*. Bernard Grasset published *Le Voleur et le sphinx* (1926), Louis Roubaud's 1925 contribution for the left-leaning newspaper *Le Quotidien*. *Reportage* also found its way into popular literature with the 1925 publication of Georges Le Fèvre's *Bagnards et chercheurs d'or* by Ferenczi et fils—a publishing house better known for its large library of crime fiction.[3]

Following the initial explosion of interest for Guyane and its prisons, a second wave crested at the beginning of the 1930s with the launch of new weekly magazines such as *Détective* and *Vu*, which were devoted to *fait divers*, *reportage* and glossy exposés of exotic places. Journalism and publishing came together in *Détective*, owned by Gallimard, which would release in edition the *reportages* published in the magazine. Whether Guyane or the spectacle of departure from Saint-Martin-de-Ré, the *bagne* and its *forçats* held pride of place in the pages of *Détective* and its rival *Police Magazine*, in particular. A final testament to the subject's success was the usage of the symbol of the *bagne* to describe other wings of the French penitentiary apparatus—the most salient example being the rise of the term *bagnes d'enfants* in investigations of juvenile penal colonies and reform institutions during this same period.

In order to locate the *grand reporter*'s Guyane in the 1920s and 1930s, we will examine, in addition to *Au bagne*, Louis Roubaud's *Le Voleur et le sphinx* (1926) and Marius Larique's *Les Hommes punis* (1933), published in *Détective* in 1931—each representing a different period of reporting on the prison system in Guyane. No longer turned towards the exterior or foreign, the *reporter*'s gaze turned inward to the inherently local but hidden aspects of French Guianese society. These investigations united the practices of travel literature and investigative

3 Sent by *Le Journal*, *Le Petit Parisien*'s direct rival, Le Fèvre announced his express intention to find an innocent man in Guyane. He claimed to have found 1,500 in three days, a statistical impossibility (Pierre, 2000, 163).

reporting by combining the exotic and the familiar, the self and the other. These myriad investigations not only (re)introduced the public to the fascinating figure of the criminal and the hidden underbelly of the French penal system, but also took readers on an exotic voyage to this colonial outpost. By modelling the emotions of compassion, disgust and outrage, the *reporters* invited their readers not only to experience Guyane in the pages of the press but also reconsider and question this place of punishment.

These journalists did not, however, all deliver the same Guyane to their readership. Roubaud rendered, if not the *bagne*, then its *bagnards* familiar for his readers. By reducing the distance between his readers and these faraway criminals, Roubaud reduced the distance between France and its distant colony. But his is only a small contribution to the representations of the *bagne* and Guyane in the 1920s and 1930s. If Roubaud kept Guyane close, Londres and Larique held Guyane and its *bagnards* at a distance. Their stories of suffering and horror kept Guyane distinctly foreign and strange. If their Guyane was at times familiar, it was an uneasy familiarity. Indeed, while the interwar *reportages* of the *bagne* destroyed certain myths, they created others. The investigations cemented Guyane as a borderland, at once distinctly French and other.

The interwar journalists were hardly entering uncharted territory. Indeed, before Albert Londres's arrival in Guyane, the myth of the *bagne*—or, more importantly, that of its *bagnards*—was inscribed in the social imaginary (Pierre, 2007). One has only to think of Jean Valjean or Vautrin, both escaped *forçats* from the Toulon work camp, or Chéri-Bibi, Gaston Leroux's famous innocent *bagnard*. As noted by Marion Godfroy, 'This rich literary history is such that when we think of Guyane we speak less of individual lives than of collective destinies and of characters instead of individual men' (2008, 17–18). The *bagne* was often associated with larger-than-life criminals who, having done their time or escaped, return to the mainland to continue their grand narrative.

If the myth of the *bagnard* was so prevalent, it was as if Guyane itself didn't exist except as an idea, as an invisible realm of punishment without any real physical form. Miranda Spieler notes that in Émile Zola's novel, *Le Ventre de Paris* (1882), 'Devil's Island is the exclusive scene of punishment, while the mainland, through which the hero escapes, is wild and empty of people' (2012, 109). Indeed, in the collective consciousness, the entire colony of Guyane could be reduced to this singular prison cell, the occupant more important than the place. The journalists of the interwar period therefore set out in part to find the reality behind the myth of Guyane—to discover the individual stories behind these collective fantasies while also mapping the invisible Guyane that these stories left out.

The Journey to 'Hell'

Reportage is first and foremost a journey, a geographical adventure, according to André Malraux (Boucharenc, 2004, 56). The voyage to Guyane is thus not without exoticism—a constant reminder to readers that they are no longer in France. Londres began his voyage on the *Biskra* (the steam liner linking the Antilles to Guyane) with the *forçats*, thereby literally insisting on the voyage with the image of the boat but also immediately introducing otherness by filling that boat with prisoners. At the same time, the presence of the prisoners underscores a certain danger. '"And if they seize the boat?" demanded with worry one of the passengers with no disposition for a life of adventure' (13). Roubaud drops his readers directly into the action but does later remind them of the difficulty of reaching Guyane and certainly the outposts away from the coast, noting: 'To come to the Crique Plomb, I travelled for twenty days on two ocean liners, three days on a steam-powered fishing boat and almost a week in a hollowed-out tree trunk' (15). Roubaud's exoticism does not come from his encounter with the prisoners; indeed, as we shall see, his investigative project was to render the prisoners familiar. The otherness for Roubaud comes both from his mode of transportation (the hollow tree trunk) and from his navigators, two Maroons whom Roubaud admires not only for their virility but also their rationality: 'The two front motors are called Lamès and Poussé. Their arms are piston rods, their paddles are propeller blades; they are regular like a machine and beautiful like a figurehead' (24).

Larique also admires the force and beauty of his Maroon navigator, who safely delivers him from the pursuit and gunshots of the penal guards. Unlike Londres or Roubaud, Larique was denied permission to visit the colony (Pierre, 2000, 170). Larique thus vividly stages his bravery in defiance of this refusal with this scene of pursuit and violence as he sped away from the leper island 'on the strength of the Boni', who easily pulled the *pirogue* out of rifle range (189). In order to see every detail and to bring the truth about the *bagne* to the reader, Larique in particular tells the story of risking his own life to visit the prisoners. He puts into play the common image of the *reporter* ready to risk his life for the authentic experience (Boucharenc, 2004, 89). Indeed, just the thought of braving these dangers gives Larique a moment of 'proud excitement' (178).

If Roubaud's and Larique's exploits seem fit for only the hardiest of adventurers, Larique reminds his readers that anyone can visit Guyane and the *bagne*. One has only to catch the ocean liner linking Saint-Nazaire to Guadeloupe and from there, catch the *Biskra*, which after several stops in the Caribbean, arrives five days later at Saint-Laurent-du-Maroni. Larique does not simply tell his readers how to get there but invites them to join him in his travels. By a process of *enallage*, in which the journalist drops the first person singular *je* to adopt the plural *nous* or 'we', he directly implicates the readers in the narrative by making them his travelling companions: 'Once we arrive, five days later in Saint-Laurent-du-Maroni, [the captain of the *Biskra*] will have possibly succeeded in putting us off quinine; he will surely have succeeded in making us regret our departure. We will be, at this moment, in Hell' (150).

The *bagne* as hell is a timeworn metaphor that dates back to the early nineteenth-century descriptions of galley slaves and also mirrors the romantic descriptions of the prisons of Victor Hugo or Eugene Sue. In order to render reality in all of its colour and horror, journalists dipped into the toolbox of fiction (Boucharenc, 2004, 67). Many journalists, Londres and Larique in particular, returned to this Dantesque image of the *bagne*, like Virgil leading his readers through the 'circles of agony' for a glimpse of the inhabitants. If Guyane and its prisons were Hell, its inhabitants were skeletons and cadavers already long gone. Guyane is not only a Hell but also a death trap. When describing Saint-Joseph island, Londres notes that 'here, living dead—in coffins—I mean cells—, men atone, alone' (99). More than the living dead, these men were at times hardly human: 'but the men are nothing but snotty, mangy, bare, anxious and abandoned animals ... Only one surprise is left: that these wretches don't walk on all fours. There is also a second: that these men speak to you when you question them and don't bark' (145). Like the romantic descriptions of the prisons, this parade of the infirm harks back to the descriptions of the *Cour de Miracles* that Hugo brought into vogue with *Notre-Dame-de-Paris*. If Londres finds this wretched scene at the Nouveau Camp, the 'garbage heap' of the *bagne* where one would believe oneself to have been transported to 'one of the most barbaric eras of humanity' (147), Larique encounters these same figures on the docks at Cayenne: 'they were pathetic, sordid, upsetting to see and painful to smell, even at a distance ... Since among them there were one-eyed, one-armed and one-legged men, I interrogated the doctor about this *Cour de miracles* that I inspected despite myself' (218).

The images are thus myriad and borrow from the lexicon and tradition of the painting of the underworld (see Kalifa, 2013). Indeed, the *reportages* were intended not only to inform but also to entertain and titillate the readers with the painting of exotic locales and characters. Both Londres and Larique make periodic use of references to hell or to the disabled wretches of a *Cour des Miracles*, but Larique completes his Guyane with all of the sensational horrors of a pulp novel. If Guyane was intended as a land of penitence, Larique instead finds a shadowy extension of the underworld with which the readers of *Détective* were so familiar. Saint-Laurent-du-Maroni was not a simple colonial outpost, but a land of outlaws seemingly drawn from a Wild West novel. It is in the commerce sector that Larique finds all of the *frissons* for his readers:

> The shadiest transactions happen in these hideouts where neither the police nor the guards venture; the most horrifying crimes are perpetuated there. It is so easy to get rid of dead bodies. The Maroni river flows right there, next to these houses from which horror oozes and which are terrifying, even in plain day. (13–14)

If Larique returns to Londres's image of death in describing the prisoners of Guyane while also borrowing from his bestiary, Larique's *bagne* is not only infirm or dead but also rotting: 'The years have passed and the *bagne* has kept its face of death, with its lightning bolts of ferocity and its exhalations of rot' (9). Like fetid breath, the odours of rot can invoke only the nausea associated with disgust. Indeed, throughout his investigation, Larique notes not only what he sees but also what he smells. In fact, it would seem that all of Guyane stinks. If we return to his image of the *Cour de Miracles*, we note that it is not only 'upsetting to see but also painful to smell'. From the humid and noxious odour of the rain in Saint-Laurent to the stench of the shacks in its commerce district, the reeking and steamy boat the *Oyapock*, as well as the dreadful odour of the lavatories and the cells, Larique passes from shivers of horror to the grimace of disgust. Indeed, his descriptions move through the lexicon of disgust and horror to describe even those images that would not usually evoke such reactions, such as the grass that grows with a *nauseating* rapidity or the death of a *forçat* that is a *ghastly* banality. The *bagne* is simply repugnant.

Moreover, if we return to his use of the word *pourriture* ('rot'), we can discern a double meaning that is illustrated throughout his travels in the colony. He not only sees and smells the physical rot but also witnesses the moral decay. In both cases, this rot refers to that which is unclean or impure and thus invokes a possibility and a fear of contamination. The atmosphere of criminality and corruption, which Larique finds to exist both inside and outside the structures of the penal administration, not to mention the rumours of homosexuality to which Larique alludes, risks contaminating even the most honest criminals: 'They live too long in a crooked atmosphere to have kept any sense of justice and the want of truth' (145). But what of the journalist's (and the reader's) own contamination? Are they not also at risk? Like indignation, disgust is a moral sentiment; disgust marks the boundaries between the pure and the contaminated, thereby signalling a moral superiority. But disgust signals a danger to our own purity since the risk of contamination is also present and feared (see Miller, 1997).

Even more so than criminals, lepers are the most polluting (and polluted) of beings for Larique and it is on his (unauthorized) visit to the leper island that he finally reaches the limits of his disgust. The horrors of infection and death come together in the image of the leper. Upon his arrival, he is greeted, not by men but by three walking cadavers: 'One no longer had hands, but instead claws, the other no longer had either a nose or teeth, the chest of the third was scaly. The third had tuberculosis' (180). After his initial reaction of fear, Larique is overwhelmed by his disgust: 'I can no longer listen, no longer look. I have exceeded … the limit of my comprehension in the horror: disgust submerges me' (189). It is less the men, however, than the conditions that Larique finds so abhorrent. It is the sight and smell of the compresses covered in pus or the revoltingly dirty hammocks that finally drive him to leave. But Larique immediately expresses his discomfort and unease about fleeing the scene, about not being able to stomach men who were simply sick. Disgust is a sign of weakness:

> Disgust signals the need to undertake further labours of purification. It is thus that disgust does not do its moral work so as to allow us unambivalent pleasure in our relative moral superiority to the disgusting other. Disgust admits our own vulnerability and compromise even as it constitutes an assertion of superiority. (Miller, 1997, 204)

Disgust would then seem to keep Larique's objects of investigation at a distance all the while assuring his readers (and himself) of their (and his) physical and moral superiority. However, Larique's disgust leads to indignation and action. While Larique expresses his disgust at the sight and smell of the *forçats*, and of the sick and infirm in particular, his disgust becomes indignation when he considers the system in its ensemble, when he considers that the penal administration has been summoned to care for these men—that the penal administration is in fact responsible for their misery. In his analysis of media representations of suffering, Luc Boltanski has identified three rhetorical 'topics' available to the spectator for his response to this suffering: sentiment, denunciation and aesthetic (see Boltanski, 1999). Larique has in fact moved from a 'topic' of sentiment or compassion, by which he finds an emotional equivalence with those who would ease the suffering of the prisoners, to a 'topic' of denunciation, by which Larique moves to identify the cause. The spectacle of suffering changes the stakes of the strictly objective investigation because it introduces a sense of urgency. Neither the journalist nor the reader can remain unaffected by the narrative. He can either choose to ignore the suffering (and risk the charge of deriving pleasure from it) or he can choose to act. For the journalist, the moment of engagement centres on the choice to write about the experience—the speech act. The *pathos* founds the *ethos*. This is an instance when the rhetorical device of *enallage* is particularly effective. The journalist implicates the readers in his own sentiments: 'But all awaken in you the sentiment of pity. We would have wanted them to succeed [in their escape attempt]' (Londres, 2007, 16).

Larique models this very engagement by narrating the expression of his outrage. His disgust has become indignation as he redirects his repugnance at the penal system and at the cause of the suffering. According to Emmanuelle Danblon, indignation is a complex emotion that is born precisely from the representation of a transgression (2005, 31). Indeed, upon his return from the leper island, he expresses his outrage to the head of the colony, Colonel Prével, who replies with a common platitude when faced with those who disgust: it's their fault. Prével reminds Larique that the *forçats* are all assassins. Larique responds with figures: the proportion of *forçats* suffering from leprosy in the course of their sentence is two per thousand, while this figure jumps to six per thousand for the *libérés* and 13 for the *relégués*. It is Guyane that has infected them. Indeed, Larique apologizes for his instinctive disgust: 'it's not their fault if I need fresh air, if I need to flee from them ... It's not their fault if their wounds are disgusting and their breath revolting' (189). It is not the men, then, who are disgusting but the system that has brought them to their current state. The penal administration has left them in a condition that 'we would not accept for our livestock' (166).

If the narration of his indignation is not enough, Larique then narrates his atonement: his moment of purification. Following the episode with the lepers, Larique expresses his shame for not daring to tell a *forçat* to attempt another escape. But his shame is such that he helps him out anyway:

> I ask forgiveness of the honest and that the Penal administration not pursue me, if it dares: I gave, that morning, to that poor wretch, against Guyanese currency, which can only be exchanged in Guyane, two thousand-franc bills from the mainland, because they can be exchanged in Brazil, Venezuela, Trinidad … (209)

Though it would seem that Larique is attempting to atone for his guilt or that he hopes to help even just one *forçat*, this scene, like that of his running from the administration's bullet, also serves to enforce his image of the journalist as hero—one who is willing to risk life and liberty to uncover the truth or to save one man from the grips of the *bagne*. In the end, was it the action that was important or the narration and spectacle of that action?

The risk, in many of these *reportages* is that the sensational overwhelms the sentiment. Though Londres's expresses his sympathy and Larique performs his disgust and outrage, both journalists maintain a distance from their subjects, preferring to describe rather than understand. The romantic metaphors build a certain wall between criminal and reader: 'The underworld marks the distance, but also blurs the ordinary convictions by showing that both the pure and the perverted exist in both places' (Kalifa, 2013, 137). As spectacle, Guyane is thus both exotic and uncomfortably familiar.

Humanizing Guyane

If Londres and Larique insist on the spectacle of suffering and on the horrors of the *bagne*, thereby keeping their subjects at a certain distance, Roubaud instead seeks to reduce the perceived distance between his readers and the subjects of his investigation by insisting on a certain familiarity and by concentrating not on the crime but on the social history of his interlocuters. He explicitly refuses the sensational images when he visits, for example, the leper colony: 'I saw faces and wounds that I won't show you out of pity for them and out of pity for you' (174). Roubaud's Guyane is not the Guyane of larger-than-life criminals, spectacular assassins, cunning thieves and facile metaphors. Roubaud's Guyane is not exotic but familiar; it is one of slaves labouring for the promises of gold, immature boys who are paying for a juvenile mistake with their lives, and criminals who are simply human beings.

Upon his arrival at the first placer mine, Roubaud meets Michel Olivier who, he finds, comes from the same region as he. Though they could communicate in the same patois, Roubaud notes that their destinies were entirely different. While Roubaud was in high school, Olivier was running barefoot in the gutters of Marseille. When the journalist left university in the evenings to find his friends at a café in Paris, Olivier was sipping absinthe in the bars of the *cité phocéenne*. 'It was maybe at the time when I was held back in my last year of university that he was pinched for the murder of Madame Langlois' (14). The importance of this citation lies in the passive construction. They both had something done to them—or, in a sense, they both got caught. The ultimate responsibility remains questionable. Though the distance between them may seem great seen from adulthood, the only thing separating the two is the circumstances of their birth—though born in the same city, the two men were born to entirely different existences or, as Roubaud says, 'destinies'. The bourgeois Roubaud was destined to an education and to success; the only real failure that he experienced was not obtaining his diploma on the first try. Michel Olivier, on the other hand, seems destined from birth to finish his days in Guyane. Though Roubaud's gaze is one of compassion, he does not engage with a spectacle of suffering. In simply describing, Roubaud moves to a topic of denunciation in his allusion to a force beyond the strict control of the criminal. However, unlike Larique, Roubaud does not present his *forçats* as different but instead renders them familiar by noting that they could be anyone. Where Larique opens his narrative by presenting 'their' capital, Saint-Laurent, Roubaud insists repeatedly on 'our' Guyane. It is not a question of them and us but of all French and, by extension, humankind.

Like the other reporters, Roubaud sets sail for Guyane to uncover the reality behind the myth. However, he doesn't begin his narrative voyage on the boat with the *forçats* or in the administrative centres of Cayenne or Saint-Laurent. Instead, Roubaud opens his narrative 'au faubourg d'Eldorado' at the Crique Plomb on the Sinnamary River. Roubaud begins his voyage where the history of French Guyane begins, with the search for the gold of Eldorado. 'For if the *bagne* is in Guyane, it is not all of Guyane, whose incoherent grandeur I perceived this night of 15 August' (21). This preliminary tour of the placer mines of the jungle allows Roubaud to posit the thesis that drives his investigation of Guyane. Behind his investigation lies an argument of economic inequality and the destructive powers of money. For Roubaud finds a Guyane filled with gold, but without any manner (or will) to exploit it: 'Our American treasure remains like a miser's cash box buried in the ground' (51).

If myth would have it that the Golden King guards his gold up in the mountains of Eldorado, Roubaud finds instead that the riches of Guyane are controlled by some civil servant in a suit. He wonders out loud if a consortium similar to the diamond consortium, which, in the interest of maintaining the value of its product, limits its production, in fact controls the gold interests in Guyane: 'I don't know of a gold consortium. Maybe it exists? Maybe I was wrong to search for the mysterious Manao, in a fairy-tale palace, at the summit of Tumuc-Humac? Maybe the Golden King lives in Paris, New York or London?' (56). In the interests of profit, Guyane flounders in mediocrity while the *forçats de l'or* continue their fruitless search for riches.

If Guyane was not an Eldorado, what about its hardened criminals? What about the famous traitors that France had sent to Devil's Island to pay for their crimes? If visions of wealth drive the numerous gold prospectors into the jungle every day, Roubaud finds that it was also a desire for wealth or possibly just the need to get by that landed those found guilty of treason on Devil's Island. In the years leading up to the First World War, when fears of threats to national security from both the interior and exterior had reached their apogee, the daily newspapers were filled with stories of insidious spies and dangerous criminals. Charles-Benjamin Ullmo was one of the more famous of these espionage cases. This flamboyant soldier was convicted of attempting to sell secret documents to a German agent in order to pay for an opium habit, gambling debts and an expensive mistress (see Datta, 2011, 179–225). Like the members of the anarchist Bonnot gang, Ullmo was also a required stop on the tour of famous criminals in Guyane. When Roubaud visits Ullmo, however, he finds neither Londres's sneaky crook nor Larique's showy film star. For Roubaud, Ullmo invites only pity. He was simply a victim of his own weakness—of an opium addiction that 'made him believe his dreams' (99).

Ullmo's plight mirrors that of Paul Gruault, also on Devil's Island for treason. Gruault's real downfall was that 'he wanted a uniform above his rank' (83). Paul was born to a single mother, but his father, who had died just before his birth, left them enough money to send Paul to high school: 'At sixteen, he had rich friends and a diploma' (83). However, while his friends went on to medical school or law school or 'out on the roads to try the new cyclecar', Paul worked white-collar jobs before becoming a salesman at a jewellery store. However, he felt his difference from his rich friends who were enjoying all of the extravagances of the Belle Époque. So when his friend who was a runner (*coulissier*) at the Stock Exchange offered him a sure thing investment, Paul stole a necklace from his employer only to lose it all when the stock didn't budge. To keep him out of jail, his mother sold the rest of her inheritance. Without money at the house, Paul searched for another scheme to get rich quick. This was 1914 and what he found were offers to spy on his country for a handy sum. With false information to sell, Gruault was entrapped by an agent from the Interior Ministry and, like Ullmo, found himself at Devil's Island for high treason.[4]

If Ullmo and Gruault could be faulted for wanting to live beyond their means, the other men Roubaud meets simply found themselves in a desperate situation and, like Gruault, turned to the foreign newspapers that offered cash for information. In relating these stories, Roubaud's gaze is one of compassion and understanding. One had a wife who spent his pay on perfume and silk stockings. Another had experienced a series of setbacks, then a bankruptcy and was no longer able to provide for his family. After a string of bad luck and when the creditors came calling, would Roubaud's readers have done any differently?

With the benefit of hindsight and in an atmosphere of anti-war sentiment, Roubaud invites his readers to consider these 'traitors' in a more indulgent light. Each of his examples demonstrates a desperate man in need of money and not a calculating one out to betray his country. Their crimes were not high treason but the lesser charge of espionage, which carried a penalty of up to five years' jail time and not imprisonment in perpetuity. The prisoners had done their time. Roubaud, however, doesn't blame the reigning sentiment of national defence that sent these men to Guyane before the war. He argues instead that as these men have changed, so too has France. Back in his office in Paris, Roubaud returns to the press clippings and the media 'parade'

4 Upon his release from the *bagne*, Gruault went to the offices of *Détective* and asked for a job. Hired by Gaston Gallimard, Gruault worked for *Détective* until 1939 and then as Gallimard's personal secretary until 1972. See Assouline (2006, 290–291).

that surrounded Ullmo's trial. An old photo falls from another file. The journalist recognizes himself but 20 years younger:

> Twenty years ago, I believe, this young man no longer resembles me. He no longer has my clothes, nor my face, nor my heart. He died twenty times! ... Does the time that erases the traits of a face and changes even eye colour conserve our mistakes? After twenty years, it seems that the punishment was wrong. The guilty is no longer there. He died twenty times like my image. (110)

While Roubaud does not excuse the gentlemen traitors whom he meets on Devil's Island, he does invite his readers to understand them.

Roubaud's investigation thus sets him apart from Londres or Larique, if not from the majority of reporting on the *bagne*. His *reportage* is fuelled not by sensationalism or spectacle but by social justice and class-consciousness. Londres and Larique modelled reporting methods in line with their place of publishing—sensational dailies or weeklies with a taste for titillation and an interest to engage the imagination. Where Roubaud could be dry and exacting, Larique was more flamboyant. It was this sensational style that would continue in the pages of *Détective*, where the *bagne* and its prisoners held pride of place in the 1930s. Aside from the spectacle of punishment, the *bagne* was also a site of adventure and exceptionalism, as Larique in particular continued his reporting on the *bagne* with narratives of heroic escapes, for instance in *Dans la brousse* (1933). Their intention, however, was the same: the denunciation of the *bagne* in Guyane. With differing methods, each journalist concentrated on the same subject—the prisoners. Guyane was the *bagne* and the *bagne* was its prisoners. Guyane was not a place but a total institution, to borrow an expression from Erving Goffman, populated by men and women who were powerless before the machine of repression:

> The *bagne* is not a punishment machine that is well-defined, ordered, invariable. It's a factory of hardship that works with neither framework nor mould. One would search in vain for the pattern that serves to shape the *forçat*. It crushes him, that's it, and the pieces land where they can. (Londres, 2007, 36)

This reporting on the *bagne* in Guyane was not without effect outside of the journalistic and literary fields. Following Londres's investigation, the Justice Ministry ceased approving authorizations for visits to the prisons in Guyane. Londres's and Roubaud's reporting also placed the *bagne* on the docket of parliamentary discussion. A first proposal for a law to end the practice of forcing prisoners to remain in Guyane after the end of their sentence was introduced in 1929 by the deputy Maurice Sibille (Sanchez, 2014). It was not, however, until 1938 that, under pressure from the Minister of Justice, Marc Rucart, Minister of Colonies, Louis Rollin, and the deputy of Guyane, Gaston Monnerville, a law was finally voted that effectively signalled the end of the *bagne* in Guyane (see Donat-Vincent, 1992). However, the last prisoners in Guyane would not return to the *métropole* until 1953.

At the same time, these reporters' investigations of the *bagne* in Guyane underlined their larger interest in repression and punishment in France. Albert Londres followed his *reportage* of Guyane with an investigation of the military prisons in North Africa: *Dante n'avait rien vu: Biribi* (1924). Roubaud joined Larique in the pages of *Détective* in 1934 and 1935 to expose the juvenile penal colonies, a subject that Larique also took up in the pages of the same magazine. Both Roubaud and Larique linked the adult penal system to the juvenile penal colonies, finding that these correctional facilities for minors were simply preparation for a life in Guyane. If these reporters had set out to locate Guyane, they were also placing Guyane and its prison within the larger French penal system.

Works cited

Assouline, Pierre. 2006 [1984]. *Gaston Gallimard. Un demi-siècle d'édition française*. Paris: Gallimard.

Béraud, Henri. 2007 [1927]. *Le Flâneur salarié*. Paris: Bartillat.

Boltanski, Luc. 1999. *Distant Suffering: Morality, Media and Politics*. Cambridge: Cambridge University Press.

Boucharenc, Myriam. 2004. *L'Écrivain-reporter au cœur des années trente*. Lille: Les Presses universitaires du Septentrion.

Danblon, Emmanuelle. 2005. *La Fonction persuasive. Anthropologie du discours rhétorique. Origines et actualité*. Paris: Armand Colin.

Datta, Venita. 2011. *Heroes and Legends of Fin-de-Siècle France: Gender, Politics, and National Identity*. New York: Cambridge University Press.

Dhur, Jacques. 1925. *Visions de bagne*. Paris: Ferenczi et fils.

Donat-Vincent, Danielle. 1992. *La Fin du bagne (1934–1953)*. Rennes: Ouest-France.

Foucault, Michel. 1975. *Surveiller et punir. Naissance de la prison*. Paris: Gallimard.

Godfroy, Marion. 2008. *Bagnards*. Paris: Tallandier.

Goffman, Erving. 1961. *Asylums: Essays on the Social Situation of Mental Patients and Other Inmates*. New York: Doubleday.

Kalifa, Dominique. 2013. *Les Bas-fonds. Histoire d'un imaginaire*. Paris: Seuil.

Larique, Marius. 1933. *Dans la brousse avec les évadés du bagne*. Paris: Gallimard.

Larique, Marius. 1933. *Les Hommes punis*. Paris: Gallimard.

Le Fèvre, Georges. 1925. *Bagnards et chercheurs d'or*. Paris: Ferenczi et fils.

Londres, Albert. 2007 [1924]. *Au bagne*. Paris: Privat/Le Rocher.

Londres, Albert. 2010 [1924]. *Dante n'avait rien vu: Biribi*. Paris: Arléa.

Miller, William Ian. 1997. *The Anatomy of Disgust*. Cambridge, MA: Harvard University Press.

Pierre, Michel. 2000. *Bagnards. La terre de la grande punition. Cayenne 1852–1953*. Paris: Autrement.

Pierre, Michel. 2007. 'Adieu Cayenne ou l'imaginaire du bagne', *Criminocorpus. Revue d'Histoire de la justice, des crimes et des peines*. http://criminocorpus.revues.org/227 (accessed 8 May 2015).

Roubaud, Louis. 1925. *Le Voleur et le sphinx*. Paris: Grasset.

Sanchez, Jean-Louis. 2014. 'L'Abolition de la relégation en Guyane française (1938–1953)', *Criminocorpus. Revue d'Histoire de la justice, des crimes et des peines*. https://criminocorpus.revues.org/2727 (accessed 18 March 2015).

Spieler, Miranda Frances. 2012. *Empire and Underworld: Captivity in French Guiana*. Cambridge, MA: Harvard University Press.

CHAPTER THREE

Kor and Karnival, the Carnal Road of Léon-Gontran Damas

'Evidence of Things Not Seen'

Kathleen Gyssels, Antwerp University

Con/text: The story of Damas's excision from the French-Caribbean canon

In the Creole language, the mother tongue of many French Caribbean poets and novelists, words that in French begin with the letter 'c' are written with 'k': *corps*, the concept of the body, is written with a 'k' (as is *carnaval*, in *karnival*) on murals and popular media. By replacing the French spelling with the Creole one in my title, I wish to emphasize the popular dimension of poetry that has been classified by many critics as 'simple'. It is indeed easy, transparent. Contemporaries of Léon Damas (Senghor, then Glissant), followed by a 'younger' generation of 'Creolists', labelled his poetry as easy to read, but they seemed to simultaneously reproach his open, violent challenge to French contestation of French supremacy, racism and European colonialism. By deeming Damas's poetry less sophisticated (than his own), Senghor damaged the other writer's posthumous reputation. As this judgement was reiterated by many later critics and authors from the (French) Caribbean, Damas disappeared from the literary scene. Indeed, Senghor's statement was repeated by Glissant,[1] who places the *aîné* (elder) Damas alongside the

1 '*The imposition of lived rhythms*. That is, orality finally recognized as a

Haitian, Jacques Roumain, from the *indigéniste* movement and the Cuban, Nicolas Guillèn. Favouring orality, these poets innerve their writing with the rhythm of their native spoken traditions. Dismissed for being insufficiently opaque, Damas's apparently simple, transparent poetry in reality opens the way to racial and gender ambiguity in a way that has gone unnoticed by French-Caribbean authors. New readings and approaches are indeed required so that this modernist avant-garde poet, with links to surrealism and dadaism, and neglected by subsequent generations of Antillanité and Créolité, can finally be rehabilitated. For Confiant and Chamoiseau, Damas is a minor poet in an inconsequential branch of literature, so much so that his name was omitted from the Index of *Lettres créoles* (1991, 191). This omission is a strange one, and perhaps signifies that they listed Damas in another kind of index—their blacklist. Writing *kor* (for *corps*/body) and karnival (for *carnaval*/carnival), Damas's openly violent and militant poetry opposed not only 'white' values and French assimilationist politics, but also the homophobia against and ostracism of a minority within a minority: the homosexual person of colour. As a matter of fact, the third cofounder of Négritude, according to Lubabu Tshitenge (2012), primarily addressed his own audience. Like Desnos, he sought to 'désintellectualiser la poésie' (to simplify poetry) so that the message could at least be understood by (local/international) readers back home. Yet that does not mean that all poems are without hidden meanings, double readings, ambiguity. Emphasising bodily discomfort and the rituals of his native Guyane which permitted (enslaved) Afro-Caribbeans to liberate themselves from the many legacies of centuries of slavery, colonialism and French supremacy, Damas appears, on the contrary, to be an extraordinary precursor. His poetry crosses the many borders which confined the coloured individual. Starting with the 'colour line' (see DuBois), he questioned the social boundaries in French society and European societies at large. 'Class' was a second battleground of the Négritude movement, as Césaire clearly stated in many of his essays. Yet the third line remained: the gender issue. It is here that Damas opened a door which many of the French Caribbeans (and Caribbeans more broadly) who followed him have not dared to discuss. Damas befriended André Gide and Langston Hughes (see Graham and Walters, 2010), was edited by Guy Lévis Mano and

forceful presence to the extent that it became the nerve centre of Damas's and Guillén's writing, thereby giving birth to the movement that would support the great thrust in Creole writing' (Glissant, 1989, 154).

inserted an epigraph by Claude McKay into his début work. For him, Black (like white) masculinity was highly determined by social and racial circumstances and constraints. Understanding 'gender' as a socio-racial construction, Damas not only favoured equality between the sexes, but also promoted the acceptance and respect of all differences, including homosexual and bisexual identities.

When Cayenne-born Christiane Taubira, as Minister of Justice, quoted from *Black-Label* (1956) and 'Grand comme un besoin de changer d'air' (from *Nostalgies*, 1966, in *Pigments. Névralgies*, 1972), reactions were glaringly absent in (French-)Caribbean (literary or other) milieux. Surprisingly, many Caribbean scholars seemed unaware of this strong defence for equal marriage by a Black female minister. Others whom I questioned, and who are familiar with Damas's poetry, warned me against jumping to conclusions. In an exchange with Christian Filostrat, in which I asked for his reaction to Christiane Taubira's quotation of Damas in the explosive context of the gay marriage debate, this personal friend of Damas responded:

> she cited '*Black-Label*' by Léon-Gontran Damas, a founding father of the Negritude cultural movement, and a native, like Taubira, of Cayenne, French Guiana. 'We the wretched, we the worthless, we the nothings, we the dogs, we the skeletons, we the Negros, what are we waiting for? What are we waiting for, to play the fools, to piss on this life, stupid and beastly, that is imposed upon us?' she asked with evocative cadence. 'Not according equality, not recognizing liberty, is the same as saying to the French people, "What are you waiting for to play the fools against this stupid and beastly life that is imposed upon you?" She could have cited the same thing about anybody who was being persecuted. It's not because she cited that during the gay-marriage debate that you think Damas was gay?[2]

In this essay I specifically argue that Damas was not 'gay', but that he nevertheless supported his friends who suffered from a 'double dilemma': being Black and non-heterosexual. His last collection of poetry, *Mine de riens*, never published during his life, although it was finished well before his death in 1978 and recited for Christian Filostrat, hinted at the last lines to cross in a White, male-dominated world. Unsatisfied with struggling to bring down the 'colour line', the Guyanais poet also wanted to move class (social) and gender lines. The collection *Mine de riens*,[3] retitled as *Dernière escale*, seems to unravel the taboos

2 Christian Filostrat, email communication, 29 August 2014.

3 Damas left a lot of unpublished and even unfinished works in Washington:

of interracial and same-sex relations, and this, indeed, even in an age of transgression (Helman, 1984).

While I am by no means claiming that Damas was gay—as one critic interpreted in a severe response to my comparison of Damas's *Black-Label* and Baldwin's *Giovanni's Room*—I propose to reread some of his most famous poems (taken from *Pigments*, *Névralgies* and *Black-Label*) from an alternative, gender-sensitive perspective. Taking into account the significant taboos surrounding interracial sex and the sexual abuses suffered by colonized men, women and children alike, I propose to look more attentively at bodily matters, gender issues and the enduring effect and impact of those on Black masculinity (due to constraints of space, I omit femininity from my discussion, although Damas was also sensitive to feminine, and even feminist, issues). Forged by the double trauma of deportation and slavery, Damas's intimate reflections allow for several interpretations: the brutal dehumanization of Black men and women implied a reversal of traditional definitions and performances of 'heterosexual' subjectivity and masculinity/femininity.

Rebelling against the establishment and against the idea of the 'Nègre gréco-latin', which became an ideal for many of his generation, Damas also fought against the ways in which oppression resulted in malaise when it came to one's behaviour in the presence of a White fe/male. While Fanon addressed this problem, he nevertheless refused to reflect upon homosexuality and other so-called 'deviations' in connection with the colonial condition (see Silverman, 2005). Arriving as an adolescent in Meaux, Damas was often confronted with the difficulties of performing Black maleness in a racist, White male-dominated world. The Cayenne poet translated this 'gender trouble' in his early poems and would tackle the question of 'trouble dans le genre', to use Butler's apt title (2005), in the collections of poetry which followed: subsequent editions of *Pigments* and *Graffiti*, and in his own *Anthology* (including 'Tu étais au bar' from *Black-Label*). Reading the famous sequence, one could argue that it evokes 'fatal attraction', the love at first sight operating between same-sex individuals:

—TU ETAIS AU BAR

et moi
—parmi d'autres—
à même la piste enduite

L'Écot de la race, a collection of poetry and *Plusieurs vie en une*, an essay, are still waiting to be published.

et patinée de steps
de stomps
de slows
de songs
de sons
de blues
   Et de la table où un Blanc à lunettes
s'ennuyait à lire un journal son journal
je te regardais boire un Canadian Club
   Fasciné peut-être
soudain ton regard
affronta le mien
mais de toi ou de moi qui déjà n'étions
qu'un seul beau désir insatisfait
je ne sais plus lequel
vint au-devant de l'Autre
alors que l'orchestre scandait
Esclavo soy.[4]

Damas realized that gender roles had been imposed upon slaves in the plantation economy in such a way as to emphasize male features in the female sex, and macho behaviour in the male sex as a compensation for the absence of authority and power in the Black man. He borrowed the *racial and cross-gender* style from his idol, Langston Hughes. From his first collection, the banned *Pigments* (1937), Damas offered elements to dismantle binaries such as male vs female, Black vs White, Africa vs Europe. One must also remember in this context that Damas claimed to be a 'Fils de trois fleuves' (the son of three rivers) and that his Amerindian background already offered explanations for different definitions and constructions of manhood and femininity. Lévi-Strauss (in a posthumous text published in *Le Nouvel Obs* in the

4 '—YOU WERE AT THE BAR / and me too / —among others— / on a level with the floor plastered / and skated with steps / with stomps / with slows / with songs / with sounds / with blues / And from the table where a White man in glasses / was bored with reading a newspaper *his* newspaper / I was watching you drink a Canadian Club / Fascinated perhaps / suddenly your eyes / sparred with mine / but of you or me that were already / but a single beautiful unsatisfied desire / I no longer know which / came towards the Other / while the band was striking / I am a slave' [Spanish in original]. Translation by K. Gyssels, Femi Ojo-Ade and Christine Pagnoulle, an unpublished translation of *Black-Label*, forbidden by the ayant droit Marcel Bibas and Sandrine Poujols, Gallimard refuses the rights to translate *Black-Label* in its entirety.

context of the equal marriage debate, 2013) and his disciple, Françoise Héritier (2003), had already paved the way for contravening dichotomies of the male-female *binôme* as a result of their ethnographic research in the Guianas. Moving beyond antagonisms of 'race', class and gender, the third man of Négritude transcends the movement's confines. Instead of being in the shadow of Senghor and Césaire, one could rehabilitate Damas for his claim, in addition to his African heritage, combined with European and Amerindian, and even Asian elements (given the Chinese features discernible in his face) something otherwise difficult to trace back in one's genealogy. Damas acknowledged his ancestry through the 'red-skinned' Galibi—'la Tigresse des hauts Plateaux' (the tigress of the high plains) living on the border of the Orénoque (*Black-Label*, 63), the 'Roucouyennes' (*Black-Label*, 21) playing 'une flûte en tibia' (a bone flute, *Black-Label*, 31) and 'flûte de bambou' (*Black-Label*, 45)—as he claimed his 'black dolls' in 'Limbé'. That poem appeared in *Negro Digest* (February 1972):

> Rendez-les moi mes poupées noires
> que je joue avec elles
> les jeux naïfs de mon instinct
> resté à l'ombre de ses lois
> recouvrés mon courage
> mon audace
> redevenu moi-même.[5]

The English translation is often given the title 'Borders', and thus does not preserve the important concept of 'Limbo', referring to the limbo-dance and the limbo-space (explored by Wilson Harris, 2008). Next to the many interpretations of this poem as a nostalgic cry for Africa, I draw your attention to the fact that the black doll is also a toy for girls, and that it refers to the non-White fe/male partner for whose company and intimacy he yearns, feeling ridiculous and small. In other words, he performs nonetheless as the 'fe/male' child who wants to play innocently with the surrogate female toy to satisfy his sensual and sexual needs.

5 'Give me back my black dolls / so that I may play with them / the naïve games of my instinct / in the darkness of its laws / once I have recovered / my courage / and my audacity / and become myself once more'.

Africa ransacked: l'afrique et l'africaine *kambriolée*

In perhaps his most famous poem (after 'Hoquet', 'Solde' and 'Limbé'), 'Ils sont venus ce soir' (*Pigments* 1972 ed.), Damas portrays the invasion of the European colonizer as a turning point in the African mind. Not only will the arrival of the 'barbarians' stop the drumbeat of African dancers and worshippers; the invasion of the White intruders will forever destroy the gatherings and ritual ceremonies of dances, songs and drums:

ILS SONT VENUS CE SOIR[6]

ils sont venus ce soir où le tam tam
roulait de rythme en
rythme
la frénésie des yeux
la frénésie des mains
la frénésie
des pieds de statues
DEPUIS
combien de MOI MOI MOI
sont morts
depuis qu'ils sont venus ce soir où le
tamtam roulait de
rythme en
rythme
la frénésie
des yeux
la frénésie
des mains
la frénésie
des pieds de statues.[7]

6 Read by Senghor at http://www.assemblee-nationale.fr/histoire/aime-cesaire/damas-photo.asp.

7 All quotations in French from *Pigments* and *Névralgies* are from *Présence Africaine's 1962* edition. The English translation by Alessandra Lillehei (2012) reads as follows: 'THEY CAME THAT NIGHT/ They came that night when the / tom / tom / rolled / from / rhythm/ to / rhythm / the frenzy / of eyes / the frenzy of hands / the frenzy / of statues' feet / SINCE / how many of ME ME ME / have died / since they came that night when the / tom / tom / rolled from / rhythm / to / rhythm / the frenzy …'. The French term *moisson* (to which Damas alludes) disappears in translation: this is a term recurrent in Damas's mind as it was indicated as the title of an unpublished anthology: *L'Écot de la race*.

The poet denounces manslaughter, ransacking and genocidal violence, and laments the unknown number of victims who have continued to fall, long after arrival of the colonizer. In the first poem of *Pigments*, Damas accuses the White invader of destroying and raping, violating and plundering the African continent and its population. Senghor very much appreciated this particular poem for its African rhythm and its evocation of communal rituals, so much so that Damas added 'To Senghor' in the final edition.[8] However, by complimenting Damas on the African beat, Senghor somewhat glossed over the actual event portrayed in 'Ils sont venus ce soir'. 'EtCaetera' also denounces the kind of spoliation and dispossession of both men and women in Africa as well as in the Diaspora. Damas in fact crosses generational and gender lines, and even those upholding the hierarchy of the French army.

In Damas's mind, the whole history of colonialism comes down to a single concept: the *cambriolage* of slaves by their masters, including the 'theft' of all types of wealth by the colonizer from the colonized. In his lexicon, *kambrioler* functions almost as the equivalent of the (English) 'F-word'. In *French Négritude Poets* by Conroy-Kennedy (1975, 39–61) and *Black Writers in French* (1991) by the Belgian, Lilyan Kesteloot, the verb *cambrioler* translates as 'ransacking'. The verb does not have the stringent corporeal meaning of *fouiller* (to frisk), nor that of *cambrioler* (to burgle). Etymologically, *cambrioler* derives from the Occitan *camber*, which means 'room' (*chambre*); it is the intimate space where atrocities take place between White master and Black slave:

> Le sauront-ils jamais cette rancune de mon cœur
> A l'œil de la méfiance ouvert trop tard
> Ils ont *cambriolé* l'espace qui était le mien. (*Pigments*, 44)

Speaking of his own private space, his own *kor*, the poet may be hinting here at sexual harassment and abuse. Consider 'Si souvent', in which the young child regrets not being able to 'sucer le pouce du sorcier en soutane' (*Pigments*), an obscure scene echoed in *Black-Label* where he portrays himself dressed as a choirboy. His innocence has been 'maculated' and spoiled by a third presence (the priest who prefers the 'enfant de chœur' 'caramel' instead of the 'white' choirboy,

8 The same poem, however, could also demonstrate the jazzy beat which Damas's friend the Belgian jazz specialist, Robert Goffin, emphasized in the new preface for the second and definite edition of *Pigments* published by Présence Africaine in 1962.

Black-Label, 38). Moreover, this lament is followed immediately by the confession that his heart (in French, *chœur*—choir—and *cœur*—heart—are homonyms) is 'marinated in the alcohol that no one wanted to touch at the table': 'mon cœur mariné dans l'alcool / dont personne n'a voulu tâter à table' (*Black-Label*, 39). As a result of mistreatment, a wounded diasporic male subject seeks consolation in rum and ruminations.

The *kambriolage*, Damas maintains in his anti-war poems, not only concerns men, but indirectly also women, as they see their husbands, brothers and fathers sacrificed in a war that is not theirs. As proof of generosity and subordination, the colonized subject is supposed to fight for the (former) colonizer's peace (still comprised of their nation, and thus their reign continues). Damas openly condemns the enrolment of coloured troops, and specifically, Senegalese soldiers in the French army. As well as speaking of the Senegalese *détachement* in general, it might well be that Damas was referring to one of the *tirailleurs sénégalais* in particular, namely Senghor. The latter replies with his liminary poem in *Hosties noires*, repudiating Damas's mistrust and pessimism: he, on the contrary, believes that the (Senegalese/African/Antillean) seeds which fell in the ground will never be futile, sown in vain, or their names forgotten. A strong divide can indeed be noted between the Francophile Senghor (the first Black member of the Académie française), falling well within the lines, and Damas, whose lifestyle, convictions and (failed) political career was ultimately relegated to the margins.

Senegal, stepmother of coloured soldiers

France's 'jewel' on the West African coast served as a machine for producing soldiers for France's war. Moreover, this 'service' was made possible by the help and complicity of Black and coloured governors (like Félix Éboué) in the highest ranks of the French colonial administration. One only has to read 'EtCaetera' and 'Ils sont venus' side by side: the invasion of Africa introduced the 'Middle Passage', the beginning of the French/transatlantic slave trade. The French colony would subsequently be used as a giant 'factory' for new slaves and serfs (before becoming a *décharge* (deposit) for waste from Europe in postcolonial times):

ET CAETERA

Devant la menace allemande, les Anciens Combattants Sénégalais adressent un câblogramme d'indéfectible attachement. (Les Journaux)

Aux Anciens Combattants Sénégalais

aux Futurs Combattants Sénégalais
à tout ce que le Sénégal peut accoucher
de combattants sénégalais futurs anciens
de quoi-je-me-mêle futurs anciens
de mercenaires futurs anciens
de pensionnés
de galonnés
de décorés
de décavés
de grands blessés
de mutilés
de calcinés
de gangrenés …

Moi je leur demande
de taire le besoin qu'ils ressentent
de piller
de voler
de violer
de souiller à nouveau les bords antiques
du Rhin

Moi je leur demande
de commencer par envahir le Sénégal

Moi je leur demande
de foutre aux « Boches » la paix.[9]

9 'In response to the German threat, Senegalese veterans send a telegram of unwavering commitment.' (The Newspapers) / To Veteran Senegalese Combatants / to Future Senegalese Combatants / to all that Senegal can birth / of future veteran Senegalese combatants / of future veteran what-did-I-get-mixed-up-in / of future veteran mercenaries / of pensioned / of tasselled / of decorated / of wretched / of gravely wounded / of maimed / of burned / of gangrened … / Me I ask them / to say nothing of the need that they feel / to pillage / to rob / to rape / to defile again the ancient banks / of the Rhine / Me I ask them / to begin by invading Senegal / Me I ask them / to fucking make peace with the "Germans"'. Damas thus identifies the White settler and the French colon as fascists who would one day 'eat' all of him and push him: 'De piller / De voler / De violer / De *souiller* à nouveau les *bords antiques* du Rhin' (*Pigments*, 79–80; emphasis added).

It seems to me that Damas indirectly hints at Senghor who, although imprisoned by the Nazis, would later still defend European values and the French 'civilisation de l'universel'. Having been colonized by the French, Senghor still thought that the Senegalese ought to be loyal to the Metropole and continue to make sacrifices, while Damas strongly opposed this idea, as well as that of Françafrique which the first president of Sénégal served so loyally.[10] For Damas, on the other hand, it was necessary to bring to light the fact that, apart from the material damage and ransacking of Africa, there was a further, lingering trauma among men and women of African descent. This was the thick knot in his throat which wanted to unravel the humiliation that Black men and women had incorporated bodily. In Damas's mind, (mother) Africa had been raped and continued to be despoiled, her children systematically dispossessed of their dignity. Men were infantilized and womanized while, on the other hand, women had to act as men in the plantation universe. Reversal and inversion became the sad reality of Africa's diaspora: women were forced to act like men and men felt obliged to compensate for their lack of 'masculinity' by acting in a masculine fashion.

The bleached and emasculated Negro

Blanchi
(Pour Christiane et Alioune Diop)
Se peut-il donc qu'ils osent
me traiter de blanchi
alors que tout en moi
aspire à n'être que nègre
autant que mon Afrique
qu'ils ont cambriolée
Blanchi
Abominable injure
qu'ils me paieront fort cher
quand mon Afrique qu'ils ont cambriolée

10 In frank and sarcastic verse, Damas protests against 'Françafrique' (a neocolonial set of arrangements involving French intervention in African affairs). After the Second World War and the dismantling of the French colonies in West Africa, Senghor would found the *Organisation internationale de la Francophonie* with President of Tunisia Habib Bourguiba and the Vietnamese king Norodom Sihanouk.

voudra la paix la paix rien que
la paix
Blanchi
Ma haine grossit en marge
de leur scélératesse
en marge
des coups de fusil
en marge
des coups de roulis
des négriers
des cargaisons fétides de l'esclavage cruel
Blanchi
Ma haine grossit en marge
de la culture
en marge
des théories
en marge des bavardages
dont on a cru devoir me bourrer au berceau
alors que tout en moi aspire à n'être que nègre
autant que mon Afrique qu'ils ont *cambriolée*.[11]

'Robbed' is not a strong enough translation for *cambrioler*, a word that hints at violent intrusion (penetration of bodily parts). *Dernière escale* recycles the traumatic and terrifying figure of the priest, an authoritarian and abusive adult who (like the schoolteacher) terrifies his pupils. A strong awareness of segregation and the imperative not to cross colour, social and gender lines are recycled in 'Je le confesse mon Révérend'. Yet Damas crossed the tenuous line of gender trouble in the Caribbean, most visibly in 'De la profonde et diffuse odeur', as well as in several poems in which he speaks in a female voice ('nos règles / nos lunes / nos périodes, nos menstrues', *Dernière escale*, 99).[12]

11 'Can it be that they dare / call me whitewashed / when everything in me / aspires only to be nègre / like my Africa / that they have robbed / Whitewashed / Abominable insult / which they will pay dearly for / when my Africa / that they have robbed / wishes for peace peace nothing but / peace / Whitewashed / My hatred grows in the fringes / of their villainy / in the fringes / of the gun shots / in the fringes / of the rolling shots / of slave ships / of the reeking cargos of cruel slavery / Whitewashed / My hatred grows in the fringes / of the culture / in the fringes / of the theories / in the fringes of the gossip / they thought they had to stuff me with in the cradle / when everything in me aspires to be nothing but nègre / like my Africa that they have robbed' (translation from Alessandra Lillehey, 2012).

12 See http://www.leondamas-mine-de-rien.com/

The knotted Negro[13]

What does the pronoun *ça* in the last line of 'Hoquet' refer to? What is the 'that' which 'mulattos' don't do? With the 'mulatto' belief of their superiority to the dark-skinned, the individual of mixed descent grows up with disdain for darker men or women. Not only do racial and sexual inequality exist in the Caribbean, but colour prejudice and miscegenation are direct and related consequences of Africa's ransacking by Europe. By repeatedly insisting on 'ransacking' and the 'robbing of' (the French *fouiller*), Damas hints at another kind of spoliation. The overt sexual connotation gives a stringent meaning to Damas's plea: a recognition of the *queer* Other, the homosexual, the bisexual or even the transgender. It seems, finally, that Christiane Taubira was reading across the lines of Damas's poetry. She slammed:

Nous les gueux
Nous les peu
Nous les chiens
Nous les riens
Nous les maigres
Nous les nègres
Qu'attendons-nous ...
Pour faire les fous
Pour pisser un coup
Sur cette vie
Stupide et bête
Qui nous est faite.[14]

In her function as Garde des Sceaux (*sceaux*, incidentally, being pronounced in the same way as *sots*—fools, madmen—a synonym for *fous*), the Minister of Justice understood that Damas was hinting at a strong taboo which had the potential to drive wo/men mad. Slamming a stanza from *Black-Label*, she explored the resonances of his surname, Damas. Indeed, the writer from Guyane, uprooted and exiled, also played verbal tricks with his surname. Firstly, in Portuguese,

13 Damas was aware that in Amerindian cultures the knot served to measure time, as in the Aztec and Mayan calendar. The knot also comes close to describing *branchement* (connection) in the sense of mixed cultures in the 'New World'. See Amselle (1990, 1999, 2001).

14 The recording of Taubira's citation from *Black-Label* (which deviated slightly from the original text) is widely available online.

the language of Guyane's neighbour, Brazil, *damas* means 'women'. Secondly, the Biblical image of the road to Damascus (in French, *Damas*) acquires additional symbolic meaning. Finally, the image of iron chains resonates in the poet's surname: the noun *damas* refers to an iron used to forge weapons, but it also links to the knots measuring distance at sea,[15] and to textile knots (*damassé*, *fibré*). The cord to hang oneself, aside from lynching and suicide, is a recurrent motif in *Black-Label*, a collection pervaded by images of death.[16]

Added to these initial wrongs were humiliation, beating, harassment and violation of the women and men brought to the countries of their masters. These additional wrongs, as Fanon argued, inspired in Africa's children immense long-term shame and distrust of themselves. Consequently, many would accept that abject condition of denying their blackness and masculinity, a result of the lingering trauma of lynching:

> 'S.O.S.'
> vous les verrez ...
> mais froidement
> matraquer
> descendre
> étendre
> et couper leur sexe aux nègres
> pour en faire des bougies pour leurs églises.[17]

In the posthumous collection, all those torments are knots interwoven in the posthumous collection *Dernière escale*. Existential crises engendered by the three lines—race, class and gender—are woven together in what his colleagues have described as simple poetry. In *Countermodernism* (see Walker, 1999, 14), Damas appears as an anthropologist,[18] poet and politician ahead of his time.

15 In *Black-Label*, Damas measures the extreme distance between him and his homeland, Africa: 'A des milles et des milles' (unpublished translation by Gyssels, Ojo-Ade and Pagnoulle).

16 The image of the *corbillard* (hearse) appears in Movement One (*Black-Label*, 27).

17 'You will see them ... / coldly beating up / knocking down / laying out / the blacks / cutting off their genitals / to make candles for their churches'. See Warner (1988, 77), which remains to date the only collection of essays devoted to Damas in English.

18 Damas's *Retour de Guyane* (1938), written following an anthropological 'mission' to Guyane, was banned by the French authorities: it did not in any way meet their expectations of a positive 'balance' with respect to the impact of French

There is a correlation between this particular poem and the defence of gay couples as voted by the National Assembly in 2014. In her speech to the Assembly in January of that year,[19] Christiane Taubira quoted further from 'Grand comme un besoin de changer d'air' to conclude her defence of *queerness* in the Republic. In doing so, she made two things clear: not that Damas was gay (as a reviewer of my comparison between *Giovanni's Room* and *Black-Label* claimed), but that he stood with his fellow men and women striving for tolerance of their queerness. ('Passing' and queering are analogous, as Butler made clear in *Bodies that Matter* (1993) when analysing *Passing* by Nella Larsen.) 'Grand comme un besoin de changer d'air' alludes to a triumph finally obtained after a long, hard battle, while images of red roses and an Eiffel Tower decorated with them point to the 'third zone' of sexual particularity. While Bhabha considers 'third space' as in-betweenness—beyond dichotomies constructed by the imperial and colonial empire—Damas adds a third race ('fils de trois fleuves'), a third class (the 'pieds-plats' and the 'pieds-nus' in the capital, strongly supportive of the *mouvement ouvrier*, *porte-parole* of the working class, independent of their colour) as a finishing touch: see his poem 'While Waiting' for a defence of the third sex.

Damas's third way was not clearly (or only) macho, like Caribbean males trained over centuries. It was instead like an effeminate and tender male who can understand the 'soul's sister'. Befriending Langston Hughes (see Shane and Waters, 2010),[20] Andrew Salkey (author of the queer novel *Escape to an Autumn Pavement* (1960), editor of the anthology *Breaklight: Poets of the Caribbean* (1973) and correspondent of Damas),

colonization in the countries concerned. Moreover, Damas became sick of the 'prénotions / notions / présomptions' and theorizing about the 'Other' in the French intellectual circles in which he had himself participated.

19 See http://www.dailymotion.com/video/xx5f7j_discours-d-ouverture-du-debat-sur-le-mariage-pour-tous_news?fb_action_ids=10151348089644064&fb_action_types=og.likes&fb_ref=.URG1EYT2sNQ.like&fb_source=aggregation&fb_aggregation_id=288381481237582#.URN9O6XWgeO.

20 In the Foreword to *Mine de riens* (posthumously published in 2012 as *Dernière escale*), Hughes writes that: 'Usually poets have their fingers on the emotional pulse of their peoples, of their homelands. Traditionally, poets are lyric historians. From the days of the bards and the troubadours, the songs of the poets have been not only songs, but often records of the most mobbing events, the deepest thoughts and most profound emotional currents of their times. To understand Africa today, it is wise to listen to what its poets say' (11).

Alain Locke, Countee Cullen, Claude McKay (*Pigments*' exergue was taken from McKay's 'To the White Fiends': see Gyssels, 2008), Damas bridged literature in different languages by Africans, Caribbeans and African Americans. It is surprising that Taubira's eloquent quoting of Damas has not elicited reactions in Martinique, Guadeloupe or Guyane. No praise for her action or resurrection of the third man of Négritude was forthcoming. This supports Murray's (2010) insights into the pervasiveness of homophobia in Antillean society, observations further confirmed by scholars and artists alike across the Caribbean.[21]

Conclusion

> Chiens pouilleux
> Chiens galeux
> Chiens dressés à se vautrer à se la manger eux-mêmes
> la queue qu'ils avaient reçue en legs. (*Dernière escale*)[22]

Ahead of his time, Damas had the courage and the obstinate audacity to address issues which were unmentionable and disrespectful. His *Dernière escale* provides further proof of the sexual ambiguities which remained one cause of frustration and alienation for Caribbean subjects in European society. Firstly, Glissant's Antillanité movement and the subsequent Créolité movement of Confiant and Chamoiseau overlooked gender imbalances and inequalities between Caribbean men and women, as if they did not want to be accused of being *macoumè* (Creole for 'homosexual'). Today, this in-between zone, or 'third sex', remains a blind spot in French-Caribbean theory, debate and fiction. For example, it is quite surprising that across the entire careers of Glissant and the defenders of Créolité,[23] alternative ways of outing one's sexual nature are not present (see Tinsley, 2010). This signifies Martinique's complicity

21 For instance, Thomas Glave, who claims in *Among the Bloodpeople: Politics and Flesh* that Jamaican gays suffer extreme violence, being publicly beaten and killed, with the complicity of the police.

22 Posthumous edition, retitled as *Dernière escale* by Sandrine Poujols and Marcel Bibas, Paris, Le Regard du Texte, December 2012, 117. Christian Filostrat has posted the entire collection of Damas's poetry at www.leondamasminesderien.com.

23 Only in *Biblique des derniers gestes* (2002) would Chamoiseau develop the theme of same-sex relations and cross-dressing with the character of Nicolas Deborah, a man disguised in female clothes.

with Fanon's statement on homosexuality, as well as a deliberate passing over of this Guyanais author who, on numerous occasions, evokes the 'crossroads' as a place of choices and doubts, a liminal space where different options and possibilities render the I/subject hesitant. While Damas's relatively small body of writing addresses the gap between the sexes and the blatantly misogynistic, masculinist dominance, the Martiniquan 'creolists' maintain a line between masculinist and feminist behaviour. Moreover, they maintain a fourth line, between male and female writing, given the exclusion of female members from their 'movement'. By doing so, they draw a line between an elitist (male) culture (Glissant) in the *départements d'outre-mer* and a more popular, rural, female culture, as Condé perceives correctly in several of her interviews. Both Césaire and Senghor, but also Glissant, were almost gender-blind or pretended to be so; they eschewed the troubles and torments of poets and artists who had to write their 'impasse double', their tenuous secrets, between the lines or on the walls. A generation oppressed by a 'double impasse'—that is, to be Black and to be non-heteronormative, was silenced. As a go-between for the African-American diaspora and the Francophone diaspora, a close friend of Langston Hughes and protégé of André Gide, Damas was aware of both this and another by-product of centuries of repression: disgust at the Black body. Beyond material deprivation in terms of the long-lasting effects of discrimination, there was also the hesitation about sexual/gender performance, and the spectre of fear of White women. It is to this taboo that Damas alludes (*Névralgies*, 133); the 'vérité terminus, terminale, terminée'.[24]

Works cited

Baldwin, James. 1956. *Giovanni's Room*, London: Albert Deutsch.

Bhabha, Homi. 1994. *The Location of Culture*. London: Routledge.

Butler, Judith. 1993. *Bodies that Matter: On the Discursive Limits of 'Sex'*. London: Routledge.

Butler, Judith. 2005. *Trouble dans le genre. Le féminisme et la subversion de l'identité*, trans. Cynthia Krauss. Paris: Editions La Découverte.

Chamoiseau, Patrick. 2002. *Biblique des derniers gestes*. Paris: Gallimard.

24 'Terminus, terminal, terminated truth'.

Chamoiseau, Patrick and Raphaël Confiant, eds. 1991. *Lettres créoles. Tracées antillaises et continentales de la littérature (1635–1975)*. Paris: Hatier.

Conroy-Kennedy, Ellen. 1975. *The Negritude Poets: An Anthology of Translations from the French*. New York: Thunder Mouth's Press.

Damas, Léon-Gontran. 1956. *Black-Label*. Paris: Gallimard.

Damas, Leon-Gontran. 1961 [1948]. *African Songs, of Love, War, Grief and Abuse*, trans. Ulli Beier and Miriam Koshland. Ibadan, Nigeria: Mbari Publications.

Damas, Léon-Gontran. 1962. *Pigments, édition définitive*. Paris: Présence Africaine.

Damas, Léon-Gontran, ed. 1966. *Nouvelle Somme de poésie du monde noir*. Paris: Présence Africaine.

Damas, Léon-Gontran. 1972. *Pigments. Névralgies*. Paris: Présence Africaine.

Damas, Léon-Gontran. 2003 [1938]. *Retour de Guyane. Suivi de Misère Noire, et autres écrits journalistiques*. Paris: Jean-Michel Place.

Damas, Léon-Gontran. 2012. *Dernière escale*, ed. Sandrine Poujols and Marcel Bibas. Paris: le Regard du Temps.

Damas, Léon-Gontran. Unpublished. *La Moisson des trois domaines (nouveaux contes)*.

DuBois, W.E.B. 1903. *The Souls of Black Folk*. Chicago: A.C. McClurg.

Glave, Thomas. 2014. *Among the Bloodpeople: Politics and Flesh*. New York: Akashic Books.

Glissant, Edouard. 1989. *Caribbean Discourse: Selected Essays*, trans. J. Michael Dash. Charleston: Virginia University Press, 1989.

Graham, Shane and John Walters, eds. 2010. *Langston Hughes and the South African Drum Generation: The Correspondence*. New York: Palgrave Macmillan.

Gyssels, Kathleen. 2008. 'Damas et McKay et les "démons blancs"', in *Harlem heritage: mémoire et renaissance*. Paris: Riveneuve, 219–227.

Harris, Wilson. 2008. 'History, fable and myth in the Caribbean and Guianas', *Caribbean Quarterly* 54.1–2: 5–38.

Helman, Albert. 1984. *Hoofden van de Oyapock!* The Hague: Nijgh & Van Ditmar.

Héritier, Françoise. 2003. 'Une anthropologie symbolique du corps', *Journal des africanistes* 73.2: 9–26.

Kesteloot, Lilyan. 1991. *Black Writers in French: A Literary History of Negritude*. Washington, DC: Howard University Press.

Lévi-Strauss, Claude. 2013. 'La Procréation assistée vue par C. Lévi-Strauss', *Le Nouvel Observateur*, 24 March 2013. http://bibliobs.nouvelobs.com/essais/20130311.OBS1499/la-procreation-assistee-vue-par-levi-strauss.html (accessed 1 July 2013).

Lillehey, Alessandra. 2012. *Pigments in Translation*. MA dissertation, Wesleyan College.

Murray, David. 2010. 'Homosexuality, society and the state: An ethnography of sublime resistance', in *Perspectives on the Caribbean: A Reader in Culture, History, and Representation*, ed. Philip Scher, 77–93. Oxford: Wiley-Blackwell.

Salkey, Andrew. 1973. *Breaklight: Poets of the Caribbean*. New York: Anchor Books.

Salkey, Andrew. 2009 [1960]. *Escape to an Autumn Pavement*, intro. Thomas Glave. London: Peepal Press.

Silverman, Max, ed. 2005. *Frantz Fanon's* Black Skin, White Masks*: New Interdisciplinary Essays*. Manchester: Manchester University Press.

Tinsley, O. Natasha. 2010. *Thiefing Sugar: Eroticism between Women in Caribbean Literature*. London: Duke University Press.

Walker, Keith. 1999. *Countermodernism and Francophone Literary Culture: The Game of Slipknot*. London: Duke University Press.

Warner, Keith Q., ed. 1988. *Critical Perspectives on Léon-Gontran Damas*. Washington, DC: Three Continents Press.

PART II

Colonial Locations: Imperialism and the Production of Place

CHAPTER FOUR

Frontier Politics

French, Portuguese and Amerindian Alliances between the Amazon and Cayenne, 1680–1697

Silvia Espelt-Bombin, University of Exeter[1]

Gomes Freire de Andrade, the Governor and *capitão-geral* of Maranhão (1685–1687), was convinced that establishing forts in Cabo do Norte, the area between the Amazon, Parú and Oyapock rivers, would help protect Portugal's interests. In a letter to the king written from São Luís do Maranhão on October 1685, he identified the old site of Torrego on the northern bank of the Amazon and the mouth of the River Araguarí as the most strategically advantageous position to build the forts. He also stated that to counteract French presence and secure the Cabo do Norte, it was key to befriend the Tucujús, the Amerindian group that lived around the location called Torrego. The Tucujús were well known to the Portuguese, to the point that they named that geographical space the 'sertão dos Tucujús' (backlands of the Tucujús). Andrade had singled them out among other Amerindians due to the fact that he considered them the bravest 'nação' and because 'sem Indios não é possível que nos

1 I am grateful to Pablo Ibáñez Bonillo, Roberto Rezende, Tomi Bartole and Mark Harris for comments on this and earlier versions of this text. This work was funded by a Leverhulme Trust Research Project Grant (RPG-2012-699), a British Academy/Leverhulme Small Research Grant (SG132847, 2014–2015) and the Sir Ernest Cassel Educational Trust Fund.

conquistem, nem nos deffendamos ...'.[2] Andrade's statement highlights three key aspects that I will address in this chapter: European rivalry over the land and rivers between the Amazon and the Oyapock; the European need for Amerindian assistance and their active pursuit of it; and the fact that the region under consideration remained mostly outside European control and, for the most part, under the influence of several Amerindian groups.

The few publications that deal with the centuries-long process of drawing the frontier between the Portuguese and French empires (Reis, 1993; Malafaia, 2002; Silva and Rückert, 2009) tend to focus on the diplomatic relations and international arbitration in regard to the establishment of this frontier, while overlooking the alliances and conflicts between Amerindian groups and Europeans, and how these interactions shaped the history of this region.[3] Were Amerindians unable to define their future and manipulated by Europeans, enslaved and decimated, or were they the main actors in French-Portuguese frontier politics in the late seventeenth century? Scholarship suggests the latter (Farage, 1986; Whitehead, 1988; Thornton, 2012, 248–311).

In this chapter I show that the history of French-Portuguese frontier initiatives and their conflicts in the Eastern Guianas (what is now the Brazilian state of Amapá and French Guiana) cannot be fully comprehended without taking indigenous agency into account. I analyse two cases of French-Portuguese-Amerindian interaction in the area between Cayenne and the mouth of the Amazon between 1680 and 1700. The first case details the establishment of a Portuguese Jesuit mission in Cabo do Norte in 1687, which lasted only a few months and ended abruptly with the murder of the missionaries and their helpers at the hand of Amerindian groups. The Portuguese attributed the intellectual planning of these killings to the French, whom—the Portuguese argued—sought thus to hinder Portuguese settlement. I question this accepted analysis by shedding light on kinship and on Amerindian decision-making gatherings, and I suggest that they may have been the masterminds behind these killings. The second case details the French

2 'without Amerindians, it is impossible to be conquered or to defend ourselves ...', Governor Gomes Freire de Andrade to the King, São Luis de Maranhão, 15 October 1685, in Reis (1993, 188–190). On the specifics of the fortifications built and planned in Cabo do Norte in the late seventeenth century, see Chambouleyron, Bonifácio and Melo (2010, 35–36). All translations are mine.

3 Reis (1993) nevertheless included sources that showed indigenous agency.

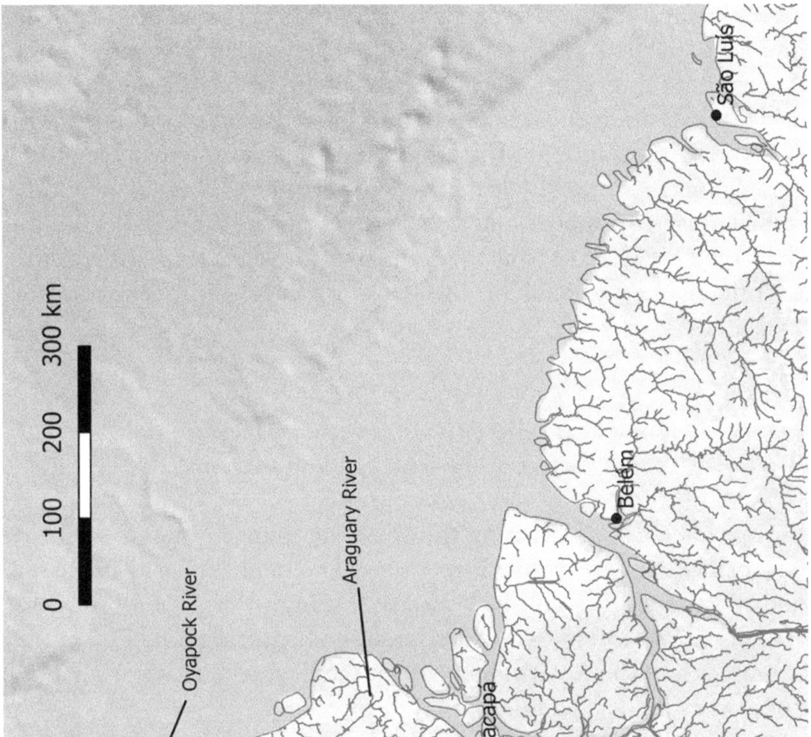

Figure 2: Map of French Guiana and Northern Brazil.

attack on and temporary occupation of the Portuguese forts of Macapá and Parú on the Amazon in 1697. My reconstruction demonstrates that Amerindian intervention was key to the French success and shows the centrality of indigenous planning and persuasion—combined with the governor's ambition—to the establishment and maintenance of French-Amerindian alliances. Ultimately, this chapter discusses why different indigenous groups positioned themselves on the French, Portuguese, or their own side, and shows the effects of the Amerindians' positioning in influencing and shaping the (lack of) European occupation of this space.

French-Portuguese rivalry over an Amerindian space between the Amazon and Cayenne

Europeans had been visiting the coastal Guianas down to the Amazon River since the early sixteenth century. The English, Irish, Dutch, French and Portuguese established either trading spots, small plantations, settlements or forts. They were intent on acquiring land and extracting resources and the Amerindians living there were not only used as labour but also as guides, paddlers and interpreters.

By the mid-1640s, the Portuguese had expelled most other Europeans from the mouth and northern bank of the Amazon delta. The area north of the Parú and Jarí rivers became the hereditary captaincy of Cabo do Norte in 1637, when it was granted to the Portuguese Bento Maciel Parente during the Iberian Union of Crowns, and consequently Portugal considered the captaincy rightfully hers when it returned to the Crown in 1693. France had only secured her colony on the island of Cayenne in 1666 (and permanently only from 1676) as previous initiatives had been unsuccessful due to Amerindian, English and Dutch attacks and takeovers. After settling in Cayenne, the French turned their attention once again to the Amazon River. France had a long-standing interest in the Atlantic coast of Brazil, having had a colony in Rio de Janeiro (known as 'France Antarctique', between 1555–1567) and in São Luís do Maranhão (1612–1615). On both occasions, France counted on Amerindian allies and lost the colonies to the Portuguese (Hemming, 1978, 119–138; Jarnoux, 1991). From the 1680s, the French and Portuguese empires expressed a renewed interest in the area between their settlements in Cayenne and Belém respectively, and their peoples travelled there to trade with Amerindians, to build forts and to establish missions, although neither had the human numbers or resources to achieve a physical settlement there.

The standard historical narrative deals with this rivalry with a clear political focus, presenting the region's past as one in which only Europeans, the newcomers, are the protagonists. Such a narrative argues that the first frontier line was drawn between France and Portugal in a provisional treaty in March 1700 which set the upper limit of the Portuguese territory on the 'River of Vicente Pinzón'. This river was interpreted as the Oyapock by the Portuguese but the Araguarí, by the French, and this divergence ignited a 200-year dispute. While this provisional treaty was ratified in the Utrecht treaties (1713–1715), it was systematically questioned until an international arbitration set the frontier on the Oyapock in 1900.[4]

According to this narrative, Europeans carved up the space and defined its cartography and its history. However, none of them would have succeeded without Amerindian knowledge and help. The region between Cayenne and the Amazon was a densely populated Amerindian space crossed by multiethnic and multilinguistic Amerindian networks which expanded beyond the Eastern Guianas before the arrival of the Europeans (Rostain, 1994, 2012, 2015; Saldanha and Cabral, 2010). Although the European colonization influenced existing networks and contributed to processes of ethnogenesis, Amerindians continued to dominate the space. However, historical research on Amerindians in early modern French Guiana and Amapá has only recently built upon the seminal works by Curt Nimuendajú (1948, 2004), Jean Hurault (1972), Pierre and Françoise Grenand (1987) and Pierre Grenand (2006), significantly with the work of Gérard Collomb (2006) and Lodewijk Hulsman (2011).[5]

Archives spread across countries, however, do hold governmental, missionary and judicial sources which, read against the grain and contrasting the data, make it possible to identify and analyse indigenous agency. Comparison of sources written in several languages helps to overcome some of the limitations imposed by documents written by Europeans for a European audience, while bringing its own difficulties, for instance regarding ethnonyms and toponyms. I have decided to retain the names that designate Amerindian ethnic groups, peoples' names and

4 See the protocol *Contesté Franco-Brésilien* (1900) among other documentation backing up that final decision.

5 Flávio dos Santos Gomes (1999, 225–318) also incidentally dealt with Amerindians in his studies of Maroon communities.

toponyms as they appear in each source's language, except when referring generically to the groups who have an agreed contemporary spelling, like Aruã and Palikur. Hence, the Amerindian groups living on the islands in the mouth and on the northern bank of the Amazon in the early modern period were the Aruas/Aroans for the Portuguese and Arouas/Aroüas for the French, and are now named Aruã (as is the extinct language they spoke). Back then, 'Aruã' may have referred to a single Amerindian group with subgroups/clans using the same name, or could have been a generic ethnic name used to refer to different groups who might have been given other names by each other or by Europeans. In any case, the archival sources clearly show indigenous involvement and the existence of Amerindian politics in addition to European politics in northern South America. Here I use the term 'politics' to refer to the initiatives that were deployed by the parties involved to defend their interests. In so doing, I argue that we need to think about this geographical space not only as a frontier space between the Portuguese and the French, but as a space inhabited by multiethnic and multilingual Amerindian groups who were not subdued by the Europeans but maintained their independence and freedom to act. Ultimately, my aim is to reconceptualize French-Portuguese-Amerindian relations by locating the region in the context of indigenous polities in northern South America and at the heart of European imperial rivalries in the Atlantic world. These two sides are interwoven in the following analysis.

The Portuguese in Cabo do Norte: a Jesuit mission and its Amerindian neighbours, 1687

In April 1680, the King of Portugal issued a law ordering the Jesuits to establish missions on the northern bank of the Amazon and in the Cabo do Norte with the double objective of securing the territory and controlling and converting its inhabitants (Leite, 1943a, 254). In the decree's own words, they were to '[tomar] noticia das paragens aptas para se porem residencias ... para por aquelle meio impedir as communicações das nações extrangeiras com os indios de seu Estado do Maranhão'.[6]

6 '[to identify] the suitable locations to establish settlements ... in order to prevent the communication of foreign nations with the Amerindians of his [the king's] state of Maranhão', in Bettendorff's contemporary *Crônica dos padres da Companhia de Jesus no estado do Maranhão* (1990, 345).

The Portuguese feared that French contact with Amerindians could lead to the French settling in Cabo do Norte, as French trading parties that exchanged goods and people in the area were so common that their presence posed a palpable threat of loss of control over the space.[7] For instance, in the expedition that explored Cabo do Norte following the king's order, the Jesuits Gonsalvi and Pfeil encountered a small French party that was returning with some Amerindians whom the French had—in the Jesuits' words—*resgatado. Resgatado* here meant that the French had obtained these Amerindians by trading with other Amerindian groups—who had held them prisoners—in exchange for goods, and the French were taking them to be sold or to be used as labour. Gonsalvi confiscated and freed these Amerindians, arguing that they had been seized in Portuguese territory and thus were free, as France could not intervene in Portuguese territory (Reis, 1993, 72; Leite, 1943a, 254–256).[8] In 1687, the Portuguese again complained about the French trading with and seizing Amerindians in the sertão dos Tucujús and the 'Ilhas dos Aroans' (islands of the Aruã) in the mouth of the Amazon. The Portuguese magnified the French threat by stating that France's intent was to settle and have Amerindian allies.[9] French traders were actually more interested in extractive resources and labour forces than in settling Cabo do Norte.[10]

The Portuguese king's orders in 1680 were not implemented until June 1687, when the Portuguese Jesuits Antonio Pereira and Bernardo

7 However, the Portuguese intention was never to kill the French traders, but simply to prevent them from entering into contact with the Amerindians. See the order from the king to the Governor of Maranhão, 24 February 1686, in *Livro Grosso do Maranhão* (70–71).

8 See Arenz (2010, 423 n. 233, Appendix 10) for the dual use of Consalvi and Gonsalvi in the original documentation.

9 On the French trading and enslaving in 1687, see Arquivo Histórico Ultramarino (hereafter AHU), Pará-Avulsos, caixa 3, doc. 267, annex, Antônio de Albuquerque Coelho de Carvalho, 19 July 1687, Belém. See also Hurault (1972, 46) and Bombardi (2014, 61–63).

10 The French found it difficult to keep Cayenne's population large enough for the creation of families, and repeatedly requested that men and women be sent there. Archives nationales d'Outre-mer (hereafter ANOM), Colonies, 14/2 Fol. 62, 29 January 1688, asking for single young women to marry; ANOM, Colonies, C14/16 fol. 241r–243r, 28 April 1734, asking for women to send to the Oyapock; ANOM, Colonies, C14/16 fol. 235r–237r, 26 February 1736, asking for single French women because settlers were marrying Amerindian women in Cayenne.

Gomes established a mission in Cabo do Norte (Leite, 1943a, 264).[11] The small island of Camunixary, located in Lake Camacary, was the chosen location, an unidentified spot west of Cape North (Cabo Norte). On the island they were welcomed by Macuraguaya/Macuraguaia, whom the Portuguese identified as the 'principal' of the village, its main authority, and he and the inhabitants of the island were said to be the Maraunizes/ Maruanís/Maruaníes.[12] Along the shores of the lake there were other Amerindian settlements, and it was these neighbouring groups who, probably in September of the same year, killed the Jesuits Pereira and Gomes, their Aruã interpreter Lopo, their pilot and two young helpers, and burned down the village of the Maraunizes (Bettendorff, 1990, 426, 430–433).

Upon learning of the killings, Captain Antônio de Albuquerque sent a military expedition and declared a 'just war' (*guerra justa*) against the Amerindian groups that had participated in the killings, justifying this attack with the Amerindians' refusal to listen to Christian teachings. Albuquerque led an expedition to capture the killers made up of 19 soldiers from the recently established fort (*casa forte*) of Araguarí nearby; 50 Amerindians, some of whom might have been Ariane; the Jesuit Pfeil, who had surveyed the area; and Nathalia, a Maraunize who served as an Aruã interpreter and was said to be the daughter of one of the most important headmen ('pincipaes') of the nation of the Maraunizes.[13] The expedition was fooled by their Amerindian guides who made them walk in circles for days. They eventually found their quarry and killed 39 Amerindians, among them the two self-confessed assassins, the 'principaes' Canariá and Amapixaba. The expedition

11 The delay was due to the exploratory voyages to survey the area and to the expulsion of the Jesuits from Belém between from 1684 until 1686, when they were allowed back with the Regimento das Missões (1686). On the eviction see Arenz (2010, 467–477), and on the Regimento das Missões see Leite (1943b, 87–94, Appendix D).

12 Leite (1943a, 258) names him as Macuraguaia. The Amerindians were *maruaníes* in AHU, Pará-Avulsos, caixa 3, doc. 267, annex, Antônio de Albuquerque Coelho de Carvalho, 19 July 1687, Belém. For the other names, see Bettendorff (1990, 425, 431).

13 Bettendorff (1990, 433–435) did not give the ethnonym of the group who had accompanied Albuquerque. However, these events happened in 1687 and in that same year Férolles had gone to the Araguarí fort and stated that the allies of the Portuguese there were the Ariane: ANOM, Colonies, C14/2 fol. 44r–45r, Férolles to Seignelay, 22 September 1688, specifically fol. 44v.

also captured other Amerindians and forcibly resettled them in villages on the southern bank of the Amazon.[14] By killing and resettling the Amerindians who had been directly or indirectly involved in the Jesuits' deaths, acts that cast doubt on the missions as state-sponsored initiatives and consequently Portuguese territorial domination, they broke kinship, exchange network and spatial ties. The ultimate aim, as stated in the king's orders, was to achieve control of the land and of the people.

Why did the neighbouring Amerindian groups kill the Jesuits and their companions, and burn down the Maraunize village? Contemporary Portuguese sources provided several explanations. Some governmental sources argued that the French instigated the killings through their agent, Lopo, the Jesuits' Aruã interpreter. These sources argue that Lopo convinced the surrounding Amerindian villages that the Jesuits were stealing from them, preventing them from continuing their cultural practices (such as polygamy) and were preparing the terrain for a Portuguese enslavement expedition; all this in addition to trying to convert them.[15] Consequently, the Jesuits were killed and the village burnt down.

Along the same lines but providing an additional insight, the contemporary account of the Jesuit Bettendorff—who had not been present but heard about it second-hand—stated that the neighbouring villagers spoke to the *principal* Macuraguaya and asked him to stop protecting the Jesuits and also to expel them from his village (Bettendorff, 1990, 428). Macuraguaya refused and left the island with most of his people because he—probably—knew what was about to happen and did not want to be associated with the killing of the Jesuits (Bettendorff, 1990, 428–429, 431). The neighbours were thus described by Bettendorff as 'barbaros' and 'inimigos' (savages and enemies), constructing the other as an enemy to those willing to be converted; this served as a justification for Portuguese retaliation against the killers and their kin, and had the

14 AHU, Pará-Avulsos, caixa 3, doc. 271, annex, Miguel da Rosa Pimentel, Belém, 27 February 1688; Bettendorff (1990, 432–435). On the relocation, its rationale and the different numbers of Amerindians who had been made prisoners, see Chambouleyron, Bonifácio and Melo (2010, 39).

15 AHU, Pará-Avulsos, caixa 3, doc. 271. See Chambouleyron, Bonifácio and Melo (2010, 41–46) for their endorsement of the role of the French in the killings, and the identification of the interpreter Lopo as a French mediator. They do, however, highlight Amerindian agency through the alliances they chose to establish with the French or Portuguese (2010, 41, 43). Bombardi (2014, 64–67) also endorses the French connection.

potential to establish an understanding of the two Jesuits as martyrs (Bettendorff, 1990, 427–428).

These two explanations present a dichotomy between good and evil, differentiating between Amerindians allied with the Portuguese (those who attacked with Albuquerque or the Maruanizes willing to be converted), and those against the Portuguese land grab, who were manipulated by the French and had no capacity of discernment (the Amerindians living in the neighbouring villages). Did the French instigate the killing of the Jesuits? Were the Amerindians defending their preferential relations with the French? My analysis suggests that the killings were an answer to decisions taken by several Amerindian groups in a collective decision without influence from the French.

Two hitherto unstudied Jesuit sources point to the relevance of ethnonyms associated with the different Amerindian groups to these questions. The story goes as follows: the *principal* of the village who welcomed the Jesuits was Macuraguaya, a Maraunize. While the killers were generically referred to as Oivanecas,[16] the two men identified as killers of the Jesuits were the *principal* Canariá, who was said to be of the Aguaraca nation, and his uterine brother, Amapixaba, also a *principal* (Bettendorff, 1990, 429). Among the other Amerindians, Goamimani was said to be an Aricoré, and Moximaré was a Maraunize. The disparity of ethnonyms is unified by a common vehicular language. The interpreter stationed with the two murdered Jesuits, Lopo, spoke Aruã, the same language spoken by the retaliatory expedition's interpreter, Nathalia.[17] They may have all spoken Aruã, or a related Arawakan language and used Aruã as lingua franca.

In addition to this linguistic connection, kinship and authority ties linked the different Amerindian villages. In 1690, the Jesuits in São Luís do Maranhão, among them Bettendorff, took declarations from three of the Amerindians who had been forcibly resettled in a nearby village. They were related to the assassin and *principal* Canariá: they were Ararû (his wife), Amâru (his sister) and a male relative of the

16 Biblioteca da Ajuda, Lisboa (hereafter BAL), 54–XIII–4, nº 77: 'Relação feita por Aloysius Conradus Pfeil da maneira como indagou as circunstancias em que foram mortos em Setembro de 1687 os Padres Antônio Pereira e Bernardo Gomes', Araguarí, 12 July 1688.

17 AHU, Maranhão-Avulsos, caixa 7, doc. 798, annex, Antônio de Albuquerque Coelho de Carvalho, 22 November 1687, Araguarí. See also Chambouleyron, Bonifácio and Melo (2010, 41).

two women, Petirî.[18] The widow Ararû was known by the Christian name of Maria and lived in a newly formed village on the River Icatû.[19] When asked why Canariá had killed the Jesuits, Ararû stated that the 'principaes' of the nearby villages had come to meet her husband, asking him to explain why his father-in-law, Macurâuaiâ (the same Macuraguaia) had allowed the Jesuits into his village. They asked him to force Macurâuaiâ to expel the Jesuits, or the 'principaes' would kill them. The reason for this—she said—was that they did not want to be friends with the Jesuits and their Catholic mass.[20]

The narrative so far is as presented by Bettendorff, but what he did not highlight is that Ararû was not only Canariá's wife but also the daughter of Macuraguaya. It is clear that the villages of Canariá, Macuraguaya and the unnamed neighbouring 'principaes' were part of an interrelated network linked by kinship and decision-making processes, despite the different ethnonyms associated with them. Their gathering and discussion suggest some type of political reconnaissance, and there is no mention of the French in any of the three witnesses' declarations. Rather, a French source of 1688 states that the place where the mission was established was frequented by Dutch and French traders.[21] It may be that the Amerindians were not specifically interested in relations with the French, but in preserving their freedom to continue with their lives and exchange with whomever they chose. This case shows how Amerindian agency and their decision-making processes prevented the permanence of Portuguese Jesuit missions, which were a fundamental part of the colonization process of Amazonia. Those Amerindians who lived in the missions were deployed to serve colonists and the colonial

18 BAL, 54-XIII-4 nº 44: 'Atestações judiciais sôbre a morte que se deu ao P. António Pereira e a seu companheiro no sertão do Cabo do Norte, Bispo do Maranhão, os quais indo prègar aos Índio foram mortos por êstes'. S. Luís do Maranhão, 22 July 1690. The Amerindians' names vary throughout the source: Canariá/Canariâ, Ararû/Araru, Amarû/Amräru and Petiry/Petiri/Petirî. Bettendorf (1990, 429) names the wife as Aracú, demonstrating that he knew about these events as he had been present on the day as attested by the document (BAL, 54-XIII-4 nº 44, fol. 1v), but in the end only selected what was relevant to his narrative.

19 BAL, 54-XIII-4 nº 44: Atestações judiciais, 22 July 1690, fol. 1v.

20 BAL, 54-XIII-4 nº 44: Atestações judiciais, 22 July 1690, fol. 4r: 'que não querião sua Missa …'.

21 ANOM, Colonies, C14/2 fol. 44r–45r, Férolles to Seignelay, 22 September 1688, specifically fol. 44v.

governments' needs, and Amerindians may have already heard about (via communication networks) or experienced the disturbances that a nearby mission could bring into their lives.

The French on the Amazon: the Franco-Amerindian takeover of Portuguese forts, 1697

Fast-forwarding ten years takes us to the French takeover of the Portuguese forts of Parú and Macapá on the northern bank of the Amazon in 1697. The existing analysis of these temporary occupations deals with the events that took place in the forts and the fact that they pinpoint the start of the negotiations which led to the provisional treaty in 1700 to settle the frontier between French and Portuguese Guianas (Reis, 1993, 88–101). My focus, in contrast, is on the French-Amerindian alliances that made the French expedition a success.[22]

Governor Pierre Éléonor de Férolles (in office 1681–1684 and 1691–1705, interim in 1688) had a strong interest in the Amazon area, and his reports are permeated by details of the benefits that controlling the land and rivers between Cayenne and the Amazon would bring to the colony of Cayenne. Already in 1687, when he was between governorships, Férolles commanded an exploratory expedition which stopped on the River Araguarí and at the Portuguese fort from which the Portuguese Governor Albuquerque's retaliation party departed in 1687, as mentioned earlier.[23] This first expedition most likely gave him Amerindian contacts *in situ* who would help him ten years later in the occupation of the forts.

In 1697, Férolles himself led the expedition to conquer the forts of Macapá and Parú. This military expedition was made up of 40 French soldiers and of 80 Amerindians. The fort of Macapá was given up without much fighting, and La Motte-Aigron was sent to take and ultimately to destroy Parú.[24] Albuquerque was taken by surprise, and told Férolles of his astonishment given that their countries were not

22 The changing Franco-Amerindian and Portuguese-Amerindian alliances between 1685 and 1697 were noted but not analysed by Hurault (1972, 37–38, 44–45).

23 ANOM, Colonies C14/2 fol. 44r–45r, Férolles to Seignelay, 22 September 1688.

24 In 1688, La Motte-Aigron had been in Cayenne for at least a decade, for in 1688 he had taken part in an expedition up the Oyapock and learnt about a land route to the Parú River (Hurault, 1972, 39).

at war. However, Férolles argued that Pope Alexander VI's division of the territory was not valid. He ordered the destruction and burning of the Portuguese houses in the forts as a means of showing Governor Albuquerque that they were not to build and settle in French territory. Incidentally, the French did not burn the Amerindians houses in the vicinity of the forts.[25] While the act of leaving the Amerindians' houses standing is that of a defending power—destroy the (Portuguese) invader but protect the locals—I argue that Férolles kept the Amerindians' residences intact because they had been instrumental to French success. Without their indigenous allies, the French lacked both the material means and the knowledge necessary to take the forts: from planning, to logistics *en route* and *in situ*, to fighting forces.

Governor Férolles had no problem acknowledging in a report sent back to France that he had been helped by several Amerindian groups along the route to the forts.[26] Rather than undermining his expedition, this demonstration of alliances with different Amerindian groups showed the minister in France that he had established durable links that would allow him to claim the contested territory, if the French king were to deem this necessary. It was, after all, a demonstration of his skills as governor of a rather small and—up to that point—unproductive colony.

Who were these Amerindian allies and what was their role? On his departure from Cayenne, Férolles travelled with 80 Amerindians in canoes, according to Bettendorff. These 80 Amerindians may have been some of the 400 Aruã who had moved from a location on the northern bank of the Amazon to the Cayenne area seeking the protection of the French some time before 1688, although they might have been accompanied by other Amerindians living in the Cayenne area.[27]

On the way to Macapá, the expedition party made up of French soldiers and Amerindians rested and provisioned themselves 'chez les Indiens Palicours'.[28] Rather than simply a stopping point on the way,

25 Letters from 3 and 19 June 1697 (Bettendorff, 1990, 624–626).

26 ANOM, Colonies, C14/3 fol. 127r–130r: 'Relation de mon voyage des Amazones en 1697', Férolles, Cayenne, 1697.

27 ANOM, Colonies, C14/2 fol. 101r–104v (copy in fol. 105r–107v), 'Mémoire des R.P. Jesuittes de Cayennes... depuis 1678 jusqu'à en fin de 1687', Jesuit Saint-Gilles. Also Jean de la Mousse mentioned the episode (Collomb, 2006, 152). Bettendorff (see note 31 in this chapter) says that Aruã came and went with the French, and that de la Mousse was their missionary.

28 'at the Palikurs' home', ANOM, Colonies, C14/3, fol. 127r–130r, 'Relation de mon voyage des Amazones en 1697', Férolles, Cayenne, 1697, fol. 127v.

the Palikurs were their true means of subsistence and support, and the French left with them those who were too ill to travel.[29]

In Macapá, Férolles stated that he had seen in the 'Indiens Aroas, Ticouyous et Arianes qui habitent sur cette côte, beaucoup de marques d'amitié pour les françois, et de joye de voir les Portugais dehors; ils me promirent de ne pas laisser manquer de vivres la Garnison que j'y laisserois'.[30] Referring back to the quotation with which I started the chapter, the Ticouyous come to the fore as the allies of the French, and they may well be some of the Tucujús whom the Portuguese had identified as those they had to befriend to defend their positions in Cabo do Norte. The Portuguese had evidently obtained some support from the Tucujús as they had established a fort in their lands, but it seems that they had lost their favour. Conversely, the Ticouyous did not actively side with the French either. Although Férolles boasted to the minister back in France that the Aroas, Ticouyous and Arianes had promised to feed the 40 soldiers he left behind upon his return to Cayenne, they certainly had not promised to defend them against the Portuguese.

Shortly after Férolles's departure, the Portuguese retook the fortress and the French soldiers were sent back to Cayenne in canoes manoeuvred by the Aruã.[31] Among them was Jean de la Mousse, a French missionary who had worked and travelled extensively in the area surrounding the coast of French Guiana and its rivers, and had reported visits from indigenous groups living close to the Amazon River.[32] His joining

29 On the contemporary Palikur see, among others, Grenand and Grenand (1987) and Passes (1998).

30 '[I had seen in] the Indians Aroas, Ticouyous and Arianes who reside on this coast many gestures of friendship towards the French, and happiness to see the Portuguese gone; they promised me they would not leave unsupplied the garrison that I was to leave there', ANOM, Colonies, C14/3, fol. 127r–130r, 'Relation de mon voyage des Amazones en 1697', Férolles, Cayenne, 1697, quote from fol. 129r.

31 'concedendo-se-lhes sómente a vida e passagem livre para Cayennas com o necessario para a viagem por mar, em canoas, como tinham vindo com o Marquez de Ferroles para o Macapá. Para isso os mandaram aos Aruans, que foram os que os levaram, indo com elles o Padre Claudio de Lamousse, seu missionario' (Bettendorff 1990, 627). Translation: 'granting them only their life and free return to Cayenne with what was required to travel by sea, in canoes, as they had come to Macapá with the Marquis of Férolles. With that purpose, they were sent to the Aruans, who took them, going with them the Father Claudio de la Mousse, their missionary'.

32 Artur argued that 'les quarante soldats se virent bientôt bloqués par cinq o six cents Portugais ou Indiens qui prirent d'abord le père Le Mousse qui était allé faire

the military expedition and accompanying the Aruã might have been significant. He may have been instrumental in establishing connections between several of the Amerindian groups, the governor and other individuals present. The fact that while at Macapá he went on a canoe trip to visit other Amerindian groups suggests the role of mediators and go-betweens in the area, and speaks to the importance of the Amerindians' role in the whole expedition.

Once clear alliances are established between the French governor and Jean de la Mousse with the Amerindian groups and French intentions, the question that remains unanswered is why the Amerindians wanted to help the French against the Portuguese. The analysis of the Ariane case might provide a partial answer.

Who were the Ariane? Were they a big Amerindian group or a small component of a larger group? The answers are uncertain. Pierre and Françoise Grenand mention them as one of the groups that appear only sporadically in written sources and did not come across them in their ethnographic work among the Palikur in Amapá and Guyane during the 1960s and 1970s.[33] However, they appear on Nimuendajú's ethno-linguistic map (1981, map, 46, 79, 87) dated 1698, which references Froger's map produced by the French that same year after Férolles's expedition.[34] Both sources locate the Ariane in a vague space close to Macapá and the sertão dos Tucujús, clearly on the northern bank of the Amazon and relatively close to the forts that were taken.[35]

According to the Jesuit Grillet, the Ariane and the Portuguese were attacking other Amerindian groups located on the northern bank of the Amazon Estuary before 1674 (Grillet, 1682, 205–206). However, this Ariane-Portuguese alliance did not last, and events show that the Ariane sought an alliance with the French. One day in February 1694, three years before the takeover of the forts, an unnamed Ariane man

une excursion chez les Indiens du voisinage', as published by Polderman (2004, 51, 215). The same sequence of events was narrated by Bettendorff (1990, 626–627) and discussed by Hurault (1972, 44–45).

33 Grenand and Grenand (1987, 19) name them 'Aririane', with a double 'ri', but it might be a mistake as Pierre Grenand names them 'Ariane' in another publication (2006, 124 – map).

34 François Froger, 'Carte du Gouvernement de Cayenne ou France Aequinoctiale', 1698, Bibliothèque nationale de France, département cartes et plans, GE DD–2987 (9566).

35 For a discussion of the Ariane and other Amerindians in the region, see my forthcoming article in *Ethnohistory* (October 2018).

arrived in Cayenne. He told Férolles that a fellow Ariane had located a mountain so bright that he could not even look at it with the sun shining, and that it was located in a northern tributary of the Amazon. Although the mineral was not named at that point, Férolles was very pleased to send this news to France.[36] In the summer of that same year, three Ariane *capitaines* visited Cayenne to invite the French to settle with them, again at an undetermined location on the Amazon.[37] As proof of their good intentions, the *capitaines* gave Férolles marcasite, a mineral[38] which they said could be obtained in three rivers located on the north bank of the Amazon.[39] Even though Férolles had deemed the quality of the mineral to be low and inadequate to make ammunition for French *fusils*, the *capitaines* assured him that the mines could produce better quality resources. What was this marcasite? In his early seventeenth-century account of the mouth of the Amazon and Guianas, Jesse de Forest mentioned the existence of a golden marcasite. However, the 1914 critical edition of his text highlights that there was another type of marcasite, white or pale marcasite, which looked like burnished steel when polished (De Forest, 1914, 275). It is probable that the marcasite the Ariane brought was the latter, given that Férolles spoke about making ammunition with it. Further, Polderman (2004, 192) states that according to recent archaeological research on the Sinnamary, flint stone ('silex taillés') were used as ammunition in French Guiana late in the early modern period up to the nineteenth century.

Both Ariane visits are linked by the marcasites, clearly establishing that the February 1694 meeting was testing the limits of French interests. The French governor was interested in much more than that, and they knew as much when they offered to settle with the Ariane on the Amazon bank. Ariane knowledge of the space of the Amazon was fundamental for Férolles, as it opened up a chance to establish a French

36 ANOM, Colonies, C14/3, fol. 29r, Férolles to the Minister, 22 February 1694.

37 ANOM, Colonies, C14/3, fol. 43r–48v, Férolles to the Minister, 14 December 1694. Were the *capitaines* the same as the 'principaes'? The sources consulted do not attribute spiritual or political status to either 'principaes' or *capitaines*, or specify the type of authority they had over their peoples or the recognition they got from them.

38 Marcasite seems to be a type of pyrite. Hurault (1972, 44) references the same source (ANOM, Colonies C14/3, fol. 43r–48v) to state that there were 'gisements d'or et d'argent', which are not mentioned.

39 ANOM, Colonies, C14/3 fol. 43r–48v, Férolles to the Minister, 14 December 1694, fol. 44v.

fort or even to envisage a settlement on the main river. From then until at least March 1695, the Ariane and other Amerindians gave to the French details of developments along the banks of the Amazon: the Portuguese attacked the Ariane villages and kidnapped their women and children, and started mining again along the northern tributaries of the Amazon. Férolles thought that these enslaving expeditions and Portuguese mining enterprises were the reason why the Ariane were looking for French protection, and indeed this might have been one of the reasons.[40] The governor considered the offer and ultimately reported to France that he had decided not to send his men with the Ariane as he feared a Dutch attack.[41]

Were the Ariane actually looking for the French to settle with them? Or was it that French presence in the Amazon would disturb the Portuguese and destroy their forts? The French expedition of 1697 suggests that the Ariane changed sides and decided to offer their support to the French, as even though the French did not settle with them, they did attack two Portuguese forts, counting on the Ariane's help—we are sure of this at least—to provide food for the soldiers after the takeover of the forts.

Conclusion

With these two cases I have analysed the complex set of alliances and conflict that developed between the French, the Portuguese and several Amerindian groups between the Amazon and Cayenne in the late seventeenth century. My aim has been to demonstrate how it is necessary to integrate all of the actors living in a specific geographical space in any discussion of the settling or establishment of international frontiers. It is clear throughout that the space between the Amazon and Cayenne remained outside the control of Europeans despite their tentative efforts to establish themselves. Amerindian groups tacked European initiatives to establish forts and missions and attack each other to their own interests, helping out those who would be more beneficial to them at specific times.

40 ANOM, Colonies, C14/3 fol. 53r–57v, Férolles to the Minister, 24 March 1695.

41 ANOM, Colonies, C14/3 fol. 49r–52v, Férolles to the Minister, 22 March 1695.

The failed Jesuit mission shows that the events that have previously been interpreted as a result of the Amerindians' lack of interest to convert to Christianity, or the French manipulation of Amerindians to gain control over a space that was Portuguese, could actually be understood as demonstrating agency on the part of the Amerindians to decide who was to settle in the space they inhabited. The fact that there was a council or gathering of Amerindians and that the different Amerindian authorities ('principaes') reached an agreement suggests some kind of decision-making process in which the Portuguese mission was ruled out. Incidentally, the Araguarí fort from which Albuquerque's retaliation party departed was abandoned by the end of the seventeenth century.

On the other side, Férolles's Amazon initiative was driven by his own ambition as much as by the motivation provided by the Ariane and the other Amerindian groups who helped the French on the way to the forts and back. It is very likely that what has been portrayed as a French initiative may instead have been planned by the indigenous people in Cabo do Norte as well as the French. It is unlikely that the Ariane invited the French into their home territory without discussing it with neighbouring or kin-related Amerindian groups beforehand. It must have been a wide-ranging decision affecting all of the Amerindians living on the northern bank of the mouth of the Amazon, a decision that ultimately led to providing help to the French throughout the trip, as they were well aware of Férolles's ambitions on the Amazon. The invitation to the French might have been a way to position themselves with the European group least capable of action at that specific moment, or the group they deemed most advantageous to their intra- or inter-group politics: playing the Europeans.

The Portuguese had actively tried to occupy the territory through missions and the construction of forts, physically establishing themselves—even if in small numbers—among the Amerindian settlements. In contrast, the French were only present through trading parties and military expeditions, always led against the Portuguese but not the Amerindians, and did not try to settle. This might have been one of the reasons why the Ariane, Aruã, Ticouyous/Tucujús and Palikurs sided with the French in 1697. Were these Amerindian groups well informed of the difficulties the French were experiencing as they attempted to develop a fruitful colony, in contrast to the Portuguese, who had been present on the Amazon for a longer period of time? France's recent establishment and still-weak position at that time, the enormity of the space and the distant presence of the Portuguese on the Amazon meant that the Amerindian groups who were living in the lands, rivers and lakes between Cayenne and the Amazon remained independent for decades, and France and Portugal struggled to physically settle and occupy the space. The frontier politics that unfolded in the Eastern Guianas at the end of the seventeenth century had multiple key actors: French, Portuguese and Amerindian groups. Any analysis of that space should incorporate all of these groups of people, including the Maroon and mixed-descent communities who would appear as actors in this context in the following decades.

Works cited

Arenz, Karl-Heinz. 2010. *De l'alzette à l'amazone. Jean-Philippe Bettendorff et les jésuites en Amazonie portugaise (1661–1693)*. Saarbrücken: Éditions universitaires européennes.

Bettendorff, João Felipe. 1990. *Crônica dos padres da Companhia de Jesus no estado do Maranhão*. Belém: Fundação Cultural do Pará Tancredo Neves, SECULT.

Bombardi, Fernanda Aires. 2014. *Pelos interstícios do olhar do colonizador: descimentos de índios no Estado do Maranhão e Grão-Pará (1680–1750)*. Unpublished MA thesis, Universidade de São Paulo, Brazil. http://www.teses.usp.br/teses/disponiveis/8/8138/tde-08012015-164954/pt-br.php (accessed 10 June 2016).

Chambouleyron, Rafael, Monique da Silva Bonifácio and Vanice Siquiera de Melo. 2010. 'Pelos sertões "estão todas as utilidades". Trocas e conflitos no sertão Amazônico (século XVII)', *Revista de História* 162: 13–49.

Collomb, Gérard, ed. 2006. *Les Indiens de la Sinnamary. Journal du père Jean de La Mousse en Guyane (1684–1691)*. Paris: Editions Chandeigne.

Contesté Franco-Brésilien. Sentence du Conseil Général Suisse dans la Question des Frontières de la Guyane française et du Brésil du 1er décembre 1900. Bern: Imprimerie St Aempfly & Cie, 1900.

De Forest, Emily Johnston, ed. 1914. *A Walloon Family in America. Lookwood de Forest and his Forbears 1500–1848. Together with a Voyage to Guiana being the Journal of Jesse de Forest and his Colonists, 1623–1625. Volume II*. Boston and New York: Houghton Mifflin Company.

Farage, Nádia. 1986. *As muralhas dos sertões. Os povos indígenas no rio Branco e a colonização*. MA dissertation, Universidade Estadual de Campinas, Brazil.

Gomes, Flávio dos Santos. 1999. 'Fronteiras e mocambos: o protesto negro na Guiana Brasileira', in *Nas Terras do Cabo do Norte. Fronteiras, colonização e escravidão na Guiana Brasileira—séculos XVIII/XIX*, ed. Flávio dos Santos Gomes. Belém: Editora Universitária/UFPA, 225–318.

Grenand, Pierre. 2006. 'Que sont devenus les Amérindiens de l'approuague? Réflexions autour d'une histoire peu documentée', in *L'histoire de la Guyane depuis les civilisations amérindiennes: actes du colloque des 16, 17 et 18 novembre 2005, Cayenne*, ed. Serge Mam Lam Fouck and Jacqueline Zonzon. Matoury: Ibis Rouge, 105–126.

Grenand, Pierre, and Françoise Grenand. 1987. 'La Côte d'Amapá, de la bouche de l'Amazone à la baie d'Oyapock, à travers la tradition orale Palikur', *Boletim do Museu Paraense Emílio Goeldi, série Antropologia* 3.1: 1–77.

Grillet, Jean. 1682. *Journal du Voyage que les Peres Jean Grillet et François Bechamel, de la Compagnie de Jesus, on fait dans la Guyane en 1674*, in *Relation de la rivière des Amazones*, by Cristóbal de Acuña, ed. and trans. Marin Le Roy de Gomberville. Amsterdam: Chez Claude Barbin, 201–255.

Hemming, John. 1978. *Red Gold. The Conquest of the Brazilian Indians*. London: Macmillan.

Hulsman, Lodewijk. 2011. 'Swaerooch: o comércio holandês com índios no Amapá (1600–1615)', *Revista Estudos Amazônicos* 6.1: 178–202.

Hurault, Jean-Marcel. 1972. *Français et Indiens en Guyane. 1604–1972*. Paris: Union générale d'Editions.

Jarnoux, Philippe. 1991. 'La France équinoxiale: les dernières velléités de colonisation française au Brésil (1612–1615)', *Annales de Bretagne et des pays de l'Ouest* 98.3: 273–296.

Leite, Serafim. 1943a. *História da Companhia de Jesus no Brasil. Tômo III, Norte 1, fundações e entradas, séculos XVII–XVIII*. Rio de Janeiro: Imprensa Nacional.

Leite, Serafim. 1943b. *História da Companhia de Jesus no Brasil. Tomo IV, Norte 2, Obra e assuntos gerais, séculos XVII–XVIII*. Rio de Janeiro: Imprensa Nacional.

Livro Grosso do Maranhão, in *Anais da Biblioteca Nacional* 5.66 (1948): 25–28.

Malafaia, Eurico de Ataíde. 2002. *O Brasil e a fronteira da Guiana Francesa: notas históricas, 1500–1900*. Lisboa: Academia Portuguesa da História.

Melo, Vanice Siqueira de. 2008. *'Aleivosias, mortes e roubos'. Guerras entre índios e portugueses na Amazônia colonial (1680–1706)*. Unpublished BA dissertation, Universidade Federal do Pará, Brazil.

Nimuendajú, Curt. 1948. 'The Aruã', in *Handbook of South American Indians*, ed. Julian H. Steward. Washington, DC: Government Printing Sources, 195–198.

Nimuendajú, Curt. 1981. *Mapa etno-histórico de Curt Nimuendajú*. Rio de Janeiro: IBGE. http://www.etnolinguistica.org/biblio:nimuendaju-1981-mapa (accessed 20 June 2016).

Nimuendajú, Curt. 2004. *In Pursuit of a Past Amazon: Archaeological researches in the Brazilian Guyana and in the Amazon region by Curt Nimuendajú*, compiled and trans. Stig Rydén and Per Stenborg. Göteborg: Elanders Infologistik.

Passes, Alan. 1998. *The Hearer, the Hunter and the Agouti Head: Aspects of Intercommunication and Conviviality among the Pa'ikwené (Palikur) of French Guiana*. Unpublished PhD Thesis, University of St Andrews, United Kingdom.

Polderman, Marie. 2004. *La Guyane française, 1676–1763. Mise en place et évolution de la société coloniale, tensions et métissage*. Petit-Bourg: Ibis Rouge Editions.

Reis, Arthur Cézar Ferreira. 1993. *Limites e demarcações na Amazônia brasileira. Vol. 1: A fronteira colonial com a Guiana Francesa*. Belém: SECULT.

Rostain, Stéphen. 1994. 'Archéologie du littoral de Guyane. Une région charnière entre les influences culturelles de l'Orénoque et de l'Amazone', *Journal de la Société des Americanistes* 80: 9–46.

Rostain, Stéphen. 2012. 'Where the Amazon River meets the Orinoco River: Archaeology of the Guianas', *Amazônica. Revista de Antropologia* 4.1: 10–28.

Rostain, Stéphen, ed. 2015. *Archéologie de l'Amazonie. Les premiers habitants de la Guyane côtière*. Oxford: Archeopress.

Saldanha, João Darcy de Moura, and Mariana Petry Cabral. 2010. 'A arqueologia do Amapá: reavaliação e novas perspectivas', in *Arqueologia Amazônica, Vol. 1*, ed. Edithe Pereira and Vera Guapindaia. Belém: MPEG/IPHAN/SECULT, 95–112.

Silva, Gutemberg de V., and Aldomar A. Rückert. 2009. 'A fronteira Brasil-França', *Confins* 7. http://confins.revues.org/6040 (accessed 8 January 2016).

Thornton, John K. 2012. *A Cultural History of the Atlantic World, 1250–1820*. Cambridge: Cambridge University Press.

Whitehead, Neil L. 1988. *Lords of the Tiger Spirit. A History of the Caribs in Colonial Venezuela and Guyana, 1498–1820*. Providence and Dordrecht: Foris Publications.

Archives

Arquivo Histórico Ultramarino, Lisbon, Portugal

Pará-Avulsos, caixa 3, doc. 267 and doc. 271.

Maranhão-Avulsos, caixa 7, doc. 798.

Archives nationales d'Outre-mer, Aix-en-Provence, France

Colonies, C14/2, C14/3 and C14/16.

Biblioteca da Ajuda, Lisbon, Portugal
54-XIII-4, no. 44 and no. 77.

Bibliothèque nationale de France, Paris, France
Département des cartes et plans, GE DD-2987 (9566): François Froger, *Carte du Gouvernement de Cayenne ou France Aequinoctiale*, Paris, Editeur de Fer, 1698. http://gallica.bnf.fr/ark:/12148/btv1b85967692/f1.zoom.r=carte%20du%20gouvernement%20de%20Cayenne (accessed 26 January 2016).

CHAPTER FIVE

Producing the Periphery

Jonna M. Yarrington, University of Arizona[1]

In the period 1800–1860, a novel source of sugar from French-grown beets offered unprecedented competition to cane sugar imports into France. This was a conjunction of two commodities: a meeting of sugars produced from two historically and pragmatically distinct production complexes. During this period, debates raged over whether French colonial cane was protectable in a national economics privileging items produced by French labour and industry. The age-old cane bloc found itself locked in a battle with the coalescing beet bloc; each asserted its own definition of economic nationalism, in differing territorial terms. Access to the national sugar market was weighed in arguments over territorial contiguity, autarky and implications for French sugar-producing colonies. Caribbean producers, specifically, seen for centuries as integral to the national interest, were increasingly positioned as external to the nation that had built them.

Guyane provides a prime case to illustrate the effects of the sugar conjunction. From its position as a relatively unsuccessful cane colony, Guyane came to be conceptualized as a territory with possibilities for French use beyond sugar extraction during the period of the conjunction. The possibility of extractable commodities from Guyane was effectively, although not entirely, eschewed by the 1850s, when French administrators

1 I would like to acknowledge feedback and encouragement from Landon Yarrington, Brackette F. Williams, Drexel G. Woodson, Mamadou Baro, Thomas Park, Richard Price and Sally Price. Thanks to Sarah Wood and Catriona MacLeod for critical feedback, and to the *Locating Guyane* conference participants.

under Louis-Napoleon Bonaparte initiated a plan that had been in the works since the 1810s, and arguably earlier, to establish a long-term penal colony in Guyane. Without assured viability of its sugar cane and as a consequence of a long history of failed settlement schemes and scams, I argue, Guyane came to be seen as a less feasible space for agriculture and more feasible for the shipment, storage and punishment—forced agricultural labour, even—of people no longer in possession of French citizenship and undesirable to the mainland.

Complexes and conjunction

To explain this argument systematically, we should start with the sugar complexes. I borrow this concept from anthropological literature and historiography of the Caribbean, and mean by it the social, economic and political institutions entwined in a system of monocrop dominance throughout a region filled with particular instantiations. Such a system of cash crops grown and harvested by slave labour, what Charles Wagley (1960) calls 'plantation America', characterized the early centuries of post-contact Caribbean society, economy and polity. The cane sugar complex, the sugar plantation system of the French Antilles, can be profitably compared with the much younger beet sugar complex of northern France.

The cane complex, as a monocrop economy, was dependent on the labour of a category of humans who were indentured and enslaved—European, African, African-descendant, and later so-called 'coolies' from Asia (see Deerr, 1949; 1950; Curtin, 1969; Adamson, 1972). The effects of the nineteenth-century sugar conjunction were major for the sugar colonies. French Antillean economies tied to sugar prices were experiencing a number of increasing pressures, compounding the effects of the new and acute competition provided by a split sugar market. These included mounting ecological disaster spurred by the overuse of land long considered to be naturally and endlessly fertile, as well as pressures from an anticipated, then realized, lack of labour following the final French emancipation of the slaves in 1848 (Tomich, 1990; Watts, 1987).

The beet sugar complex was much younger than the cane sugar complex, beets only being planted for sugar in certain areas of northern France in the early nineteenth century. Despite the myth of a *sucre indigène* wrought by the genius of *la patrie*, beet sugar was seriously experimented with first by a Prussian, Andreas Marggraf, in the late 1740s, and was developed later by his student Franz Karl Achard, a Prussian of French Huguenot descent.[2] Sugar beets were later adopted in a research programme by French scientists working on the cutting edge. A group of scientists called themselves the Société d'Arcueil and included Claude Louis Berthollet, Jean-Antoine Chaptal and Pierre-Simon de Laplace among its membership.[3] Patronized by Napoleon I himself, they studied the scientific and technological possibilities of various kinds of commodities, only one of which was sugar, that French people wanted to consume but were struggling to acquire due to the trade blockade established by Napoleon.[4]

Beet sugar was not a commodity prised from the fields and factories only by French hands. The labourers were usually migrants from Belgium, Italy, Switzerland, and as far as Poland, who would work for cheap wages (Châtelain, 1976, 637ff.). Beet sugar was part of the new kind of industrial agriculture: what Marc Bloch (1966, 216) called the 'agricultural revolution'. Furthermore, planting beets for sugar was not a national phenomenon, since planting was really only concentrated in the north, in particular in the Pas-de-Calais and Picardy (Clout and Phillips, 1973; cf. Châtelain, 1976).

2 Secondary literature on beet sugar development includes historical accounts such as Hélot (1900), Rolph (1917), Baumont (1931) and Coons (1949). Primary documents on early beet sugar development include Marggraf's series of reports (1762) and Achard's report (1812). N.B. Marggraf's surname is sometimes spelled 'Margraf'. Achard publicly described beet sugar as 'European sugar' with the explicit potential to free Europe from dependence on imports (Crosland, 1967, 33). Once sugar from beets became an established possibility, many others were interested in learning about it. Thomas Jefferson's library at Monticello, for example, included books on beet sugar (for example Parmentier, 1812) and his correspondence includes letters to French contacts asking for information on processes to make sugar from beets. These letters explicitly refer to the capacity of such a procedure to change the colonial relationship (Jefferson to A.M. Rochon, 14 December 1813; Jefferson to A. Thoüin, 14 December 1814).

3 Three volumes of the Société d'Arcueil papers were published, none of which includes reports on beet sugar experiments (Société d'Arcueil 1807; 1809; 1813). See Crosland (1967) for background.

4 The continental blockade (*blocus continental*) was one measure in a developing system of national protection, which historians generally take to begin with the physiocrat philosophers in the late eighteenth century and, although changing, becoming eclipsed by free trade policy only after 1860. See Clough (1964) on national economy and Baugh (1998) and Sloane (1898) on the blockade.

From initial discovery in 1747 by Marggraf in Berlin to proof of profitability and early production designs in 1812—a 65-year period—beet sugar went from a European daydream openly acknowledged as the end of tropical dependence to a reality of mass production.[5] It was science, said politician-scientist Jean-Antoine Chaptal (1821, 3), that saved France during its commodity crisis, a time of blockade and isolation, of 'exile by sea'. He credited inroads in chemistry and industry for lifting the 'yoke of the New World' from France, releasing it from dependence on tropical production of sugar. The exile to which Chaptal referred was a possible double reference—to the self-imposed exile during Napoleon's *blocus continental* and the increasing costliness and inefficiency of the French sugar colonies.

Although the separate elements of the two sugar complexes, such as labour, are incomparable in themselves (see Mintz, 1977), the complexes themselves are comparable analytically, especially in light of the fact that, although very distinct systems, they produced an identical commodity that split the French national sugar market. The period of the complexes' coexistence and market competition within a system of national economic protection was characterized by bitter debates, alive to contemporaries invested in either and both sides of the splitting sugar market, one of the most famous among them Mathieu de Dombasle (1822), a proponent of beet sugar and tariff protections.[6] Charles Forbin Janson (1840) provides a further example of an outspoken yet complicated position on the sugar question, in his person embodying the interests of a sugar refiner who was invested to some degree in both beet and cane ventures. The debate was over protection, as in the case of many other types of commodities at the time, such as tobacco, cotton and textiles (see Clough, 1964). In the case of sugar, however, the state had incentivized the technology and industry for mass production of new, non-tropical sugar and faced

5 Proof of mass production and profitability is attributable to Benjamin Delessert. Delessert was a banker, philanthropist and amateur botanist and chemist. In 1801, he established a beet sugar factory in Passy, now part of Paris (Redlich, 1948, 138, 144–145; Bruguière, 1980, 667). Delessert's workers introduced a new machine that cut and pulped the beet tuber to extract its juice, significantly improving if not actually establishing the economic viability of mass production (Clout and Phillips 1973, 106).

6 Yarrington (2018) further historicizes the splitting of the French national sugar market, finding the changes of the 1848 revolution and abolition to be the primary political-economic turning point for both sets of sugar interests and their advocates in Paris.

the dilemma of whether to continue to protect and support its mainland production in the face of the cane complex it had constructed centuries earlier. Both cane and beet sides claimed the right to protective policies, while only beet interests could claim unequivocally to be located territorially within the Hexagon. From the perspective of the colonies, 'the very monopoly which had built up the Caribbean was now trained against it' (Williams, 1970, 383).

In a wide view, the conjunction could be defined as the first 60 years of the nineteenth century, but would more narrowly be defined as occurring between 1812 and 1860, based on the dates of viability of mass production and the equalizing of tariff rates and concomitant shift to a free trade policy. The conjunction occurred because of scientific, technological and entrepreneurial advances that allowed identical sugar commodities, at various degrees of possible refinement, to be profitably mass-produced from two botanically different plants.[7] The political and economic stakes were high for both sides during the conjunction: beet and cane exponents were categorized most commonly as protectionists (for the former) or, for the latter, early versions of free-traders. Pamphlets and newspapers on the question flooded Paris and the large port cities in the 1820s and 1830s, with both sides claiming a right to be favoured exclusively by the state. The year 1840 was particularly explosive, with proposed equalization of tariff and bounty rates, and thus equalization of symbolic citizenship for both beet and cane interests. Beet interests and the strong protectionist ideas of the nationalist Prime Minister, Adolphe Thiers, obstructed the move that year to equalize duties (see Todd, 2008, 307–327). By the end of 1840, each side was calling outright for the prohibition of the other, meaning the liquidation of an entire industry and indemnity paid by the state to its owners. It was unclear how that would work for an entity as huge and pervasive as the cane complex in the French Caribbean, which was by then a society organized on the principle of cane sugar production.

The outcome of the conjunction was tied to French ruling-class politics of the mid-nineteenth century. In 1848, Louis-Napoleon Bonaparte exercised his coup overthrowing Louis-Philippe, which had the important additional effects of producing thousands of political prisoners needing prisons, the final abolition of slavery and the breakdown of the Caribbean

7 See Smith (2006) for the history of the development of business investment practices in France, which contributed directly to financing sugar interests. Redlich (1948) provides an older and shorter account.

cane lobby in Paris (Yarrington, 2018). In 1852, Louis-Napoleon became Emperor Napoleon III. With this political upheaval and return to the authoritarianism of an empire, Louis-Napoleon was able to enact certain changes over the next few years that had been slow in coming since Waterloo. Two of those changes are crucial for the argument at hand: the emancipation of the slaves in the French Caribbean in 1848, a feat accomplished quickly and led by politician-scientist François Arago and abolitionist Victor Schoelcher, and Louis-Napoleon's quiet but conclusive and official switch of the state's political orientation to free trade in 1860, away from the protectionism that had been his uncle's prized policy and which had in fact characterized French trade since the mid-1600s in the form of *l'Exclusif.* In 1860, Napoleon III put the full force of the state behind a treaty secretly signed with Great Britain which, upon becoming public, startled French industry.[8] Trade between the two nations was to be open and completely reciprocal. Decades removed from Napoleon I's open war of financial attrition, there was full commitment to peace and entirely reciprocal trade relations. In 1902, the free trade of sugar between nine nations, including Great Britain and France and their colonies, was solidified in an international free trade agreement for sugar, the Brussels Sugar Convention (Guyot, 1902; Martineau, 1904; see also Clough, 1964; Haight, 1941).

Guyane at the conjunction

What did the sugar conjunction and its outcome mean for the French Caribbean and Guyane, specifically? The jewel of the French Antilles had been Saint-Domingue. It was lost to France in 1804, becoming the nation of Haiti, largely before beet sugar became a political factor. Guadeloupe and Martinique, France's two major cane sugar-producing colonies, were both devastated by the same mid-nineteenth-century changes, including ecological disasters, surrounding the entrance of beet sugar on the market. The most illustrative case, it seems, of the sugar conjunction's effects on the Caribbean is that of Guyane, a colony characterized

8 The treaty was negotiated by the free trade ideologues Michel Chevalier and Richard Cobden. See Daumard (1976) and Kindleberger (1975). Louis-Napoleon, before he became Napoleon III, himself wrote on the sugar question, siding ultimately with the free trade ideas influenced by a strain of Saint-Simonian philosophy. See Bonaparte (1842).

by the possibilities of the cane complex, set up sparsely with plantations peopled in part by African slaves and their descendants as well as by indentured labourers. The cane sugar complex in Guyane was never as widespread or as successful as that in Martinique or Guadeloupe. In this way, compared to the practical effects on the existing productive infrastructures in Martinique and Guadeloupe, Guyane provides a relatively open field for the exploration of the effects of beet sugar on the concept of colony and a colony's uses, both for and outside of a national sugar market.

Despite its geographic marginality as a mainland colony when grouped with the contingent of Antillean island colonies, Guyane can be considered socially, politically and economically connected to and characterized by the French Antillean cane complex during the period of conjunction. Continual efforts to establish sugar operations indicate more strongly the drive to maintain and extend the cane complex in Guyane. The cane complex was one means by which the French could establish sovereignty over the territory between the Oyapock and Maroni rivers, perhaps even further into the Guiana highlands and Amazon rainforest, although that territory could never be contiguous with the French mainland. In this way, Guyane provides a means to question economic concepts such as markets, duties and tariffs that reify territory as national or, alternatively, outside of the nation.

In 1851, the French state established a penal colony in Guyane. This had been planned as far back as 1831, when the legislature made deportation a legal punishment, as an alternative to the hulk ships that had housed convicts off of French port cities (Forster, 1991, 147; see also Spieler, 2012). But it was not until Louis-Napoleon's coup supplied both authoritarian change and tens of thousands of political detainees—crucially, at a time when the conjunction was hitting the cane complex hardest, hot on the heels of emancipation—that the plans for a penal colony were actualized in the territory of Guyane.

During the heyday of the cane complex, the Antilles, along with Guyane, had been conceptualized as useful in their proximity to the European mainland. Following 1851, Guyane especially was conceptualized instead for its distance, as a place where felons stripped of their citizenship were exiled by the state (Spieler, 2012, 23). In other words, conditioned by the seeming emptiness of the space in terms of exportable produce before and during the conjunction, Guyane's use as the territory for a penal colony indicates the reverberations of French economic nationalism and the influence of the French sugar market on colonial ideologies. The albatross of colonial sugar, once lifted from France's neck by the possibility of metropolitan beet sugar, allowed Guyane's relevance as a geographically distant place, useful in imperial logic for the storage of undesirables. This logic was long-held but, with emancipation and the decline of cane sugar in a market favouring beet sugar, Guyane could now be realized as a penal destination.[9]

The French colonial relationship with Guyane comprised a series of efforts to people and develop infrastructure and production of that territory, beginning in the 1600s. The repeated encounters and projects were, as noted, types of schemes and scams for increasing the population and the productive capacity of the region. The plans for development reveal ways in which Guyane was characterized as Antillean and colonial, supposed to function in the same mode that was so prosperous in Saint-Domingue, Guadeloupe and Martinique. These efforts at development and peopling also reveal, in practice, that this colonial categorization did not necessitate successful results for the development of agriculture or sugar production. Nonetheless, from an ideological standpoint, ideas for the colony's use-value relied on the same processes that had set conditions for the cane sugar complex across the French Caribbean. To understand the repeated disjunction of French schemes for use and the practical outcomes of projects, it is critical to keep in mind the many failed schemes implemented before 1809, when the British and Portuguese began their military occupation of Guyane (Lowenthal, 1952; Traver, 2011). One must consider the details of the catastrophic Kourou expedition in the 1760s (Epstein, 1984; Rothschild, 2006) and the other, smaller-scale expeditions and activities during the pre-occupation period, which show French conceptualization of Guyane as a space of as-yet-untapped possibility.

The period of conjunction of the sugar complexes (1812–1860) coincided with the last years of British-Portuguese occupation and the French resumption of control over the territory. During this time, a second series of development schemes and scams co-occurred with the sugar conjunction, such as the establishment of settlements like 'Laussadelphie' (Boromé, 1967) or Mère Javouhey's colony at Mana (Curtis, 2008). This co-occurrence was influenced and, to some extent,

9 For French colonial ideology before 1789, see Confer (1964). It is important to note that another penal colony was established in New Caledonia in the South Pacific. A similar question to that asked here might be posed of that venture. See Forster (1996) and Toth (2006).

predetermined by the ways in which the cane complex had established Guyane's use-value as a contributor to the French national economy.

Locating the periphery

To show that the sugar conjunction influenced the selection of Guyane as a site for a penal colony, the most important question is that of direct and indirect causes linking the sugar conjunction and resultant shift in the conceptual status of Guyane as a colony for the uses of the French state. The penal institution was established in 1851–1852. With its use-value pitted against criteria based in the Antillean cane complex, debates about territory and differential rights of access to French markets were directly related to the resulting use of the colony for the detention of criminals. By conviction, these former Frenchmen no longer had any rights of access to French citizenship (Spieler, 2011; 2012; Krakovitch, 1990). A tentative analogy may be made to the diminishing rights of exclusive protection of cane sugar producers in the French West Indian territories. In other words, the meaning of colonial citizenship was in flux. Without French dependence on tropical, colonial cane sugar, the status of colonists and colonies was destined for revision, a revision in which the potential profits of sugar production were less important than other potential uses for a distant, hard-to-develop territory. Development was thus overtaken by punishment in Guyane; colonists and freed slaves were bound to live alongside the outcasts of French mainland society.[10]

Work remains to be done on this topic. Any historical consensus on the connections between settlement schemes, relations with the French national sugar market, and the establishment of the penal colony is implicit at best in the existing historiography. Secondary analyses do not concentrate on causal connections between overseas sugar production, metropolitan sugar production and Guyane's political-economic circumstances. The effects associated with the cane complex, or any Guyanais

10 The effect of this ideological revision and revaluation on social stratification for extant positions in Guyanais society is deserving of a complete historical study. Spieler (2011; 2012) and Toth (2006) address the penal colony's beginnings and functioning, while Jennings (2001) provides a view of Guyanais politics in the face of emancipation. No study has considered the colonial revaluation's effects specifically on stratification within Guyanais society. Comparable examination of status differentials changing elsewhere in the colonial Caribbean has been made in the work of Barbara Bush (1981), among others.

agricultural production for that matter, have not been central to most socio-historical analyses. In the service of beginning to fill these gaps, my attention here is devoted to this causality in Guyanais history and what may be said of its contribution to conditions that set the course for continued development of this place as a French territory.[11] My intention has been to glean what the existing literature can be made to show about the direct and indirect causal influence of the competition between beet and cane sugar complexes on ideologies of national autarky, as well as on shifts in the conceptualization of belonging to and right of participation in the French nation—as both positive participation in markets and negative exclusion from society.

Developments in Guyane during the period 1800–1860 can be shown to result in part from shifts in the meaning of 'the colonial', beginning with reliance on the viability of Antillean cane sugar and shifting as that viability began to wane. When state officials in France reconsidered Guyane for further settlement and development, the sugar question and existence of beet sugar as a possibility changed the conceivable options as to what the colony could produce, consume and symbolize for the French nation. That the penal colony was established near the end of the conjunction speaks to a shift in the state's operating concept from production of proximity—in modes of production and exchange—to a production of distance in the transport of undesirables abroad. It is in this way that we might be able to address the historical state interests at work in setting this 'peripheral' or 'marginal' status of Guyane from well before the establishment of the penal colony.

Here and elsewhere (Yarrington, 2014; 2018), I have tried to show how Guyane was made marginal. As a sociocultural anthropologist engaging in history, I find it unsatisfactory to imply that Guyane's marginal status during and after this period was somehow natural or logical to the French, inherent in its location or its geographic proximity. I attempt to show and explain this contributing aspect to its marginality, which I maintain must be culturally and ideologically produced. Sugar had a part in determining the borders of France, whether in the Antilles or in the beet fields of the Pas-de-Calais. In this sense, changes to the sugar market meant changes in locating the most marginal places of the French empire and in repositioning those edges both in ideology and in practice.

11 A similar project is noted by Gritzner (1964), writing on the effects of the penal colony on the infrastructure and political development of the territory.

Works cited

Achard, F.C. 1812. *Traité complet sur le sucre Européen de betteraves*, trans. D. Angar. Paris: M. Derosne.

Adamson, Alan H. 1972. *Sugar without Slaves: The Political Economy of British Guiana, 1838–1904*. New Haven: Yale University Press.

Baugh, Daniel A. 1998. 'Withdrawing from Europe: Anglo-French maritime geopolitics, 1750–1800', *The International History Review* 20.1: 1–32.

Baumont, Maurice. 1931. 'Les Origines du sucre de betterave', *Annales d'histoire économique et sociale* 3.10: 280–81.

Bloch, Marc. 1966. *French Rural History: An Essay on its Basic Characteristics [Les Caractères Originaux de l'Histoire Rurale Française]*, trans. J. Sondheimer. Berkeley: University of California Press.

Bonaparte, Louis-Napoléon. 1842. *Analyse de la question des sucres*. Paris: Administration de Librairie.

Boromé, Joseph A. 1967. 'When French Guiana sought American settlers', *Caribbean Studies* 7.2: 39–51.

Bruguière, Michel. 1970. 'Finance et noblesse: l'entrée des financiers dans la noblesse d'empire', *Revue d'histoire moderne et contemporaine* 17.3: 664–670.

Bush, Barbara. 1981. 'White "ladies", colored "favourites" and black "wenches": Some considerations on sex, race and class factors in social relations in white Creole society in the British Caribbean', *Slavery & Abolition* 2.3: 245–262.

Chaptal, Jean-Antoine. 1821 [1815]. *Mémoire sur le sucre de betterave*. 3rd ed. Paris: Huzard.

Châtelain, Abel. 1976. *Les Migrants temporaires en France de 1800 à 1914: histoire économique et sociale des migrants temporaires des campagnes françaises au XIXe siècle au début du XXe siècle. Vol. 2*. Lille: Université Lille-III.

Clough, Shepard Bancroft. 1964 [1939]. *France: A History of National Economics 1789–1939*. New York: Octagon Books.

Clout, Hugh D., and Anthony D.M. Phillips. 1973. 'Sugar-beet production in the Nord Département of France during the nineteenth century', *Erdkunde* 27.2: 105–119.

Confer, Vincent. 1964. 'French colonial ideas before 1789', *French Historical Studies* 3.3: 338–359.

Coons, George H. 1949. 'The sugar beet: Product of science', *The Scientific Monthly* 68.3: 149–164.

Crosland, Maurice. 1967. *The Society of Arcueil: A View of French Science at the Time of Napoleon I*. Cambridge, MA: Harvard University Press.

Curtin, Philip D. 1969. *The Atlantic Slave Trade: A Census*. Madison: The University of Wisconsin Press.

Curtis, Sarah A. 2008. 'Missionary utopias: Anne-Marie Javouhey and the colony at Mana, French Guiana, 1827–1848', in *Views from the Margins: Creating Identities in Modern France*, ed. Kevin J. Callahan and Sarah A. Curtis. Lincoln: University of Nebraska Press, 21–52.

Daumard, Adeline. 1976. 'L'état libéral et le libéralisme économique', in *Histoire économique et sociale de la France, Vol. III*, ed. Pierre Léon and Fernand Braudel. Paris: Presses Universitaires de France, 137–159.

De Dombasle, C.-J.-A. Mathieu. 1822. *Faits et observations sur la fabrication du sucre de betteraves et sur la distillation des mélasses*. 2nd ed. Paris: Huzard.

Deerr, Noël. 1949. *The History of Sugar, Vol. 1*. London: Chapman and Hall.

Deerr, Noël. 1950. *The History of Sugar, Vol. 2*. London: Chapman and Hall.

Epstein, David M. 1984. 'The Kourou expedition to Guiana: The genesis of a black legend', *Boletín de Estudios Latinoamericanos y del Caribe* 37: 85–97.

Forster, Colin. 1991. 'French penal policy and the origins of the French presence in New Caledonia', *The Journal of Pacific History* 26.2: 135–150.

Forster, Colin. 1996. *France and Botany Bay: The Lure of a Penal Colony*. Victoria: Melbourne University Press.

Gritzner, Charles E. 1964. 'French Guiana penal colony: Its role in colonial development', *Journal of Geography* 63.7: 314–319.

Guyot, Yves. 1902. 'The sugar industry on the continent', *Journal of the Royal Statistical Society* 65.3: 419–446.

Haight, Frank Arnold. 1941. *A History of French Commercial Policies*. New York: The Macmillan Company.

Hélot, Jules. 1900. *Le Sucre de betterave en France de 1800 à 1900*. Paris: Fernand and Paul Deligne.

Janson, Charles Forbin. 1840. *Examen impartial et solution de toutes les questions qui se rattachent à la loi des sucres*. Paris: Le Normant.

Jefferson, Thomas. 1813a. 'Thomas Jefferson to Alexis Marie Rochon, 14 December 1813', in *The Papers of Thomas Jefferson, Volume 7: 28 November 1813 to 30 September 1814*, ed. J. Jefferson Looney. Princeton: Princeton University Press, 53–54.

Jefferson, Thomas. 1813b. 'Thomas Jefferson to André Thoüin, 14 December 1813', in *The Papers of Thomas Jefferson, Volume 7: 28 November 1813 to 30 September 1814*, ed. J. Jefferson Looney. Princeton: Princeton University Press. 54–55.

Jennings, Lawrence C. 2001. 'Associative socialism and slave emancipation in French Guiana, 1839–1848', *Outre-Mers* 88.330–331: 167–188.

Kindleberger, Charles. 1975. 'The rise of free trade in Western Europe, 1820–1875', *The Journal of Economic History* 35.1: 20–55.

Krakovitch, Odile. 1990. 'Les Antillais et les bagnes de Cayenne: nouvelle approche de la répression dans les Caraïbes', *Revue Historique* 284.1: 89–100.

Lowenthal, David. 1952. 'Colonial experiments in French Guiana, 1760–1800', *The Hispanic American Historical Review* 32.1: 22–43.

Margraf, A.S. 1762. *Opuscules chymiques*. Paris: Vincent.

Martineau, George. 1904. 'The Brussels Sugar Convention', *The Economic Journal* 14.53: 34–46.

Mintz, Sidney W. 1977. 'The so-called world system: Local initiative and local response', *Dialectical Anthropology* 2.4: 253–270.

Parmentier, Antoine Augustin. 1812. *Aperçu des résultats obtenus de la fabrication des sirops et des conserves de raisin, dans le cours des années 1810 et 1811, pour server de suite au traité publié sur cette matière, avec une notice historique et chronologique des corps sucrants*. Paris: Imprimerie Imperial.

Redlich, Fritz. 1948. 'Jacques Lafitte and the beginnings of investment banking in France', *Bulletin of the Business Historical Society* 22: 137–161.

Rolph, George M. 1917. *Something about Sugar: Its History, Growth, Manufacture, and Distribution*. San Francisco: John J. Newbegin.

Rothschild, Emma. 2006. 'A horrible tragedy in the French Atlantic', *Past and Present* 192: 67–108.

Sloane, William M. 1898. 'The continental system of Napoleon', *Political Science Quarterly* 13.2: 213–231.

Smith, Michael Stephen. 2006. *The Emergence of Modern Business Enterprise in France, 1800–1930*. Cambridge, MA: Harvard University Press.

Société d'Arcueil. 1807. *Mémoires de physique et de chimie, de la société d'Arcueil, Vol. 1*. Paris: Bernard.

Société d'Arcueil. 1809. *Mémoires de physique et de chimie, de la société d'Arcueil, Vol. 2*. Paris: Bernard.

Société d'Arcueil. 1813. *Mémoires de physique et de chimie, de la société d'Arcueil, Vol. 3*. Paris: Bernard and Klostermann.

Spieler, Miranda F. 2011. 'The destruction of liberty in French Guiana: Law, identity and the meaning of legal space, 1794–1830', *Social History* 36.3: 260–279.

Spieler, Miranda F. 2012. *Empire and Underworld: Captivity in French Guiana*. Cambridge, MA: Harvard University Press.

Todd, David. 2008. *L'identité économique de la France: libre-échange de protectionnisme, 1814–1851*. Paris: B. Grasset.

Tomich, Dale W. 1990. *Slavery in the Circuit of Sugar: Martinique and the World Economy, 1830–1848*. Baltimore: Johns Hopkins University Press.

Toth, Stephen A. 2006. *Beyond Papillon: The French Overseas Penal Colonies, 1854–1952*. Lincoln: University of Nebraska Press.

Traver, Barbara Jean. 2011. *After Kourou: Settlement schemes in French Guiana in the Age of Enlightenment*. PhD dissertation, Washington State University.

Wagley, Charles. 1960. 'Plantation America: A culture sphere', in *Caribbean Studies: A Symposium*, ed. Vera Rubin. Seattle: University of Washington Press, 3–13.

Watts, David. 1987. *The West Indies: Patterns of Development, Culture and Environmental Change since 1492*. Cambridge: Cambridge University Press.

Williams, Eric E. 1970. *From Columbus to Castro: The History of the Caribbean 1492–1969*. London: André Deutsch.

Yarrington, Jonna M. 2014. Droits *and* frontières*: Sugar and the edge of France, 1800–1860*. MA dissertation, University of Arizona.

Yarrington, Jonna M. 2018. '*Sucre indigène* and *sucre colonial*: Reconsidering the splitting of the French national sugar market, 1800–1860', *Economic Anthropology* 5.1, 20–31.

CHAPTER SIX

A School in Boniville?

Political Skills and 'Primitives' in Guyane (1930–1969)

Edenz Maurice, Centre d'Histoire de Sciences Po, Paris[1]

In 2009, the school in Maripasoula, Guyane's largest town,[2] celebrated its twentieth anniversary. This school was the first secondary school to be founded in the Upper Maroni region, mostly populated on its French side by the Boni (or Aluku).[3] The Boni, who settled in French Guiana in the late eighteenth century, are one of the three main Bushinengue (Maroon) societies present in the territory today (Bilby, 1990; Price and Price, 2004; Collomb and Jolivet, 2008; Moomou, 2013).[4] They are also the only Bushinengue to have opted for France in the late nineteenth

1 This study originates from ongoing research on social and political change within the Guyanais school system between 1930 and the late 1970s and would have been impossible without the support of the Region of French Guiana and the National Research Agency (France) which funds the 'Autochtom' project under the leadership of Benoît Trépied. I wish to thank Romain Bertrand, Gérard Collomb, Elissa Maïlander and Simone Montin for their comments and suggestions.

2 Covering 18,360 square kilometres, Maripasoula is therefore also the largest French *commune*, almost as large as Wales.

3 Note that 'Aluku' is what the Boni call themselves, after a prominent historical chief. The appellation has become increasingly common in recent years, especially in Maripasoula.

4 The Bushinengue (from the English *Bush Negroes* or the Dutch *BosNegers*) are the descendants of rebellious slaves who formed autonomous societies. While

Figure 3: Gran Man Difou in official dress (second from the left) in Boniville in 1964 (Screenshot. Guiana Triptych, 1964 Ina.fr).

century (Moomou, 2013, 477–501).[5] The school was named after the man who embodied their highest political and spiritual authority between 1937 and 1967: Gran Man Difou.

they prefer to be called Bushinengue within Guyanais political space, the words 'Maroon' or 'Maroon black' are still widely in use.

5 The Ndyuka, whose territory lies mainly over the Tapanahony Basin in Suriname, were in 1760 among the first Bushinengue to sign a peace treaty with the Dutch colonial authorities. The latter then recognized Ndyuka independence and their authority system but demanded in return their support in the fight against all other Bushinengue groups, especially the Boni. Indeed, the Boni were fighting the Dutch in the Cottica region, north of the junction which connects Albina, a border town located at the mouth of the Maroni, to Paramaribo, the capital of the colony. War eventually broke out between Boni and Ndyuka, at the end of which the Ndyuka killed the Boni chiefs and subjected the Boni to strict supervision. It was only in 1860 that the Boni broke free of this vassalage. With the support of the French governor, they obtained from the Governor of Suriname the official recognition of their independence and the right to sail freely on the Maroni. Since then, the Boni have seen themselves as French *protégés*.

The Boni were nevertheless relegated to the status of 'primitives' until the late 1970s, as much by the French colonial and then prefectural authorities and the Creoles (Jolivet, 1982)[6] as by ethnologists who built up in Guyane an aura of expertise on the issue of indigenous people. The former considered them 'savages' with a rudimentary lifestyle, resisting civilization; the latter as representatives of early humans, the last custodians of a 'pure race' whose social organization and lifestyle had to be protected. Both agreed that the Boni lacked political skills and awareness of key colonial (and postcolonial) state institutions despite—admittedly irregular and sporadic—contacts with the 'white' world during more than a century until the late 1960s.

The school's principal took advantage of its twentieth anniversary to stress that the Boni's real integration into the French school system had only taken place as late as 1969, when a government decree ended the traditional colonial division between coastal and inland Guyane.[7]

In the principal's opinion, the key players in this integration process were Robert Vignon, Maripasoula's senator-mayor and former prefect of Guyane (1947–1955), and Gran Man Tolinga who, for the first time

6 'Creole' is a self-referential word used by people born in Guyane denoting descendants of slaves emancipated in 1848, and immigrants who joined that initial group.

7 Between 1930 and 1969, Guyane was divided into two separate areas. In the north, along the coastal strip, was the colony of Guyane itself. 'Departmentalized' in 1946, that is to say transformed into a French department, until recently it has mainly been inhabited by Creoles. Beyond this coastal area lay the 'Inini'. This territory, first a colony under direct administration created by the decree of June 1930, then a departmental district under emergency law from 1951 to 1969, was predominantly populated by Amerindians and Bushinengue. For example, the district of the Inini had an autonomous budget prepared by a sub-prefect and voted by a *conseil d'arrondissement* (borough council) with the powers of a municipal council. This *conseil d'arrondissement* was composed principally of the sub-prefect, two councillors of the department and two notables. Nine municipal circles were also created within the district. Municipal functions were carried out by officers of the *gendarmerie*, designated by the prefect. These administrative units had no individualized budget; it was up to the Sub-prefect to divide up the funds between them. In sum, until the late 1960s, the Prefect of Guyane and the Sub-prefect of Inini wielded in the district of Inini the powers available to the Governor of Guyane. In March 1969, a government decree ended this emergency law. The district of Saint-Laurent was substituted for the district of Inini and municipal circles were transformed into fully functioning municipalities, including Maripasoula (see Figure 4).

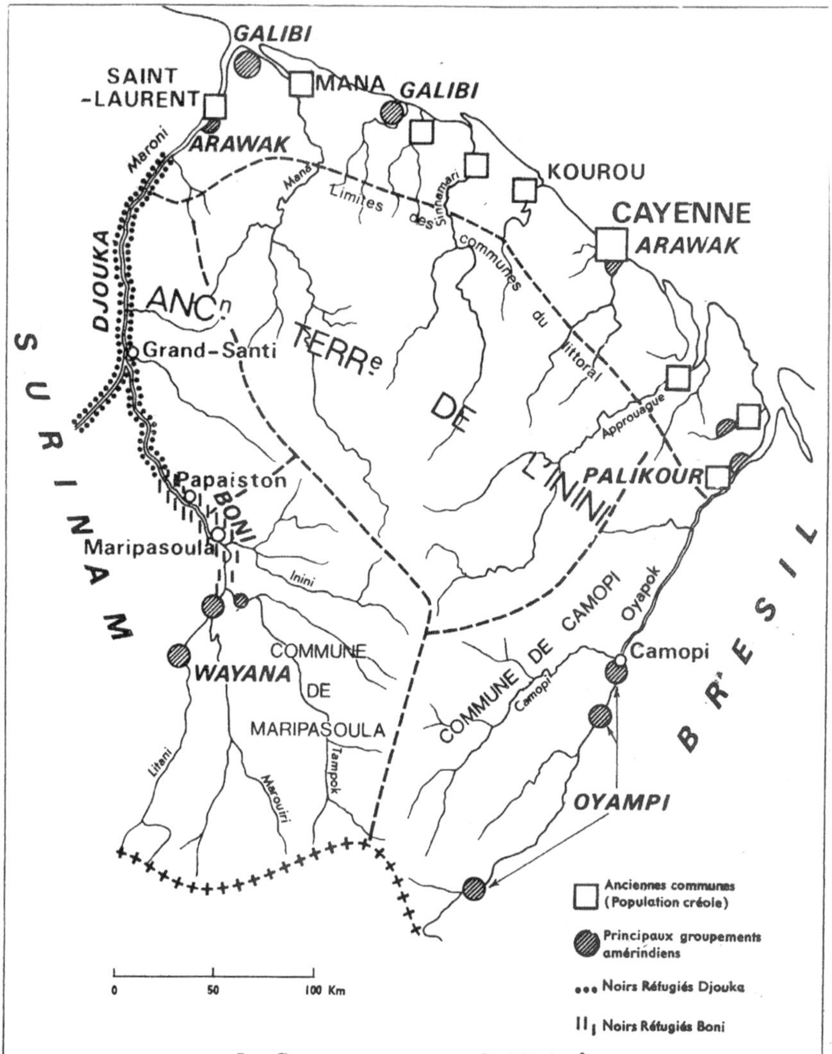

La Guyane francaise : 91 000 km^2

1656 : fondation de la colonie ; 1677 : l'amiral d'Estrée la reprend aux Hollandais ; 1763 : Choiseul tente de la coloniser ; 1852 : création du bagne ; 1968 : installation de la base du Kourou

Figure 4: Map of Guyane in 1970 (Le Fait public, No. 16, March 1970).

Figure 5: Boniville in February 1953 (from D. Bougot's private archives).

between 1969 and 1989, was both Gran Man and Mayor of Papaïchton.[8] However, the principal conceded that the first experience of the Boni with schools had been the Akaba School located in a *kampu* downstream of Boniville, then capital of 'Boni country'[9] in the 1960s, at the end of Difou's rule.

8 Born around 1908, Emmanuel Tolinga was recognized as Gran Man of the Boni from 1965/1967 until his death in 1990. At his request, the village of Papaïchton was elevated to capital of the Boni.

9 Boniville, formerly known as Agodé, was made Boni capital after Difou's accession to power, recalling the Boni's territorial rights, recognized by the French colonial authorities, over that village. The former name Agodé was actually derived phonetically from Louis Albert Grodet (1891–1893), first Governor and then Deputy of Guyane (1910–1919), who officially recognized the Boni settlement on the French bank of the Maroni—the reason for that settlement being the internal dissent caused by Gran Man Ochi's appointment (1892–1917), obliging him to leave the Dutch village of Cottica, until then the Boni country's capital and, as a result, to found another one on French territory. Boniville-Agodé's status remained unchanged until Gran Man Tolinga's accession to power. The *kampu* (from the Portuguese *o campo* or the Dutch *kamp*) is in fact a family-based habitat close to the village, where slash-and-burn agriculture is practised. It remains under its founder's authority: so the Akaba Kampu, near Boniville, belongs to Gran Man Difou.

This study proposes to review the principal's position, until now considered as established truth.[10] It was actually in the 1930s, not in the 1960s, that Difou was the key actor in a school project in Boniville involving several participants, including the Maroni Catholic Mission incumbent and the Inini district sub-prefect. Each of these immediately assigned it political objectives that could easily have clashed. From the mid-1950s, the alliance between Difou and Father Yves Barbotin, the Maripasoula incumbent, prompted a strategy which ensured that most Boni interests were met. In fact, the Boni considered an educational institution within their own society long before their *de jure* integration into the French Republic in the late 1960s. More broadly, the creation of a school in the Upper Maroni region also resulted from the context of the age-old rivalry between France and the Netherlands in a coveted region, which was 'neither French, due to the population dynamics originating from Suriname, nor Surinamese because set up in opposition to slave society' (Piantoni, 2002, 13). Consequently, the Bushinengue played a crucial role as economic intermediaries between the coast and the hinterland and as cultural go-betweens. In other words, this chapter aims to locate Guyane in a relational space characterized by dynamics and conflicts, on the local scale just as much as on the regional and imperial.

Implementing an 'histoire à parts égales' of that colonial situation, that is, a narrative that 'provides equal documentary dignity to the different formulations involved' (Bertrand, 2011, 14), requires both analysis of European institutional and private archival sources, and semi-open interviews with Boni from Maripasoula, Papaïchton and Cayenne. This methodological approach raises at least two issues. On the one hand, European archives are key sources to help piece together the Boni perspective on schools but can only offer a partial and distorted view. On the other hand, even though oral tradition has helped, thanks to abundant anthropological and historical research (Price, 1983; 1990), to provide the Boni with a relevant historical framework, this study reveals that the tradition reported today by the 'sabiman' ('the ones who know')[11] obscures Difou's leading role in founding and operating a

10 No historical analysis supports that position which, according to the school principal, was based on Tristan Bellardie's body of research, although the latter focused on the eighteenth and nineteenth centuries. Gustave Ho-Fong-Choy's MA dissertation (2003) remains the only study written about Upper Maroni schools (albeit from a Eurocentric perspective).

11 *Sabiman* is a position, but not a title, which comes with seniority and is recognized by the whole of society, in this case, the almost-centenarian and

school in Boni country, although that role was definitely acknowledged by many minor Boni players. This analysis reminds us that writing a plurivocal narrative of a single colonial situation cannot exempt us from contextualizing oral narratives. Colonized societies are indeed fraught with rivalries, tensions and ambitions. Therefore they do not hesitate to use or manipulate the resources of the colonial power in local political interactions (Naepels, 2013).

Therefore, this analysis allows us to study the Boni's political skills from the late 1930s in reclaiming an institution—in this case a school—despite the European players' insistence that the Boni were unable to perceive the school as political. This last point is decisive in so far as the Boni's thought-action repertoire lay beyond European direct knowledge. The end of Difou's rule in the mid-1960s corresponded, according to Jean Moomou, to the end of 'Maoudo Nengué téin' (the 'time of marauding Negroes') (Moomou, 2007, 51–82). This period, beginning in 1860, was characterized by increasing wealth linked to heavy river traffic to and from Guyane's coastal towns, prompted by the need to supply the industrial plants on the Upper Maroni. It confirms the ability of the Boni and the other Bushinengue peoples to mobilize forces in order to maintain control of river traffic, in particular through strong industrial action (Scholtens, 1994, 72–73, 76–80). Rethinking the role of the Boni in the field of Guyanais education, by confronting two different types of source, allows us to rethink the history of this territory on the basis of a shared chronology and a 'full and complete contemporaneity of actors' (Bertrand, 2014, 142), whatever their categorization during the colonial era.

Founding a school in Boniville

The project of a French state school in the Boni region first appeared in a March 1938 report on the management of the Maroni district by its chief, R. Augeau. According to Bourgeois-Gavardin, the colonial inspector, this project represented 'one of Difou's main requests' shortly after he became Gran Man. Accordingly, Bourgeois-Gavardin asked Augeau to clarify the necessary conditions to carry out the project, adding that the school could only achieve formal status if an administrative

therefore oldest Boni, Galmot Saïfa (Interview, Galmot Saifa, 25 October 2014, Papaïchton).

employee's post were established in the Upper Maroni area, and stating that classes would have to include 'general educational grounding and a significant amount of craft and agricultural education'.[12] If the Boni were to build the school, they should build it inside their Gran Man's village, Augeau specified, strongly recommending that a Creole instructor be appointed, as only a Creole could adapt to the Boni ways and learn the language.

The school was built in 1939 but never thrived due to a lack of instructors, and promptly fell into ruin. From 1947, the Boni benefited from the Guyanais clergy's support, specifically that of Father A. Bessac, the Upper Maroni incumbent who asked his bishop to help nominate a Guadeloupe Creole to the teaching post. This potential candidate was a war veteran whose chief quality was his ability to speak 'taki-taki', perceived to be the local pidgin (Price and Price, 2004, 29). However, according to Father G. Le Cam, Father Bessac's successor since the early 1950s, Difou had opposed the rebuilding of the school; the Boni were supposedly offended that the school had never opened, ten years after their request, despite the colonial and then the prefectural administration's promises.[13]

According to Jean Hurault, the school eventually opened in the mid-1950s (Hurault, 1972, 37).[14] And yet in February 1959, Sub-prefect J. Mathivet reported that 'he would propose the creation of a school to the Inini District Council' only if the prefect agreed to the appointment of a young Apatou Boni instructor, in which case Mathivet even considered entrusting Hurault with selecting the necessary textbooks.[15]

Although sources might disagree over when the school was (re) opened, many oral or written ones testify to its (sporadic) functioning in the 1960s. Two witnesses vividly remembered the complete commitment

12 Overseas National Archives (henceforth ANOM). GUY CORR 148. Report by Bourgeois-Gavardin, colonial inspector, and explanations provided by R. Augeau, Maroni District chief (53 pages), 22 March 1938.

13 Bishopric of French Guiana Archives. Letter dated 10 June 1953, Father Le Cam to Monseigneur Marie.

14 Jean Hurault, an engineer-geographer, was gradually considered from the 1950s to be the only scientific expert known and recognized by sociocultural groups inside Guyane.

15 Departmental Archives of Guyane [from now on AD 973]. Series WP. Letter dated 27 February 1959, Sub-prefect to warrant officer Saboly, Maripasoula circle manager and letter dated 28 February 1959, Maroni inspection tour report, sub-prefect to prefect.

of the first appointed instructors—a Creole couple from Saint Lucia.[16] Hurault argued that the school was more or less regularly attended by about 20 pupils (Hurault, 1972, 37), which Sub-prefect Mathivet confirmed in a 1961 report.[17] Lastly, in 1965, Father Raux from Maripasoula underlined the need to go into Boni country to 'prepare several Boniville schoolchildren to receive baptism'.[18]

In summary, despite their persistent 'primitive' status, the Boni demonstrated sufficient political skill to build a school in the Gran Man's village and to manage it between the late 1930s and the late '60s. In other words, education played a major political role for the Boni, especially as it took place in their capital. Moreover, the tribulations of the Boni school project, partly caused by a lack of actors from the Guyanais educational field, demonstrated that the Boni's access to schooling was a political rather than educational issue beyond local interests. The improvement of 'indigenous well-being', a notion developed by the progressive circles around Robert Delavignette[19] and invoked by Guyane's colonial administration from the mid-1930s onwards, never included native 'educational development'.

Diverging political goals

In 1938, Governor Veber assigned the Boniville school project a 'political rather than educational goal'.[20] The factors were threefold. First, anchoring the Boni on French territory was vital—in order to help the Maroni region develop economically, within the twin context of an ageing Creole mining population and the end of penal transportation in 1938, the Boni represented a very promising type of labour: perceived as physically sturdy, they constituted the largest local group with the most children.[21] They moved freely from one bank of the Maroni to the other,

16 Interview, Emile Joseph, 17 April 2014, Cayenne; interview, Béatrice Youssou, 27 October 2014, Papaïchton.

17 AD 973. Series WP. J. Miguet, Inini sub-prefect. Report on Guyanais tribal populations. Studies and proposal for a new status. 30 June 1961 (12 pages).

18 Bishopric of French Guiana Archives. Letter dated 31 April 1935, Father Raux to Monseigneur Marie.

19 Head of the Parisian Ecole Coloniale from 1937 to 1946.

20 ANOM. GUY CORR 148. Answer from the governor to the Bourgeois-Gavardin Report, August 1938 (10 pages).

21 According to R. Augeau's estimates, the Boni made up a third of the Maroni

according to the advantages offered by the different European administrations, such as the school at Cottica—the oldest Boni village—on the Dutch side across from Boniville, which underwent major renovations in the 1930s (Moomou, 2007, 66). The fear that a growing number of Boni would settle there, chiefly to enrol their children in the local school, was a major argument for creating a school in Boniville. The border region of the Maroni was marginal within the French and Dutch colonies yet it represented a space that was coveted by the two colonial powers. Thus, when an international mission arrived to define the border, Governor Veber advised R. Augeau to work on his 'contacts and [make them] as constant and progressive as possible, in order not to offend the Boni'. The support of the Bushinengue in this mission was essential for both colonial powers, be it for the material necessities of the operation (canoeing and porterage, for instance) or for its strategic aspects:

> information concerning the topography of the place, testimonials relative to the presence of such and such a village, to the allegiance of its inhabitants, the visit of such-and-such an authority, to the passage of such-and-such a mission. It is undeniable, according to the Governor, that the natives can, without being aware of it, play a first-rate intelligence role and create an atmosphere that will be favourable or unfavourable to the cause of either of the parties involved.[22]

From the same perspective, furthermore, it was crucial to strengthen French prestige. The Dutch had already founded three schools in the Upper Maroni region in the 1930s; there were none in the French Maroni district and, according to Augeau, the Cottica schoolteacher led an anti-French campaign, telling Boni children that 'they were not French, but Dutch by descent'.[23] Consequently, the third and last political goal was to tighten anew the French-Boni alliance formed in the late nineteenth century by

district population in 1938 (ANOM. GUY CORR 148. Bourgeois-Gavardin, colonial inspector's report and explanations by R. Augeau, head of the Maroni district (53 pages), 22 March 1938). According to a census conducted 20 years later by two policemen, 36% of the populations of the Maripasoula circle were Boni (AD 973. Series WP. Report by Police Officer J. Sallares and Deputy Police Sergeant R. Claire on a mission to the Franco-Surinamese border region between 12 and 24 January 1959 (52 pages)).

22 AD 973. Séries W. 660 E. Letter dated 27 August 1937, Governor Veber to R. Augeau, Maroni district head.

23 ANOM. GUY CORR 148. Colonial Inspector Bourgeois-Gavardin's report and explanations provided by R. Augeau, Maroni district head (53 pages), 22 March 1938.

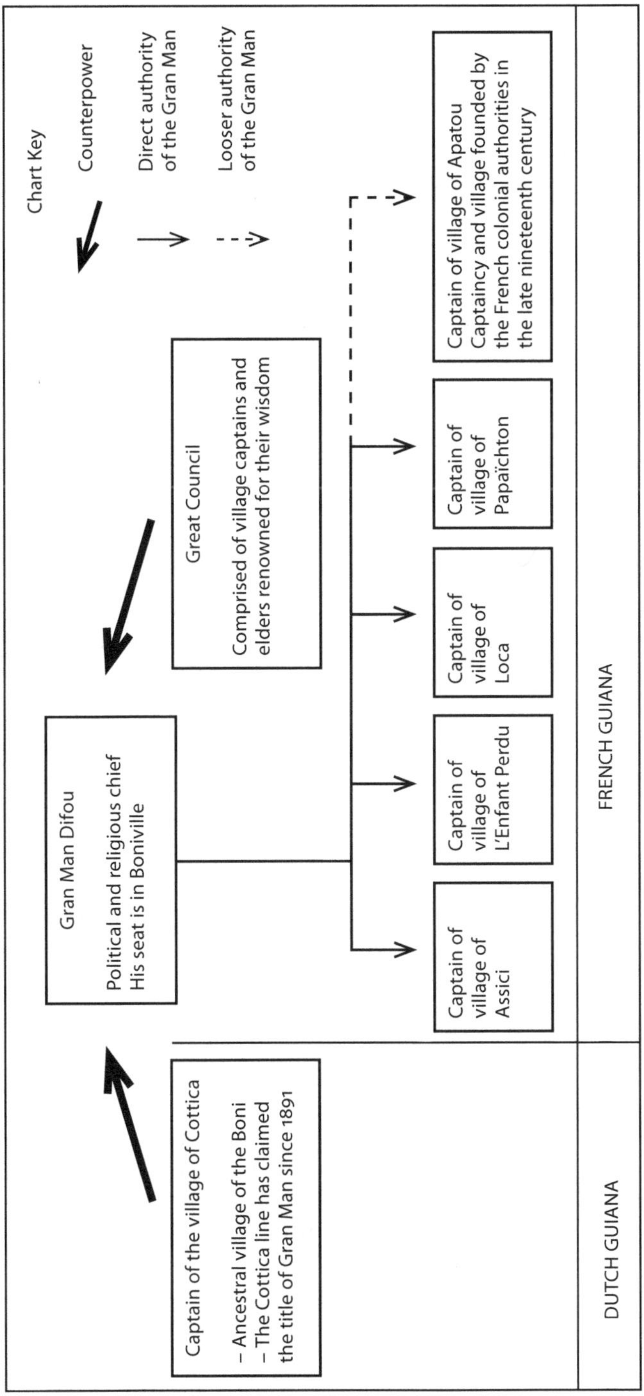

Figure 6: Boni society's political organization under Gran Man Difou

strengthening the new Gran Man's authority.[24] Inspector Bourgeois-Gavardin lamented the vagueness of the Gran Man's influence and the means of exerting it, especially in cases of dispute, considering Difou's authority 'still very weak, chiefly over his captains and village or minor local chiefs …, some of whom seem rather too influential'.[25] The Boni who had settled down in Cottica to enrol their children in the local school were thus perceived as members of a dissident movement fomented by Captain Doua, the Captain of Cottica connected to the Dutch authorities (Thabouillot, 2012, 196). Furthermore, according to Moomou, Difou's appointment revived Doua's expectations—his clan had been claiming the position of Gran Man since 1891 (2013, 307–308). Augeau, the first French colonial civil servant who attended and described the designation ceremonies of the Gran Man of the Boni, thought a school would attract and increase Boniville's demographic weight relative to other Boni villages, and thus Difou's authority over his subjects.[26]

The three political reasons for establishing a French school in Boniville—anchoring and controlling the Boni on the Maroni's French bank, strengthening French imperial prestige and securing the Gran Man's loyalty—were also put forward by the religious actors. On the one hand, the Guianese clergy's support has to be seen within the wider context of an old but renewed rationale of evangelization: the school wished to train young Boni as catechist primary school teachers. On the other hand, the Guyanais church had to cope with Dutch Protestant missions in the Maroni border region, widely subsidized by the Surinamese colonial government to ensure the academic and spiritual education of the so-called primitive populations.

From the Boni perspective, let us first note that until the late 1960s, no statutory text obliged them to enrol their children in school. Such practices were governed by a contract between the Gran Man and the colonial authorities or clergymen. Moreover, the Gran Man did not have

24 In a letter to the colonial office, the governor wrote: 'the old chiefs asked for my advice. They will most likely choose a certain Dufou, one of Awensaïe's nephews, a young man still, active and devoted to our cause. He would appear to be a useful ally' (AD 973. Governor to the colonial minister, 13 March 1937).

25 ANOM. GUY CORR 148. Colonial Inspector Bourgeois-Gavardin's report and explanations provided by R. Augeau, Maroni district head (53 pages), 22 March 1938.

26 ANOM. GUY CORR 148. Colonial Inspector Bourgeois-Gavardin's report and explanations provided by R. Augeau, Maroni District Chief (53 pages), 22 March 1938.

the authority within Boni society to force one of his captains to create a school in his village (Moomou, 2013, 310); captains had to seek the whole maternal family's consent before enrolling a child.[27] Within this general framework, the school was more of a lobbying tool in order to gain new and immediate symbolic and material advantages to improve Boni living conditions, and to reaffirm their territorial autonomy and specific allocation within the Guyanais space, both at the level of society and at village, clan or family levels (Price, 1990, 43–53).

Second, the absence of a school on the French side of the Maroni meant the Boni had to enrol their children in Cottica, so that many of them 'suffered in their dignity and their French identity'.[28] Inspector Bourgeois-Gavardin's report also mentioned 'that Difou demanded a school, the Dutch having given one to the Bosch'. Until a school opened in Akaba in the 1950s, the Boni were actually the only Bushinengue not to have schools on their territory. Richard Price points out that education provided by missionaries settled in their villages appeared among the Bushinengue populations' claims when the first treatises were concluded with the Dutch in the second half of the eighteenth century. Very early, education was seen as a way to better integrate and understand the *bakaa*[29] world, in order to efficiently negotiate the concession of material goods (Price, 1990, 66–68). More generally, the Boni, like many colonized African societies, were conscious of their indirect and sporadic knowledge of the colonial power (Cooper, 1994, 1516–1545). The lack of schools was thus long perceived as a disgrace by the Boni settled in France.[30] That feeling of shame increased when, on the Surinamese side, many Cottica Boni started attending secondary school in Paramaribo, after attending primary school in Cottica, and even got involved in Surinamese political life in the 1950s and 1960s (Scholtens, 1994, 103–109). The Boniville school thus aimed at legitimizing the Boni's choice of a French allegiance, unique among the Guianese Bushinengue societies.

27 Boni society is matrilineal so that children belong to their mother's clan and are placed under their maternal uncles' authority.

28 ANOM. GUY CORR 148. Colonial Inspector Bourgeois-Gavardin's report and explanations provided by R. Augeau, Maroni District Chief (53 pages), 22 mars 1938.

29 *Bakaa* means 'white'. The word is historically linked to the colonial world of slave plantations and, more broadly, to the coastal colonial societies of both Dutch and French Guiana.

30 Interview, Emile Jospeh, 17 April 2014, Cayenne.

Third and last, according to the priest Barbotin, in the late 1950s, the Boni refused to be despised by the Creoles any more.[31] As early as 1958, Gran Man Difou and his council claimed not only French nationality and voting rights, but also Boni representation at the General Council of Guyane,[32] which Sub-prefect Mathivet interpreted as an expression of the Boni's desire to belong to the common law system.[33] These political and academic claims clearly expressed Difou's dual vision: on the one hand, his desire for his people to better integrate into the departmental system and hence for the interconnections between their authority system and departmental representative institutions to be redefined, and, on the other, his perspective on the French Boni model confronted with the Bushinengue societies from the Surinamese territories. This was demonstrated by the testimony of B. Youssou, a former Akaba school pupil. She remembered Difou popping into school every Friday afternoon, encouraging her friends to learn 'well' in order to help him accomplish his mission.[34]

In short, the issue of a school in Boniville was definitely more political than educational. The 'Boni perspective', although we can deduce it less from 'oral tradition' than from European sources, was overall directly opposed to that of the institutional actors confronting them. For the latter, school was both a necessary tool in the violent age-old struggle between France and the Netherlands and a way of controlling a population who never considered the Maroni to be the watertight border imagined by the two rival administrations and churches. For the Boni, school and education were political concerns because they raised the double issue of their collective identity and their future within the Maroni region and Guianese space. At the local level, the creation of a school at the heart of the Boni region was all part of the age-old rivalry with the Ndyuka and, ultimately, about legitimizing their choice to settle down in Guyane in the late eighteenth century and accepting, a century later, some sort of French suzerainty. On a larger scale, Difou's school project underlined the Boni's awareness of their social and civic

31 Bishopric of French Guiana Archives. Letter dated 5 November 1958, Father Barbotin to Monseigneur Marie.

32 Bishopric of French Guiana Archives. Letter dated 29 November 1958, Father Raux to Monseigneur Marie.

33 AD 973. Series WP. J. Miguet, Inini sub-prefect. Report on the tribal populations of Guyane. Studies and proposals for a new status, 30 June 1961 (12 pages).

34 Interview, B. Youssou, 27 October 2014, Papaïchton.

interests within the context of a decolonizing process. On the Dutch side, Suriname gained considerable political autonomy in 1954 and in the process attempted a political integration of all the Bushinengue. On the French side, departmental authorities promoted the increased *francisation* of inland Guyane's native populations.

Were the conditions for opening a school in the second half of the 1960s part of Boni tactics?

Around the mid-1950s, the issue of a school in Boniville generated deeply divisive debates about the tactics (de Certeau, 1990, 59–63) to implement. These debates opposed, on the one hand, Gran Man Difou, backed by his friend Father Barbotin, to members of his council and his 'brother-in-law' Tolinga,[35] and on the other hand, Mathivet, the Inini sub-prefect, backed by Jean Hurault, to the Guyanais religious authorities.

We should first remember that the Boni school issue arose within a disturbing context for the French actors, at a time when an autonomous Suriname exerted great influence over the Maroni border region. In 1954, the Surinamese government decided to build a large administrative structure on Stoelman Islet, where the Tapanahony and Lawa intersect to form the Maroni. Opened in 1956, the Stoelman structure included a school, a boarding school, an agricultural centre, a modern hospital, many very well-stocked shops and an airport. Administrative staff belonged for the most part to the powerful Protestant congregation of the Moravian Brothers. In short, the Stoelman centre quickly structured itself as the well-maintained showcase of an autonomous Suriname, aiming to integrate Maroni Bushinengue.

In 1957, Father Barbotin submitted a new proposal to the Boni, providing temporary accommodation for a few Boni children within his presbytery to allow them to attend the Maripasoula state school. The project was twofold, first addressing the colonial and prefectural authorities' constant argument that the Boniville school failed to open for lack of an instructor;[36] second, its provided a response to the municipal authorities who, because they could not refuse the Boni children access

35 Tolinga was married to the daughter of Gran Man Awensaï (1917–1936), Difou's uncle.

36 Bishopric of French Guiana Archives. Letter dated 3 April 1955, Father Barbotin to Monseigneur Marie.

to school, objected to sharing school supplies and food costs. Difou approved the project but had to get his council's approval first.[37]

At least two trends appeared through individual positions or actions between those who opposed the principle of a school in the name of their traditional society's survival and those who considered it, as we have seen, a powerful tool for rethinking their political autonomy and collective identity. According to Father Barbotin, Captain Adisso from Assici, one of the council's key members, belonged to the first trend.[38] The Boni collective memory relates that the captain articulated the perspective of those for whom the school threatened both their religious system and their social structure. In other words, school was considered as a *bakaa* institution that might jeopardize the future of a society for which its ancestors had fought hard.[39]

According to E. Joseph's testimony, the drafting of the 1957 Difou-Barbotin project aroused marked opposition from Tolinga, who nevertheless belonged to the above-mentioned second trend. Tolinga was adamant about opening a school in Boniville, even without the Prefect's consent—which Difou objected to fiercely—as he thought that too much time had already been wasted. Thanks to his mastery of the Upper Maroni's several languages, Tolinga had been attending the many missions organized by Hurault since 1947. He was appointed in 1959 as the Maripasoula municipal circle's official interpreter and as such received an allowance almost equal to that of the captains[40] (although this did not stop him from allegedly being forbidden by Difou to leave his village for five years and to trade with Maripasoula).[41]

In spite of internal opposition, Difou wrote to Monseigneur Marie in 1958, on behalf of all the captains that: 'All Boni … realize that education is necessary'.[42] He later entrusted Father Barbotin with six boys, including his own son and two of Tolinga's nephews, for them to attend school at Maripasoula, and also asked for a girls' boarding school. It was then that Sub-prefect Mathivet, availing himself of the

37 Bishopric of French Guiana Archives. Letter dated 13 December 1957, Father Barbotin to Monseigneur Marie.

38 Bishopric of French Guiana Archives. Letter dated 13 December 1957, Father Barbotin to Monseigneur Marie.

39 Interview, Galmot Saïfa, 25 October 2014, Papaïchton.

40 AD 973. Series WP. Prefect's Maroni Inspection tours, 7–14 March 1959.

41 Interview, Emile Joseph, 17 April 2014, Cayenne.

42 Bishopric of French Guiana Archives. Letter dated 13 August 1958, Gran Man Difou to Monseigneur Marie.

Figure 7: Tolinga and his wife in Tolinga's village, September 1952 (from D. Bougot's private archives).

combined support of the population director, the Maripasoula circle manager and the geographer Hurault, wrote to the Prefect to counter the project, which he considered as the beginnings of a 'Boni home'[43] devoted to the Boni's evangelization and their accelerated assimilation.

43 In Guyane, 'home' is the name given to a boarding school managed by a Catholic religious congregation whose aim is to educate and evangelize so-called 'primitive' populations.

Relying on educational arguments for the first time, such as the risks offered by a type of education modelled on metropolitan schools, he suggested that a 30-year-old man from Vaucluse—who held only the first part of the *baccalaureat*—be appointed the primary school inspector for the 'primitive populations' and that a Boni instructor from Apatou be posted to the Boniville school.[44]

In the mid-1960s, the Boni finally obtained both a functioning school in Boniville and the enrolment of their most powerful families' children into the departmental school system, and a rudimentary educational system in the Upper Maroni. These results were achieved through a Boni strategy implemented—not without conflict—by Gran Man Difou, their highest authority within both his own society and the *bakaa* world, in conjunction with administration and Catholic authorities. In other words, well before the administrative reform of 1969, Gran Man Difou had developed the political awareness and skills necessary to meet what he considered to be specifically Boni needs: schooling in both Boniville and Maripasoula.

In conclusion, the Boniville school narrative followed an epigenetic process, 'developing through a series of unpredictable steps over time' (Veyne, 2007, 263). This process involved various actors from the scientific, religious and political realms, who interacted on the one hand with Gran Man Difou and, on the other, with local authorities, both across Guiana and in the Maroni basin specifically. Each actor promoted his own political vision for the project and, ultimately, his own field of competence and expertise. The process also implied an ongoing reformulation of relations between those actors, thereby revealing opposition, avoidance and alliance strategies beyond the colonial socio-racial dividing lines and reflecting the mistake of analysing a colonial past based on obvious disruptions and based only on French political history. This analysis shows both the limitations and uncertainties of the colonial and postcolonial state in a peripheral space, and the various areas for mediation and specific strategies offered by a situation as an indeterminate and coveted border.

First, after he was designated Gran Man, thereby causing internal dissent, Difou was the key promoter in introducing a state school in the Boni region. In the late 1930s, he won the French colonial authorities approval to open a school in Boniville, as he was indeed a key ally in

44 AD 973. Series WP. Letter dated 28 February 1959. Maroni Inspection tour Report from the sub-prefect to the prefect.

the French conflict against the Dutch colonial power. Second, taking into account all interactions between the local situation and the different actors' various and sometimes contradictory interests, allows us to identify the circumstances surrounding the Boni's introduction to the French schooling system in the second half of the 1950s. Finally, the issue of schools demonstrates the Boni's ability to take over a colonial institution and to adapt it to their own needs (although not without tensions), and consequently their early awareness of the sociopolitical challenges of education in France. The Boni were among the first Guyanais sociocultural groups between 1930 and the late 1960s to rethink the nature of their political and cultural integration into this territory, and consequently into the French Republic, in the name of an affirmed dual identity: both regional *and* national, Boni *and* French.

An analysis of Boni political skills in the educational realm also reveals the limits of traditional, 'official' oral tradition which is, in many ways, a matter of partial and situated history. Partial, because it could not fully reflect until now the significance of Difou's instrumental role in implementing an educational project which had nevertheless been thought out as early as the late 1930s. In 2011, in an article recommending innovative teaching methods for Bushinengue pupils, Serge Anelli, a former Boni Director of *collège* Gran Man Difou's 'adapted' general and vocational educational streams—and since 2014, mayor of Maripasoula—wrote: 'Emmanuel Tolinga, the future Gran Man, was the one who would do his utmost to allow Bushinengue pupils to attend school .... He even succeeded in sending three young people to continue their studies in Cayenne' (Anelli, 2011, 190). Oral history can also be considered partial because it tends to hide the various Boni authorities' diverging opinions. It is therefore situated history. Wishing to conceal dividing lines could be interpreted as a desire not to offend a defeated village's sensibilities, a clan's claims or such-and-such a family's honour in order to safeguard Boni social cohesion, especially when faced with a foreign interlocutor. The narrative told by the *sabiman* is therefore more akin to a certain Boni elite's perspective. In short, although Boni history from a Boni viewpoint has experienced a significant revival, the complexities of local politics and their resulting dividing lines—and consequently the capacity for action of the 'lowest of the low', to quote an editorial in *Politix* ('L'Etat colonial', 2004, 12)—remain major historiographical challenges.

Works cited

Anelli, Serge. 2001. 'Ajuster l'aide pédagogique aux élèves de langue maternelle Bushinengué dans les Segpas à l'ouest de la Guyane', *La Nouvelle revue de l'adaptation et de la scolarisation* 54: 185–197.

Bertrand, Romain. 2011. *L'histoire à parts égales. Récits d'une rencontre Orient-Occident*. Paris: Seuil.

Bertrand, Romain. 2014. 'Au milieu du gué. Situation(s) de l'anthropologie historique du fait colonial', *Genèses* 97: 140–148.

Bilby, Kenneth. 1990. *The Remaking of the Aluku: Culture, Politics and Maroon Ethnicity in French South America*, Ph.D., Baltimore: Johns Hopkins University.

Collomb, Gérard and Marie-José Jolivet, eds. 2008. *Histoires, identités et logiques ethniques: Amérindiens, Créoles et Noirs Marrons en Guyane*. Paris: CTHS 18.

Cooper, Frederick. 1994. 'Conflict and connection: Rethinking colonial African history', *American Historical Review* 5, 1516–1545.

de Certeau, Michel. 1990. *L'invention du quotidien. 1. Arts de faire*. Paris: Gallimard.

'L'Etat colonial', *Politix* 66, 2004: 11–13.

Ho-Fong-Choy, Gustave. 2003. *La Mise en place de l'école de la République sur le fleuve Maroni: l'exemple de Maripasoula*, MA dissertaion, Institut d'Etudes Supérieures de la Guyane, Cayenne.

Hurault, Jean. 1972. 'La Scolarisation des populations tribales en Guyane française', *Minorités. Bulletin du groupe d'études pour les minorités ethniques* 1: 29–38.

Jolivet, Marie-José. 1982. *La question créole. Essai de sociologie sur la Guyane française*. Paris: ORSTOM.

Moomou, Jean. 2007. 'Les Bushinenge en Guyane: entre rejet et intégration de la fin du XVIIIe siècle aux dernières décennies du XXe siècle', in *Comprendre la Guyane d'aujourd'hui. Un département français dans la région des Guyanes*, ed. Serge Mam Lam Fouck. Cayenne: Ibis rouge, 51–82.

Moomou, Jean. 2013. *Les Marrons Boni de Guyane. Luttes et survie en logique colonial (1712–1880)*. Cayenne: Ibis rouge.

Naepels, Michel. 2013. *Conjurer la guerre. Violence et pouvoir à Houaïlou (Nouvelle-Calédonie)*. Paris: Editions de l'EHESS.

Piantoni, Frédéric. 2002. 'Les Recompositions territoriales dans le Maroni: relation mobilité-environnement', *Revue européenne des migrations internationales* 2: 11–49.

Price, Richard. 1983. *First Time. The Historical Vision of an African American People*. Baltimore: Johns Hopkins University Press.

Price, Richard. 1990. *Alabi's World*. Baltimore: Johns Hopkins University Press.

Price, Richard and Sally Price. 2004. *Les Marrons*. La Roque d'Anthéron: Vents d'ailleurs.

Scholtens, Ben. 1994. *Bosnegers en overheid in Suriname. De ontwikkeling de politieke verhouding. 1651–1992*. Paramaribo: Adeling Cultuurstudies/minov.

Thabouillot, Gérard. 2012. *Un projet politique et administratif pour l'arrière-pays de la Guyane française: le territoire de l'Inini (1930–1969)*. PhD dissertation, Paris: Université Paris-IV.

Veyne, Paul. 2007. *Quand notre monde est devenu chrétien (392–394)*. France: Albin Michel.

CHAPTER SEVEN

Reclaiming Félix Éboué

Departmentalization and the Politics of Commemoration in Guyane, 1944–2012

Sarah Wood, University of Connecticut[1]

Félix Éboué was born in Guyane in 1884, at a time when slavery had been formally abolished for over three decades but forced labour continued within the confines of the penal complex which still dominated the colony. Éboué, whose great-grandparents had been enslaved, was a scholarship boy. As Weinstein (1972) recounts, he crossed the Atlantic in 1901 to attend *lycée* in Bordeaux before moving on to the Parisian École coloniale in 1905 and entering the colonial administration in 1908. This rapid social ascent landed him in the highly mobile and élite category of administrators whose lives spanned the continents covered by the Third Republic empire (Hélénon, 2011). As they developed intellectual and social exchanges in the interwar years these administrators helped constitute both an old-boy network around the École nationale de la France d'outre-mer (known as the École coloniale before 1934) and

1 Research for this article was funded by the University of York, the University of Manchester, the Arts and Humanities Research Council and the Society for the Study of French History. Photographs of the Éboué monument are reproduced here with the kind permission of their owners: Frédéric Lesimple, Marie-Odile Delaunay and Philippe Delaunay. I am grateful to Jessica Field and Barbara Lebrun for their careful readings of the chapter and their helpful comments. I also thank Nicola Carpentieri for his help with the classical references. Translations from French into English are my own unless otherwise stated.

a 'transnational black public sphere' as described by Edwards (2003) and Wilder (2005). Aided by friends and colleagues across both these networks, as well as by his participation in the Socialist Party (SFIO) and the freemasons, by his wife Eugénie Tell-Éboué and by the support of Marius Moutet during the Popular Front government, Félix Éboué climbed the hierarchy of the colonial administration.[2] He gained renown in 1940 as the first French colonial governor in Africa to declare support for Charles de Gaulle rather than for Vichy, allowing the Free French to take control of much of French Equatorial Africa (AEF) and enabling the Allies to gain a key, strategic foothold in the region. That year, promoted by de Gaulle, Éboué became Governor-General of AEF, the first person of African descent to hold such a position.

Hero of the Free French and lynchpin of the colonial administration, Éboué has symbolized republic and empire, liberation and domination, humanism and heroism. Assuming that these concepts must compete where they coexist, historians have sometimes struggled with—and often sidestepped—his legacy. Others have paid straightforward homage to a 'great man' of (*majuscule*) History (Alexandre, 1984; Degras, 2004). More recent scholarship has begun to take as its starting point the idea that 'republican imperialism' is not necessarily an oxymoron and that Third Republic France was, in Wilder's formulation, an 'imperial nation-state' (2005) in which 'France and its colonies' were 'one internally variegated unit' (Forsdick, 2009, 270). If empire has always been in the Republic's DNA, then historians are no longer bound to see the coexistence of empire and Republic as a puzzling contradiction to be resolved. The way is therefore open to more nuanced assessments of the 'heroic reputation' of a life made 'exemplary' (Cubitt et al., 2000) of empire, of Republic and of 'Black France'.

This chapter locates Guyane within a network of commemorative activity for Éboué, whose geography was largely Atlantic and which was bound up with negotiations over the French empire's future after the Second World War. Politicians, writers and others who publicly 'remembered' Éboué sought—for a variety of reasons—to link together local, national and pan-African political and cultural visions via this figure who might be deployed to embody all of these. The chapter traces his afterlife through three public acts of commemoration, asking

2 After beginning his career in the Oubangi-Chari province of Equatorial Africa, he later worked in Martinique, in French Soudan and, as governor, in Guadeloupe and then from 1938 in Chad.

what the repeated iterations of Éboué—and the occasional disavowal of him—can tell us about how certain Guyanais located themselves, and about how Guyane has been envisaged, amid the wider, shifting imperial formations of the Fourth and Fifth French Republics. Commemoration of Éboué, it argues, has played an important and overlooked part in the ongoing story of Guyane's incorporation into the French Republic as an overseas department, its 'departmentalization'. The chapter thus spans the period from the first acts of posthumous 'remembrance' (1944–1949), via the 1957 inauguration of parallel statues in Cayenne and Brazzaville prior to the referendum on the constitution of the Fifth Republic the following year, up to a twenty-first-century iteration of Éboué at the newly renamed airport in Matoury, near Cayenne. On all these occasions, those invoking Éboué were staking claims on his legacy in order to symbolize and reinforce the interrelatedness of Guyane and France. Each new 'site of memory', however, with its different composition of materials, symbols and functions (Nora, 1984, xxxiv), called upon a different idea of France. That certain individuals and groups have so consistently resorted to reclaiming the Guyanais who—so the story goes—'saved' France in 1940 indicates ways in which the purportedly sturdy and natural bond of departmentalization has been intentionally and repeatedly renewed and strengthened throughout the latter half of the twentieth century and into the twenty-first, usually by these very same individuals and groups, and often at the same time as French imperial dominance was challenged elsewhere.

Staking a claim: Éboué in living memory

After Éboué's early death in March 1944, writers and politicians across France and its African and American colonies celebrated his life in newspaper columns, prefaces and dedications: a nationalistic variation, perhaps, on the practices common to the transnational 'public sphere' of black intellectuals described by Brent Hayes Edwards (2003). Central to the posthumous reputation that commentators constructed for Éboué was the assertion that he had come 'first' in two domains: first 'Black' colonial governor, and 'first Resistant of overseas France'.[3] Few at

3 See, for example, the dedication in Delavignette (1946, 5). Éboué was described in such terms in newspapers including *Libération*, *L'Aurore*, *Le Monde* and *L'Humanité* (GM19/1). However, Eric Jennings's work on the African Free

the time expressed qualms about the interrelatedness of empire and Republic within this legacy, although there were variations in the emphases used. De Gaulle referred to Éboué in a 1944 speech as a 'great African Frenchman' ('grand Français africain', cited in Capdepuy, 2015, 7) and at a 1947 rally in Bordeaux called upon his memory to proclaim the necessity of a 'strong state' and a 'strong Union' (F22/23). As the centenary of 1848 approached, political actors invoked Éboué in rhetoric as the ultimate justification of the abolition of slavery. In this paternalistic narrative, French actions in liberating the slaves were vindicated by a descendant of the latter as he responded to the call of an ideologically pure, 'true France' and helped liberate it. In a more Atlanticist variety of panegyric, however, some writers—particularly in the United States—claimed Éboué as a black American, and sometimes as a socialist hero: a descendant of slaves who had chosen to act as a principled—even internationalist—humanist. These articles and obituaries depicted a 'great' man 'devoted to the ... ideal [of]: "One World" of freedom and unity'.[4] Thus, while New York claimed Éboué for black internationalism, de Gaulle and his retinue carved him a protagonist's role in the myth of French 'puissance par l'empire coloniale' (Agéron in Gildea, 2002, 19, 286). In an example of what Nelly Schmidt (2012, 106) refers to as the peculiarly French 'mythmaking' associated with the abolition of slavery, Gaullists wrote the figure of Éboué into a narrative of colonial-humanist triumph. This attempt to seal the imperial bonds between France, Africa and the Americas was contemporaneous with the negotiations described by Cooper (2014) over the existence and nature of 'French Union'. The competing and sometimes overlapping claims on Éboué in the transatlantic public sphere echoed debates being had between 1944 and 1946 among, on the one hand, politicians who sought to reform

French demonstrates why the heroic narrative which has sometimes emerged—in which Éboué, true to pure ideals, almost single-handedly enables Allied success in Africa—is far from the full story. In the first place, Jennings demonstrates how the success of the African campaign depended upon ordinary Africans and indeed upon politicians and administrators other than Éboué himself. Moreover, he explains that Éboué had also been presented with pragmatic, tactical reasons as to why he should support the Allies from Chad—such as the promise of oil supplies (2014, 31). Shipway, meanwhile, emphasizes the influence of Éboué's colleague Henri Laurentie in the decision to 'rally' (2011, 225–226).

4 These include an obituary in *Africa Today and Tomorrow*, issued by the African Academy of Arts and Research in New York, and the *Pittsburgh Courier*, June 1945, from which this quotation is taken (GM19/1).

the empire to better preserve it and, on the other, the 'small group' of 'elected deputies'—described by Cooper (2014) as 'African' but among whom Guyanais and Antillais were prominent—who tried to 'prise open the cracks in the imperial edifice of France' (ix) by arguing for more inclusive—even truly universal—definitions of citizenship.

The first wave of commemoration culminated in 1949 with the ceremonial placing of Éboué's ashes in the Panthéon along with the remains of anti-slavery campaigner Victor Schoelcher. In her classic essay on the Panthéon as 'lieu de mémoire', Mona Ozouf identified this Parisian site as a locus of national debate which has, since its creation, challenged the 'capacity of the French to reunite around their great men' (1984, 139). More recently, Charles Forsdick (2012) has deepened understanding of the processes of 'Pantheonization' and their instrumental functions, particularly with regard to the 'memory' of slavery and its abolition. The 'Pantheonization' of Éboué beside Schoelcher demonstrates well how, as Watts (2009) claims, questions of 'race'—and with them, of empire—reached the 'centre of public discourse' in post-war France. Indeed, the ceremony consolidated their place centre stage, as it sought to stage-manage the presentation of these questions in service of national and imperial unity. The newsreel of the ceremony and radio broadcast of accompanying speeches also meant that listeners and viewers across the French-speaking world might be privy to the occasion.[5] As for the Guyanais, they could not reclaim the physical ashes of their 'native son', but as long as his legacy was prominent in Paris, they might claim a symbolic place for Guyane at the heart of the new Fourth Republic. Few understood this better than the Guyanais politician Gaston Monnerville—then President of the Conseil de la République (the parliamentary second chamber)—who orchestrated the 'Pantheonization' of his friend and compatriot. Monnerville worked alongside former Free French leaders, including René Isambert, General Koenig and René Pleven,[6] to campaign for Éboué to be granted formal, national recognition. Their Comité colonial (later the Comité national) Félix Éboué evoked personal memory and sentiment as well as more patriotic ideals as it sought to gain governmental and popular support for these plans.

5 See http://www.ina.fr/video/AFE85003085/transfert-des-cendres-de-felix-eboue-et-de-victor-schoelcher-au-pantheon-video.html.

6 Isambert was then the chief colonial administrator as well as secretary of the national Éboué committee; Koenig was president of the committee at this time (GM19/1).

This Paris-based campaign was only one manifestation—albeit the best-mediatized—of a movement which also encompassed French Equatorial and West Africa, the Antilles and Guyane. Smaller-scale commemorative campaigns arose at municipal level: in Paris, it was the municipality which instigated the renaming of Place Daumesnil in the twelfth *arrondissement* as Place Félix-Éboué, while Cayenne's municipal authorities named Guyane's new *lycée*—its first—after Éboué in 1944, along with the street where he was born. Soon afterwards, local notables set up a *comité d'initiative* to raise funds for a statue. Similar monument committees were also founded in Guadeloupe, Brazzaville, Fort-Lamy and Bamako as well as Paris.[7] Cayenne's committee had first persuaded the Governor of Guyane to act as honorary president, and later brought the new President of the Conseil de la République, Gaston Monnerville, on board (GM19/1). The official information service also participated by publicizing the committee's efforts daily in its local bulletin. As they were listed here, the names of those who populated the committee were familiar from the local sections of the Ligue des droits de l'Homme et du Citoyen, the Red Cross Committee and Guyane's two masonic lodges, suggesting a secular, republican, bourgeois and/or socialist make-up. Founding members were often war veterans, and like the 'national' committee's membership, many had credentials as *compagnons de la Libération*. They presented a broad church, however, and also attracted donations from schoolchildren, associations, trade unions and the Bishop of Cayenne (ADG1J56, 1J57). More often than not, members of Éboué committees were the same people who constituted local Schoelcher committees. In the run-up to the centenary of the 1848 abolition of slavery, the Schoelcher cult—which Brown describes as variously 'imposed by colonial or national authorities' and 'created from the bottom up' (2002, 95)—was particularly strong in the French American territories; the 1949 Pantheon ceremony ensured that the same was true in 'metropolitan' France. On the day, representatives of the local Éboué and Schoelcher organizations held parallel ceremonies

7 Guadeloupe had hosted Éboué as its governor between 1936 and 1938. Brazzaville had served as the Free French capital in Africa from 1940, and was the site of the 'Brazzaville conference' of 1944—in which he participated before his death—the result of which, as Gildea (2002, 20) recounts, was a prevailing sense among the government that the future of the empire would continue to be French. Fort-Lamy (now known as N'Djamena) was the capital of Chad, the colony that Éboué had been governing in 1940. Bamako (now in Mali) was a key city of French West Africa.

in Cayenne, reaffirming the participation of local elites—despite their fierce internecine political rivalries of other kinds—and of the wider population in this transatlantic commemorative network.[8]

In a speech broadcast on national radio in 1949 (but not, apparently, made at the ceremony itself), Monnerville described Éboué as a result of Schoelcher's acts and proof positive of their worthiness. France, he implied, had been saved by a 'product' of abolition: a Black man from the colonies 'elevated' to a position of national responsibility via the humanistic colonial education system of the Third Republic. But he also reminded the French that, as was the case during the Second World War, they had depended upon Africans—and Guyanais—for their national survival. In this way, Monnerville helped advance a political vision by which imperial reform—even the end of colonialism—would be achieved through the eventual promulgation of equal citizenship across the territories of the empire.[9] As Nick Nesbitt (2007) has explained, this vision had been partly realized by the law of March 1946 converting the four *vieilles colonies* ('old colonies') into 'overseas departments'. Monnerville had been one of the key architects of this 'departmentalization', along with Léopold Bissol and Eugénie Tell-Éboué (who entered politics in 1944 as women were enfranchised) for Guadeloupe, Aimé Césaire for Martinique and Raymond Vergès for La Réunion.[10] When Monnerville made his 1949 broadcast, the Fourth Republic had for three years been remodelling the empire as the 'French Union', with the participation of deputies and senators such as the above-named, as well as Amadou Lamine Guèye, deputy for Sénégal-Mauritanie, and Léopold Sédar Senghor (who at this stage was Félix Éboué's son-in-law, having married Ginette Éboué in 1946). French West African territories such as theirs were not 'departmentalized', but some of the deputies' attempts to 'democratize colonial political structures' (Nesbitt, 2007, 33) had

8 For instance, although no love was lost between Monnerville and the poet-cum-politician Léon-Gontran Damas (Deputy for Guyane 1948–1951), both supported the Éboué committee's efforts. On the significance of local rivalries see Wood (2015).

9 This vision was a longstanding one among politicians in French West Africa and the French Americas. The 'four towns' of Saint-Louis, Dakar, Gorée and Rufisque had, like the four 'old colonies', sent deputies to the National Assembly since 1848 and those who were from these *communes* possessed limited citizenship rights. These rights were renegotiated by Éboué's friend Blaise Diagne (the 'first Black deputy') in 1915–1916. See Fogarty (2008, 239) and Wilder (2005, 129–131).

10 *Journal Officiel*, 12 March 1946.

borne fruit, for example with the law introduced by Guèye's Overseas Territories Commission according French nationality to French West Africans.[11] Debates continued over the extent to which France's many and varied imperial subjects would be represented in government, the 'overseas departments' being one of a variety of ways in which these relationships were formulated (Cooper, 2014).

Many 'overseas' deputies, along with a number of colonial troops, were present at the Pantheonization ceremony, and the event was widely reported as marking recognition of the Black contribution to the liberation of France. Yet the front line of the cortège seems to have featured no ostensibly African or Caribbean faces, and the Minister for Overseas France, Paul Coste-Floret—rather than, say, Monnerville or the Guyanais deputy Léon-Gontran Damas—made the only speech at the ceremony. Even as the occasion stood for some, as Damas wrote afterwards in the journal *Le Populaire*, as the 'symbole de la réconciliation des races et de la fraternité universelle', it was nevertheless choreographed in such a way as to present a more conservative hierarchy, with de Gaulle and other political leaders of European France, such as Coste-Floret, in the foreground and verbally interpreting the *sens* of Éboué's life.[12] Monnerville's speech, although widely broadcast, was made from an invisible position behind a radio microphone. If the Pantheon ceremony were a 'site of memory' (Nora, 1984), it was one at which the contestations over the idea of the Republic were evident, as different parties vied with one another for centre stage. The fact that Éboué was Pantheonized in the first place is testament to the efforts of those, such as Monnerville and Tell-Éboué, who attempted to write French Africans and French Americans into the post-war republican order. Yet de Gaulle and Coste-Floret's leadership of the Pantheon procession may be seen as indicative of how, by 1949, the more conservative preference for a Paris-centred federation—over the community of true equals espoused by Senghor and his ilk—was winning the political struggle taking place in Paris over the future of the empire.

Nevertheless, a number of contemporary commentators viewed France's treatment of Éboué and of Guyane in a positive light. The

11 See Assemblée Nationale, 'Amadou Lamine-Guèye'.

12 'symbol of the reconciliation of the races and of universal brotherhood … peoples are defined by their soul, and not by their race'. The term *sens* here means 'meaning' but also 'direction'; it was used in a report on the ceremony in *Le Figaro* (GM19/1).

Trinidadian politician and historian Eric Williams (1955), for example, wrote that departmentalization and the Pantheonization were concomitant statements of anti-racism on the part of the French state, and that they were felt in the Caribbean as 'the most dramatic gesture in the field of racial equality'. Given that Monnerville had been instrumental in both processes, a reassessment of his intellectual and practical role in the making of 'Black France', and of the post-war French imperial order, is overdue. Monnerville's political successes of the late 1940s—in ensuring near-egalitarian treatment of the 'old colonies' by their departmentalization and in conveying an anti-racist image of France abroad—were preceded in the 1930s by energetic promotion of Guyane, which he had represented in the National Assembly since 1933. In 1935, Monnerville instigated and directed celebrations of the tricentenary of Guyane's 'attachment' to France, and for the rest of the decade, he campaigned for the legal 'assimilation' of Guyane—which since the late nineteenth century had been ruled by direct decree from the executive head of state (Nesbitt, 2007, 33)—into metropolitan administrative norms.[13] Before Damas condemned governmental neglect of the colony in his polemical tract *Retour de Guyane* (1938), Monnerville had prefaced an inventory that was more optimistic in tone, *La Guyane méconnue* (1936), written by his friend Gabriel Bureau—an inventory of Guyane's natural resources and industrial possibilities in the hopes of attracting investment. When negotiations over the future of the 'old colonies' eventually took place, Monnerville's participation ensured that Guyane was included in the 1946 departmentalization law when doubts were expressed about its suitability (Alexandre, 1999, 206).[14] In this light, his leadership of the campaign to Pantheonize a Guyanais compatriot may be seen as pragmatic as it was ideological: a continuation of a PR campaign for his native land as well as an expression of *schoelcherisme*. It reaffirmed the place of Guyane in the Republic that had been sought by its local bourgeoisie since at least the late nineteenth century and obtained in legal terms in 1946.[15]

13 See ANOM/AGEFOM/286/2 and Assemblée Nationale, 'Gaston Monnerville'.

14 Certainly, the existence of uncounted Maroon and Amerindian populations in the so-called *territoire de l'Inini*, claiming to be 'represented' to the administration and government via 'customary chiefs' in the manner of sub-Saharan African 'indigenous' populations of the empire, might have been perceived as an obstacle to Guyane's immediate assimilation as a department of the Republic.

15 Guyane's deputies to the National Assembly, Gustave Franconie (1879–1898 and 1906–1910) and Henri Ursleur (1898–1906) advocated 'l'harmonisation des

The Guyanais who perpetuated the heroic Éboué myth did not do so merely out of patriotism. As they lobbied the governor (and then the prefect) and applied for financial and symbolic governmental support, they claimed moral legitimacy and purpose in the immediate aftermath of the Allied victory in which Éboué had (they affirmed) been so instrumental. They reminded all 'French' compatriots—especially the distant central government with its changing priorities—that France owed a debt to 'their' South Americans as much as to the African Free French and to other 'colonial' troops who had paid the French 'blood tax' (Cooper, 2014, 17). Recognition of Éboué might offer Guyane its best chance to reap its dues and redress the perceived centuries of French harm and neglect (Damas, 1938).

'Remembrance' of Éboué between 1944 and 1949 was thus in equal parts about ensuring Guyane's visibility in Paris and about materializing—and trying to shape—French power in Guyane. Still, this power had to be moulded in a certain image, and even though they did garner much popular support, the socio-professional make-up of Éboué's most prominent advocates in this 'first wave' of commemoration—largely colonial administrators and bourgeois professionals—bore a striking resemblance to Éboué himself. Name changes and centenary celebrations, Dubois (2000) reminds us, are part of a self-perpetuating, often self-aggrandizing, French-Caribbean politics of commemoration of both local and national (lone, male) heroes. In Cayenne, as across the transatlantic memorial network, the social world of the mobile, bourgeois professional was a small one, and many of those who first 'remembered' Éboué did so literally as well as symbolically, since they had known or come into contact with the man during his lifetime. The longer-term legacy of the hubris attached to Éboué in 1944—and the extent to which it would be associated with patriotic nationalism or internationalist idealism—was bound up with the future of this specific network of actors: their ability to keep their own position, their relationship with wider society and their capacity to perpetuate through time and space the *sens* (a certain interpretation of an individual's trajectory and the meaning of his choices) that they attributed to Éboué's life.

institutions républicaines ... égalité politique et legislative' ('the harmonization of republican institutions ... political and legislative equality') (Alexandre, 1999, 230)—and these ideas also found favour among the General Council, the Chamber of Commerce and the masonic lodges.

French (dis)union: reclaiming Éboué in tropical America and Africa

By 1950, the year after the Pantheon ceremony, Guyane's statue committee had reached the peak of its powers. It had raised almost a million francs and gained the support of local and national authorities on the basis of Éboué's 'souvenir [qui] contribue ... à resserrer les liens puissants qui unissent les fils de ce Département d'Outre-Mer à ceux de la France continentale'.[16] However, by 1955, the statue not yet built, preparatory sculptures and engineering works that had already been commissioned were being wound up due to an apparent lack of money. The departmental administration had cut by 80% the funds initially promised to the project.[17] Popular support faded as disillusionment grew with departmentalization and its unkept promises, while the Cayenne committee itself grew fractious and disunited. Autonomist ideas were gaining traction locally, and Éboué's reputation became tarnished due to his association with colonial administration. At the national level, Éboué's former associate de Gaulle was undergoing his 'crossing of the desert' following the demise of his Rassemblement du Peuple Français (RPF) from 1953 and his departure from party leadership (Pierce, 1954, 97). Broadly put, by the mid-1950s, the cosmopolitan vision that played a role in negotiations over the Fourth Republic and French Union had faded, in Cayenne as in Brazzaville. Central government, preoccupied with bloody entanglements in Indochina and Algeria, did not give priority to 'remembering' the solidarity between metropolitan and colonial elites that Éboué represented. Both Éboué the individual and Éboué the hero had receded from recent memory—and lost legitimacy.

Nevertheless, the monument was finally completed and inaugurated in 1957, one year before the referendum in which the Guyanais, like the voters of other territories of the Union, would decide whether or not to retain their association with France. The timing was not entirely coincidental; it appears that high-level input—as well as the tenacity of Éboué's family members—helped the project along in its final stages (F22/23/1). De Gaulle visited Guyane in 1956, the year before its completion, while André Malraux, soon-to-be Minister of State for Cultural Affairs (on

16 His 'memory [which] contributes to tightening the powerful bonds uniting the sons of this Overseas Department with those of continental France'. Letter, Prefect of Guyane to the Minister of the Interior. ADG/1J57.

17 Letter, Horth to the Prefect of Guyane, 24 October 1955. ADG/1J57.

Figure 8: A group of schoolchildren gathers to read the text on the plinth of the Félix Éboué monument in the Place des Palmistes (photograph by Frédéric Lesimple, 2007).

which see Lebovics, 1999), corresponded with Eugénie Tell-Éboué and Ginette Éboué, who were also in touch with Monnerville as the statue was being prepared. The final product occupied—and continues to occupy—the most central spot in central Cayenne, in the Place des Palmistes. This public square of palm trees, surrounded by administrative buildings, remains a civic focal point: the location of many a carnival, festival and political demonstration. Malraux, de Gaulle and Jacques Chirac, among others, have chosen to stand next to it to address the Guyanais public. In September 1958, as de Gaulle completed his tour of Africa to campaign for a 'yes' vote in the forthcoming referendum—including a stop at the newly inaugurated Éboué statue in Brazzaville—Malraux took a parallel tour of the Antilles, appealing to the Guyanais to keep the departmental status quo, which they subsequently did (Malraux, 1968, 130). On both sides of the Atlantic, then, Éboué became a figure of dual usage in 1957–1958. In the sense that local support for the statue existed and that it served—in Cayenne at least—as a local rallying point for contestatory demonstrations (Malraux, 1968, 123–129), Éboué served to remind French politicians of Guyanais and African 'contributions'. On the other hand, the monuments provided rhetorical fuel to those same politicians as they attempted to persuade the inhabitants of Guyane and Congo that their Frenchness was beyond question.

If both monuments' use as civic focal point and patriotic symbol has been somewhat conventional, the Cayenne sculpture—created by Paris-based artist Maurice Gardon with the approval of Félix's widow and daughter—is unusual in aesthetic terms. The text engraved on its stone plinth reproduces words from the plaque dedicated to Éboué in the Pantheon. In classic Third Republic style, its words hark back to a heroic, classical past, as do the friezes on the sides of the arch. The archetypical classical hero, as Drayton (2011, 33) recalls, is a man who distinguishes himself by wartime actions, and on the monument, this description is attributed to Éboué. The plinth's text, written first in ancient Greek, then French, accords him an epitaph which connects his actions to those of a small group of Spartans who supposedly held off an attack by a large Persian army at the battle of Thermopylae in 480 BCE. This text is associated with an ancient Greek lyric poet, Simonides of Cos, although on the plinth in Cayenne it remains unattributed, as if it were common knowledge.[18] Underneath, a longer passage in

18 The Greek text reads: 'Ὦ ξεῖν', ἀγγέλλειν Λακεδαιμονίοις ὅτι τῇδε κείμεθα, τοῖς κείνων ῥήμασι πειθόμενοι'. The original has been translated into English

Figure 9: The text carved in stone on the statue's plinth (photograph by Marie-Odile and Philippe Delaunay).

French—attributed to Malraux—reinterprets the Greek, applying its laudatory words to Éboué. In order to interpret the text on the plinth, then, one must follow this convoluted chain of citation from ancient Greece to Africa via Paris, which requires both knowledge of classical literature and awareness of Éboué's actions. In Guyane, a place where a French education is touted as something to aspire to but where, in practice, classical scholars are scarce, this linguistic act may well be highly symbolic of the (classical) civilizing mission of the French education system, but it is nevertheless deeply impractical.

At the same time as it claims a Greek heritage for Éboué, however, the statue also constitutes an example of a more irreverent tropical modernism, and in this way it gestures towards an emerging, common language of cosmopolitanism that might be recognizable across South America, West and Equatorial Africa and Europe. The immense, concrete-block arch cites the Arc de Triomphe in Paris, but it also precedes the Grande Arche de la Défense, constructed three decades later. The rendition of Éboué in bronze reflects Graeco-Roman heritage, but its rather unflattering, exaggerated rotundity echoes the work of the Colombian artist Fernando Botero, who had worked in Paris during the 1930s and, according to Pau-Llosa (2012), was beginning to attract fame

(William Lisle Bowles cited in Schmidt, 2005, 239) as: 'Go tell the Spartans, thou that passest by, that here, obedient to their laws, we lie'. The first French translation on the monument reads: 'Etranger, va dire à Lacédémone que ceux qui sont morts ici sont tombés dans sa loi'.

Figure 10: A closer view of the statue
(photograph by Marie-Odile and Philippe Delaunay).

by 1958.[19] All in all, the work materializes a striking idea of what sort of monument could possibly be appropriate in tropical America for a heroized colonial governor, at a moment when France stood on the cusp

19 Little is known about Gardon, but archived correspondence indicates that he was present in Paris during the early 1950s; it is likely that he encountered Botero's work and perhaps the artist himself.

between old imperialism and a new but unknown future. Erected as it was a year before the Fifth Republic's constitution was finalized, this statue suggested that, although this future may or may not be 'decolonized' (to paraphrase Kristin Ross, 1996), it would certainly be reordered. This idea of modernity was common to the 1950s iterations of the Gaullist hero: in Fort-Lamy, according to Lebovics (2004, 60–74), there was a project to build a modernist Maison de la Culture designed by Le Corbusier, in honour of Éboué, but it went unrealized as Chad elected to separate from France. The Brazzaville statue, lacking the Latin American-style aesthetic of the Cayenne figure, was nevertheless of comparably modern design, as was the football stadium in front of which it stands. Both statues stand as fascinating remnants of the twilight of the French Union, as political leaders and then voters first clung to, then hesitated between reaffirming and disavowing, the empire. The Gardon monument, with its meeting of tropicalist, pan-African, Classical and French cultural referents, belongs in a sense to the French-influenced but cosmopolitan utopia of 'Universal Civilization' imagined by proponents and successors of Négritude such as Senghor, the one-time husband of Ginette Éboué (they divorced in 1956). Influenced by Surrealism and by abstract, communist ideals of universal brotherhood, Senghor claimed to 'believe, for the future, in *la Francophonie*, or to be more precise, in *Francité*, but it must be integrated into *Latinité* and, beyond that, into a Universal Civilisation, where Negritude has already begun to play a fundamental role' (quoted in Murphy, 2009, 168). After Éboué's 1940 'rallying' to the Free French, Senghor wrote a poem, 'Au gouverneur Éboué', in praise of his actions and reclaiming him for Africa. Already the subject of this lyric panegyric, in 1958 Éboué—ever the versatile signifier—was materialized in bronze, stone and concrete, erected and sanctioned as the embodiment of a Senghorian dream of 'universal civilization' in Cayenne's public space. By comparison, his Pantheonization in 1949 appears as part of the practically consequential but ultimately limited 'discursive universalism' (Denoyelle cited in Tumblety, 2003, 484) promulgated by metropolitan French political elites after the Second World War, in which colonial subjects, like women, would be enfranchised as a reward for their contribution rather than because of 'inalienable rights'.

Yet the 1957 monument still arose out of political circumstances as much as artistic vision: after the Cayenne committee lost its impetus and funding, government officials and Éboué's family had to intervene for the monument to finally take physical form. Concrete commemoration in public space remained the preserve of a limited network of privileged actors, and the state legitimacy granted to these statues by Malraux and de Gaulle—evident in the auspicious timing of their completion—indicates that attempts were being made to reclaim Éboué for distinctly Gaullist purposes once again in 1957–1958. This time, however, commemoration in Guyane was less a product of popular activity than a top-down statement of political will. When events in Algeria led to the in-out referendum on belonging to the French Union in 1958, Gaullists were able to take advantage of the monument's aesthetic to make their appeal to the Guyanais. Its tropical modernism served to lend visual weight to de Gaulle's promise/ultimatum that a modern future for the African and American territories of the Union might (only) be secured under French tutelage.

Éboué relocated: the renaming of the airport

Éboué and his story faded into relative obscurity after 1958 as Cayenne's press and political culture refocused around lively debates about autonomy (Mam Lam Fouck, 2006). Although municipal politics were dominated by Gaullists in the late 1950s and early '60s, many Guyanais turned their attention to the Parti socialiste guyanais and its charismatic leader, Justin Catayée. Comparable to Césaire in political outlook, Catayée was, like the Martiniquan politician, a former member of the SFIO who abandoned communism in the late 1950s to form a new socialist party responding to local specificities on his return to his 'native land' following studies in Paris (Wood, 2015, 85–93). Éboué thus blended into the changing intellectual and political background, as well as the increasingly modern architectural surroundings, of 1960s–1970s Cayenne.

However, in January 2012, then President Nicolas Sarkozy countered any forgetfulness when he arrived at Matoury (near Cayenne) to inaugurate the newly renamed Félix Éboué Airport. The airport had been constructed by US forces during the Second World War to provide a refuelling point for planes flying to Africa, yet the commemorative gesture of its renaming paid little attention to the African connections of Éboué nor of Guyane (and even less to any part played by the US in the territory's history). Instead, it emphasized the French identity of both. As a gesture to Franco-American friendship, the airport had previously been named after Rochambeau, a *maréchal* of the French expeditionary forces who fought in the American War of Independence. In 1999, however, Christiane Taubira—then deputy for Guyane in the

National Assembly—called for the name to be changed. She pointed out that the son of Rochambeau had been involved in the brutalization of Haitians, and that the name was offensive in this part of the world, not least in Guyane, where thousands of Haitians were residing as refugees and migrants. Taubira did not, in 1999, suggest a specific replacement, and local associations soon initiated discussions and consultations in order to choose a new dedicatee. But, according to the Guyanais news site Blada, Taubira did launch a competition to elicit a new name from among the Guyanais population, and in 2003 this was won by a group of local schoolchildren, who chose that of Sépélu (in French, Cépérou), a Ka'lina native leader who had resisted European colonization ('Félix Eboué ou Cépérou' 2010). In 2009, the children's choice was rejected following counterpetitions and lobbying by the local 'Éboué circle'. This circle comprised local intellectuals, politicians and members of the Chamber of Commerce, thus recalling in no small measure the Éboué committee of the 1940s. As in the 1940s, Éboué was again claimed as a consensual figure by elites exercising their power to assign names: this time, however, they had competition rather than consent for their choice of hero.

As the airport's name changed, its premises underwent renovation and a small monument, mirroring in design the 1957 original in the Place de Palmistes, was erected outside the main doors. Glass panels displaying an assemblage of texts were placed above the main entrance and exit. Instead of Malraux's classical grandiloquence, they featured extracts from the poetry of Damas and Senghor. The symbolic associations of Éboué seemed at first glance to have been altered so as to refer to the literary movement of Négritude as much as—or more than—to commemorate wartime heroism, thus celebrating 'black' writing rather than that of Malraux and his Hellenic referents. On closer inspection, however, it appears that the cumulative message of the texts at the airport differs little from those of earlier commemorations; indeed, if anything, an even less subtle version of masculine heroism emerges. The excerpts selected contain almost no reference to 'blackness' or to Négritude's pan-African dimensions. This apparently colour-blind patriotism was not typical of Guyane in the 2000s, where an Association des Amis de Léon-Gontran Damas has since the late 1990s undertaken to revive local 'memory' of Damas in a way comparable to—and perhaps rivalling—the Éboué circle's activity. At around the same time as the airport was renamed, pupils and teachers painted the poem *Blanchi* by Damas, with its references to Africa, blackness and whiteness, on the wall of their French state school in Cayenne (see Wood, 2015, 78). The poems redacted at the airport, by contrast, function as an uncritical, nationalistic recuperation of Négritude on the part of the Chamber of Commerce and airport authorities as much as being a (literal) elevation of the words of 'black' writers. The carefully chosen words attribute an assertiveness to Damas and Senghor which bears little relation to the ambiguity of their original literary works (see Gyssels, this volume) nor to the fluid Négritude of Aimé Césaire, which—famously—'n'est pas une pierre' (1994). The Senghor poem on display indeed equates Éboué with *la pierre* and celebrates his erectness—'tu es debout'—suggesting militaristic masculinity and uprightness in the face of capitulation or apathy. On the small monument opposite, Éboué's own words, from the 1937 speech given in Guadeloupe, appear to incite readers to 'jouer le jeu' ('play the game'): to play the hand one is given by harmonizing external discipline ('responsabilités') with personal will and action (GM 19/1). The story of Éboué as told in its new incarnation is still one in which republican virtue and moral fibre best reveal themselves when employed in the service of the nation. The literary expression of Senghor and Damas has elsewhere been interpreted as emphasizing a 'black' contribution to universal humanity—'a challenge to an ethnocentric view of Frenchness as the expression of white, metropolitan, French culture' (Murphy, 2009, 165)—but here it is deployed to serve a masculinist, martial, rhetorical agenda and, in practical terms, to herald the tightening of the ties between Cayenne and Paris.

The recuperation of Négritude at the airport gains a new significance when we take into account the gradual disassociation of Guyane—via its international airport—from non-French destinations. When the airport was first built, flight paths linked Cayenne to countries of the Americas, Europe and Africa.[20] In 1949, as Éboué's remains entered the Pantheon, these connections were paralleled by the French Union's attempts to consolidate political and cultural connections between these continents. However, flights from Cayenne in the twenty-first century chart a rather different map, serving almost exclusively to convey passengers to and from Paris and Martinique (Socie, 2004, 8–9). Likewise, the

20 In 1939, the US company Panam ran flights to Cayenne from San Juan (Puerto Rico) via Port-of-Spain (Trinidad) and Georgetown (then British Guiana). After the Second World War, which saw Cayenne connected to Africa for military purposes, Air France linked Cayenne into a Caribbean archipelago which included San Juan and Curaçao. By 1961 it was operating a Miami-Cayenne arc and the flight to Paris from Cayenne passed via Lisbon (Chardon, 1987, 1–68).

commemorations at the renovated airport offer a rather uncosmopolitan presentation of nationalistic heroic virtue and a celebration of discipline and morality in a way that implicitly consigns France's African dimensions to the past, and with them the cosmopolitan visions of the 1940s and '50s. If, as Murphy (2009, 164) claims, 'Negritude might loosely be defined as the cultural "revolt" of a colonized elite against the path that the colonial system had laid out for it', then the commemorations at the airport try to claim not only the *sens* of Éboué's life but also that of Senghor's and Damas's Négritude. At the key point of arrival and departure for the state functionaries, politicians, business people and students who regularly make the pilgrimage to and from Paris, the elite mythmakers behind Éboué's 2012 incarnation constructed a public face and identity for Guyane on the basis of a direct link to Paris which, over time, has allowed for fewer and fewer detours.

Conclusion

The afterlife of Félix Éboué remains, to cite Cooper (2005, 11), a 'space of empire': a 'terrain where concepts' are 'imposed' but also 'engaged and contested'. So it was at the Pantheon in 1949, so it was in Guyane's public spaces in 1944 and 1957 and so at the airport in the early twenty-first century. For the Guyanais politician Taubira (2012), the instigator of the recent name change, French political space was the locus of personal and political 'combats', as it was for Monnerville (see Mouralis, 2005, 101)—and indeed Éboué—before her. Like many Guyanais and French individuals, they used rhetorical, visual and material languages of commemoration within a certain political arena in which they knew these might gain recognition and legitimacy. In doing so, these actors identified and explored both mechanisms of oppression and, at the same time, tools with which they considered that emancipation from oppression might be achieved. Taubira obtained the removal of Rochambeau's name from the airport on the grounds of its association with imperialist violence. Yet the local renaming committee was still bound to choose a replacement which could acquire national legitimacy, and did so in the context of the apparent 'resurgence' in the mid-2000s of colonial 'questions' in national discourse, the furore surrounding the 2005 law referring to alleged 'positive' aspects of colonialism being a case in point (Coquio, 2008, 11). Hence the committee chose perhaps the only legacy in which French elites across the political spectrum might find some common ground: in short, that of a man who confuses by his status as both 'colonized' and 'colonizer' but who might be claimed as a 'hero' by either Sarkozy or Taubira. Celebrating an exemplary life of 'Black France', however, entailed ignoring the choice expressed by Guyane's children to elevate a Ka'lina hero. Rather than accepting a mascot of resistance to French colonization, local elites—interpreting Éboué's 1937 exhortation to 'play the game', perhaps, as they assigned this same text to the new monument—chose to play Guyane's historical trump card in order to reinforce its French identity.

Change is afoot, however. Since the postwar period, Guyane's demographics have changed considerably, high birth and immigration rates meaning that by 2012, INSEE could count more people in Guyane who had been born outside the department than within its borders ('Migrations, famille et vieillissement', 2012). The sociological composition of the Cayenne-based elite social and political circles, meanwhile, has—excepting the increasing numbers of women in political roles—remained little changed since 1944. The state's reach has always been limited in Guyane, and in this context, demographic change has aggravated existing social fault lines and brought new ones. Cultural, economic and linguistic gaps appear to be widening and hardening between those who embody and assert Guyane's Frenchness—usually enabled to do so only because they have left Guyane—and those without access to the geographical, cultural and social mobility on which 'Frenchness' depends in South America. Worried by the porosity of borders they perceive as under-protected by a distant central state, many voters in the traditionally socialist constituencies of Guyane have turned to more conservative forces and in 2007 a small majority gave their approval to Sarkozy's Union pour un Mouvement Populaire.[21] Yet in September 2016 as he campaigned to return to executive office, revelations in the press about contemptuous remarks Sarkozy had allegedly made in 2008 regarding cultural and intellectual life in Guyane indicated that Guyanais voters' support for him was not reciprocated by any interest in or understanding of them on his part.[22] Nevertheless, it was ultimately from Sarkozy—who, as president, set himself up as

21 In the first round of the 2017 presidential election, almost a quarter of the Guyanais vote went to Marine le Pen ('Présidentielle', 2017).

22 In September 2016, a former advisor to Sarkozy revealed that in 2008 the latter had expressed dread at the prospect of spending the night in Guyane and disparaged half of its population as 'illiterate'. See 'Sarkozy selon Buisson' (2016).

gatekeeper of the national narrative—that those seeking to rename the airport had to gain approval for their choice. In this context, it is perhaps unsurprising that they invoked Éboué since he provided the most powerful and indisputable referent of Guyane's—and indeed 'Black France's—claim to recognition and legitimacy.

With departmentalization in 1946, Monnerville sought for Guyane the path of 'emancipation' from colonialism but without state sovereignty: something, perhaps, like the utopian visions of Senghor and Césaire described by Wilder (2015). The airport's renaming in 2012 was testament to forms of neocolonial dependence that have, in practice, taken shape since 1946, when Éboué's legacy was used to help obtain Guyane's 'departmentalization'. Nevertheless, the future of Guyane's relationship with France remains open. Against a background of official nationalism propagated by elites used to the transatlantic, Paris-Cayenne paths of mobility, Guyane's children—more likely to be mobile within Caribbean and Amazonian South America—chose Sépélu, a native Ka'lina, as their emblem. In doing so, they demonstrated what Gilroy (2004) has described as the 'conviviality' that is possible after empire in multicultural societies. The utopian futures dreamed of at the end of the Second World War have been described as 'impossible', but Guyane's on-the-ground cosmopolitanism offers glimpses of them.

Works cited

Alexandre, Rodolphe. 1984. *Hommage à Félix Éboué*. Guyane: Conseil Régional.

Alexandre, Rodolphe. 1999. *Gaston Monnerville et la Guyane, 1897–1948*. Guadeloupe: Ibis rouge.

Assemblée Nationale. *Amadou Lamine-Guèye*. http://www2.assemblee-nationale.fr/sycomore/fiche/(num_dept)/4314 (accessed 23 November 2014).

Assemblée Nationale. *Gaston Monnerville*. http://www2.assemblee-nationale.fr/sycomore/fiche/(num_dept)/5348 (accessed 23 November 2014).

Brown, Laurence. 2002. 'Monuments to freedom, monuments to nation: The politics of emancipation and remembrance in the eastern Caribbean', *Slavery and Abolition* 23.3: 93–116.

Bureau, Gabriel. 1936. *La Guyane méconnue*. Paris: Fasquelle.

Capdepuy, Arlette. 2015. *Félix Éboué: De Cayenne au Panthéon (1884–1944)*. Paris: Karthala.

Césaire, Aimé. 1994 [1939]. *Cahier d'un retour au pays natal*. Paris: Présence africaine.

Chardon, Jean-Pierre. 1987. *L'avion dans les Antilles: géographie des transports aériens des îles de la Caraïbe*. Bordeaux: Centre de Recherches sur les Espaces Tropicaux.

Cooper, Frederick. 2005. *Colonialism in Question: Theory, Knowledge, History*. London: University of California Press.

Cooper, Frederick. 2014. *Citizenship between Empire and Nation: Remaking France and French Africa, 1945–1960*. Princeton: Princeton University Press.

Coquio, Catherine. 2008. 'Retours du colonial?', in *Retours du colonial? Disculpation et réhabilitation de l'histoire colonial*, ed. Catherine Coquio. Nantes: L'Atalante, 9–43.

Cubitt, Geoffrey. 2000. 'Introduction: Heroic reputations and exemplary lives', in *Heroic Reputations and Exemplary Lives*, ed. Geoffrey Cubitt and Allen Warren. Manchester: Manchester University Press, 1–27.

Damas, Léon-Gontran. 1938. *Retour de Guyane*. Paris: José Corti.

Degras, Jean-Claude. 2004. *Félix Eboué. Le gouverneur nègre de la République (1936–1944)*. Paris: Editions le Manuscrit.

Delavignette, Robert. 1946. *Les Constructeurs de la France d'Outre-Mer*. Paris: Editions Corrêa.

Drayton, Richard. 2011. 'The problem of the hero(ine) in Caribbean history', *Small Axe* 34: 26–45.

Dubois, Laurent. 2000. 'La République Métissée: Citizenship, Colonialism, and the Borders of French History', *Cultural Studies* 14.1: 15–34.

Edwards, Brent H. 2003. *The Practice of Diaspora: Literature, Translation, and the Rise of Black Internationalism*. London: Harvard University Press.

'Félix Eboué ou Cépérou: Deux noms pour un aéroport qui en a déjà un', *Blada*, 8 April 2010. https://www.blada.com/jodlas/5332-Felix_Eboue_ou_Ceperou_deux_noms_pour_un_aeroport_qui_en_a_deja_un.htm (accessed 6 September 2016).

Fogarty, Richard. 2008. *Race and War in France: Colonial Subjects in the French Army, 1914–1918*. Baltimore: The Johns Hopkins University Press.

Forsdick, Charles. 2009. 'Colonialism, postcolonialism and the cultures of commemoration', in *Postcolonial Thought in the French-Speaking World*, ed. Charles Forsdick and David Murphy. Liverpool: Liverpool University Press, 271–284.

Forsdick, Charles. 2012. 'The Pantheon's empty plinth: commemorating slavery in contemporary France', *Atlantic Studies* 9.3: 279–297.

Gildea, Robert. 2002. *France since 1945*. Oxford: Oxford University Press.

Gilroy, Paul. 2004. *After Empire: Melancholia or Convivial Culture?* London: Routledge.

Hélénon, Véronique. 2011. *French Caribbeans in Africa: Diasporic Connections and Colonial Administration, 1880–1939*. Basingstoke: Palgrave Macmillan.

INSEE. 2012. 'Migrations, famille et vieillissement: défis et enjeux pour la Guyane', *Antianéchos*. http://www.insee.fr/fr/themes/document.asp?reg_id=25&ref_id=19085 (accessed 28 September 2014).

Jennings, Eric. 2014. *La France libre fut africaine*. Paris: Editions Perrin.

Lebovics, Herman. 1999. *Mona Lisa's Escort: André Malraux and the Reinvention of French Culture*. London: Cornell University Press.

Lebovics, Herman. 2004. *Bringing the Empire Back Home: France in the Global Age*. London: Duke University Press.

Malraux, André. 1968. *Antimemoirs*. London: Hamish Hamilton.

Mam Lam Fouck, Serge. 2009. 'L'Union du Peuple Guyanais et l'invention du nationalisme en Guyane française (1955–1965)', *Outre-mers* 93: 259–292.

Mouralis, Bernard. 2005. 'René Maran et Gaston Monnerville: entre négritude et radicalisme', *Francofónia* 14: 101–122.

Murphy, David. 2009. 'Léopold Sédar Senghor: Race, language, empire', in *Postcolonial Thought in the French-Speaking World*, ed. Charles Forsdick and David Murphy. Liverpool: Liverpool University Press, 157–170.

Nesbitt, Nick. 2007. 'Departmentalization and the logic of decolonization', *L'Esprit Créateur* 47.1: 32–43.

Nora, Pierre. 1984. 'Entre mémoire et histoire. La problématique des lieux', in *Les Lieux de mémoire 1. La République*, ed. Pierre Nora. Paris: Gallimard, xvii–xlii.

Ozouf, Mona. 1984. 'Le Pantheon. L'École normale des morts', in *Les lieux de mémoire 1. La République*, ed. Pierre Nora. Paris: Gallimard, 139–166.

Pau-Llosa, Ricardo. 2012. 'Botero and sculpture', *Sculpture* 31.8: 26–31.

Pierce, Roy. 1954. 'De Gaulle and the RPF: A post-mortem', *The Journal of Politics* 16.1: 96–119.

'Présidentielle 2017: Guyane', *Le Monde*. http://www.lemonde.fr/guyane/guyane,973/elections/presidentielle-2017/ (accessed 18 June 2017).

Ross, Kristin. 1996. *Fast Cars, Clean Bodies: Decolonization and the Reordering of French Culture*. London: The MIT Press.

'Sarkozy selon Buisson: la Guyane "200 000 habitants dont la moitié d'analphabètes"', *France Info: Outre-mer 1ère*, 29 September 2016. http://la1ere.francetvinfo.fr/sarkozy-selon-buisson-la-guyane-200-000-habitants-dont-la-moitie-d-analphabetes-401635.html (accessed 12 November 2016).

Schmidt, Michael. 2005. *The First Poets: Lives of the Ancient Greek Poets*. New York: Alfred A. Knopf.

Schmidt, Nelly. 2012. 'Teaching and commemorating slavery and abolition in France: From organized forgetfulness to historical debates', in *Politics of Memory: Making Slavery Visible in the Public Space*, ed. Ana Lucia Araujo. London: Routledge, 106–123.

Shipway, Martin. 2011. 'Thinking like an empire: Governor Henri Laurentie and postwar plans for the late French colonial "empire-state"', in *The*

French Colonial Mind Volume I: Mental Maps of Empire and Colonial Encounters, ed. Martin Thomas. London: University of Nebraska Press, 219–250.
Socie, Michel. 2004. *Etude et propositions concernant la desserte extérieure de la Guyane*. Paris: Ministère de l'Équipement, des Transports, de l'aménagement du Territoire, du Tourisme et de la Mer.
Taubira, Christiane. 2012. *Mes météores: combats politiques au long cours*. Paris: Flammarion.
Tumblety, Joan. 2003. 'Responses to women's enfranchisement in France, 1944–1945', *Women's Studies International Forum* 26.5: 483–497.
Watts, Richard. 2009. 'Negritude, Présence Africaine, race', in *Postcolonial Thought in the French-Speaking World*, ed. Charles Forsdick and David Murphy. Liverpool: Liverpool University Press, 227–237.
Weinstein, Brian. 1972. *Éboué*. London: Oxford University Press.
Wilder, Gary. 2005. *The Imperial Nation State: Negritude and Colonial Humanism between the Two World Wars*. London: University of Chicago Press.
Wilder, Gary. 2015. *Freedom Time: Negritude, Decolonization, and the Future of the World*. London: Duke University Press.
Williams, Eric. 1955. 'The contemporary pattern of race relations in the Caribbean', *Phylon* 16.4: 367–379.
Wood, Sarah. 2015. *Tensions of Development and Negotiations of Identity at the Periphery of France: Guyane française since 1946*. PhD dissertation, University of Manchester.

Archival sources

Archives du Centre d'Histoire du Vingtième Siècle, fonds Gaston Monnerville
GM19
GM21
GM26

Archives de la Fondation Charles de Gaulle
F22/22
F22/23

Archives départementales de Guyane (ADG)
1J56
1J57

Archives Nationales de l'Outre-Mer (ANOM)
AGEFOM/286/2

PART III

Relocating Culture: Language, Art and Identity

CHAPTER EIGHT

Palikur, a Language between Two Worlds

Antonia Cristinoi and François Nemo, Université d'Orléans

The Palikur people occupy several territories in the Brazilian state of Amapá and in Guyane, an ambiguous situation which has a strong impact on their present life in terms of identity, education, language and citizenship. This situation is the product of a long and complex history stretching back to the beginning of the sixteenth century—in 1500, Vincente Yañez Pinzon first mentions a 'Costa de Paricuria'—and marked by the Treaty of Utrecht (1713), which ultimately resulted in the Swiss arbitration (1900) that ended the dispute between Brazil and France over the possession of Amapá.

Based on our 15 years of fieldwork in Guyane, spent conducting lexicographical work for a Palikur-French dictionary and sociolinguistic surveys, we shall discuss how the Palikur linguistic situation in Guyane is influenced by permanent contact and movements between this French *département d'Outre-mer* and Brazil, and how these factors contribute to defining and locating the identity of this moving population in contemporary Guyane. This analysis of the linguistic situation of the Palikur people and of the political, religious and social realities associated with it will also show that the linguistic and symbolic borders of Guyane go far beyond the current political borders.

We focus here on the place that a Native American language can hold in a highly multilingual context. In this case, it is exposed to the two national languages of French and Portuguese and to two French-based Creoles: French Guianese Creole and Karipuna. Specifically, we consider the ways in which the Palikur language can be preserved, both through a slowing of the creolization process (a process which may otherwise have led to the disappearance of the language) and through the transition towards a written form, entailing the creation of language documentation resources and of dictionaries to fight lexical erosion, as well as the standardization of spelling. This transition has been imposed by mandatory schooling and hastened by the use of modern communication devices.

The Palikur people and language

The Palikur language belongs to the Arawakan family. It possesses a complex grammar, including one of the richest classifier systems in the world (Green 1994; Aikhenvald and Green 1998; Cristinoi 2014). This complexity, combined with linguistic contact with 'simpler' languages, can in itself constitute a reason for language loss, as has been seen in numerous situations of language endangerment. For example, as far as number expression and numeral classifiers[1] are concerned, the French forms are preferred to the Palikur ones and the Palikur classifier system is presently declining. It is quite difficult to know the exact number of Palikur speakers but our data clearly shows that the population is experiencing high demographic growth. Since Nimuendaju counted 188 speakers in Brazil and 49 in Guyane in 1926, the situation has changed dramatically: 1,293 Palikur people were registered in Brazil in 2010 by the Indigenous Educational and Research Institute and even though there are as yet no exact numbers for Guyane (due to the fact that the state does not collect statistics of this kind and to the incessant population flow between Guyane and Brazil), several estimations—of 720 (Passes, 1998), between 700 and 1,000 (Launey, 2009) and over 1,200 (according to our own census conducted in 2011)—indicate that the evolution is fairly straightforward.

It is quite difficult to consider Palikur as a written language since written resources are scarce. At the time of writing, they consist of: a translation of the Bible into Palikur, a Palikur-Portuguese dictionary based on the Bible translation (Green and Green, 2010), several school manuals in Brazil, a Palikur grammar by Michel Launey (2003) and

1 Morphological devices used to express number depending on the nature and the shape of the object designated by a noun. In Palikur there are, for example, 20 different morphemes corresponding to the English numeral *one*.

several books containing traditional stories in Guyane. The complex writing system developed by Harold and Diana Green is neither generally used nor standardized and most Palikur speakers are unable to use it.

The Palikur people consider their native land to be the River Urucaua (Aukwa in Palikur) in northern Amapá, from which several waves of migration towards Guyane have occurred since the Swiss arbitration on the border issue in 1900 (Grenand and Grenand 1987; Grenand 2009). In 1925, Nimuendaju mentioned one important settlement in Brazil (Arucaua, 186 inhabitants) and four in Guyane, along the Oyapock or its affluents: Yuminã, Crique Marouan, Coumancouman and Montagne Bruyère. Several other territories were later occupied and then deserted for various reasons, including religious ones (Passes, 1998) and we can presently count three major settlements in Brazil (several villages on the River Urucaua, one village on the road between Oiapoque and Macapá and several families in and around the village of Oiapoque) and three in Guyane (the villages Espérance 1, Espérance 2, Savane and Gabaret in Saint-Georges-de-l'Oyapock, two villages near Macouria and one in Regina). On the French side we can add the small community of the village Favard near Roura and two families in the village of Trois Paletuviers, communities which are seldom mentioned in the relevant literature but are quite actively involved in conservation issues.

The interactions and movements among all these villages are constant and permanent but linguistic dynamics vary noticeably according to a combination of factors, such as isolation, contact, ecology, religion and schooling.

Fieldwork and methodology

In the early 1980s, the anthropologists Françoise and Pierre Grenand began to undertake fieldwork towards a Palikur-French dictionary. Their project has been continued since 2000 by a team of linguists from the Laboratoire ligérien de linguistique, and this chapter arises from these 15 years of fieldwork. The lexicographical fieldwork was performed mainly in Saint-Georges-de-l'Oyapock but also in Macouria, and surveys dedicated to the sociolinguistic reality of the Palikur were conducted in all the Palikur settlements in Guyane, with the exception of Favard (Cristinoi and Nemo 2013; Nemo and Cristinoi 2016). In 2011, surveys (reinforced by participant observation) were conducted on the languages spoken by the Palikur population and in 2014 others were conducted on lexical erosion, with speakers aged from seven to 60. Participant observation was also an important part of the study: on two occasions, in 2012 and 2014, Antonia Cristinoi lived for six months with the family of Clarisse Labonté in Espérance 2. We also undertook shorter field trips—mainly forest expeditions—with different groups of informants, testing lexical erosion and linguistic competence for the biolexicon.

The findings of this complex fieldwork are related to:

- the languages used and the context of use for each (family, casual social interaction with people speaking other languages or with Palikur speakers from other villages, administration, school);
- how language use evolved over the past 30 years (by comparing our own work with that of previous researchers, such as Françoise and Pierre Grenand);
- the contexts of language preservation;
- the speakers' relationship to their native language, especially in Guyane;
- lexical dynamics in various settlements in Guyane and the factors that have an influence on them;
- the speakers' relationship to writing in general and to the writing system that is used in Brazil and has been more or less imported to Guyane;
- the political stakes of language conservation and documentation.

The Palikur people and multilingualism in Guyane and Brazil: languages used and sociolinguistic context

Even if numerous contacts and cases of population migration are noted between Guyane and Brazil, the linguistic situations in the two countries are different. Determining exactly which languages people use and in what contexts requires great patience and, although surveys are certainly helpful, participant observation is ultimately the most effective methodology. Surveys may indicate what people think of their linguistic practices, but observation shows actual practices, and sometimes the two techniques can give different results. The conclusions presented here refer to actual linguistic practices and not to alleged ones.

Palikur people in Guyane speak four languages: Palikur, firstly, is spoken in family contexts, in religious (evangelical Protestant) contexts and, rarely, in schools through the system of cultural and bilingual mediators (Alby and Léglise, 2006); French Guianese Creole is used in current spoken interactions with other people in Guyane, such as Creoles or other Native American groups and in Catholic religious contexts; Karipuna Creole serves in daily interactions with other indigenous people from Brazil (namely Galibi Marwono and Karipuna); and, finally, French is the language of school, administration and television. It must be noted, however, that younger generations (those under 40) born in Guyane and living in inland settlements such as Macouria and Régina do not speak Karipuna, as they have no contact with indigenous populations other than Palikur from Brazil. The Palikur people in Brazil are slightly less multilingual than those from Guyane, and use mainly three languages: Palikur with family, in church (again evangelical Protestant), and in primary school education; Karipuna Creole in daily interactions with other indigenous people from Brazil (namely Galibi Marwono and Karipuna) and Guyane; and, finally, Brazilian Portuguese, the language of school, administration and television.

The linguistic situation of Palikur speakers in Guyane has evolved significantly over the last 30 years. Even though some linguistic and cultural elements have been lost forever, we have noticed that, over the last ten years, linguistic dynamics have somehow been reversed, allowing for a more optimistic perspective on language documentation and conservation in Guyane. The data used to illustrate this point come from researchers including Pierre and Françoise Grenand (unpublished fieldwork and personal communications), Gabriel Bergounioux (unpublished fieldwork on Palikur phonology), Passes (1998), Alby and Léglise (2006), Leconte and Caitucoli (2003) and from our own fieldwork between 1999 and 2014.

Before 2000, the Palikur language was steadily declining as communities underwent a strong process of creolization. Some of the older speakers no longer see the point of language transmission, their language and culture being considered inferior, unimportant and useless (the language of education being French and the language of interethnic communication Creole), and there are visible tensions between the various communities. Younger generations claim not to see the point of learning the language (as social success can only be ensured by speaking French) and the increasing presence of neo-Protestant religions coming from Brazil does not really serve language and culture conservation.

Demographic growth is rather limited in certain settlements, such as Saint-Georges, due to their isolation. Despite the creation of new settlements, there is no trace or recognition of indigenous languages in schools, where French is compulsory, both during the educational process (classes) and during breaks (in Saint-Georges, the use of French in the schoolyard is mandatory).

Since 2000, the number of speakers has increased progressively and Palikur is used on a wider scale, including in school contexts due to the bilingual mediator system Intervenant en Langue Maternelle (ILM).[2] The language acquired a higher status and wider transmission, and the proclamation and defence of a Palikur identity became an important issue for the community (interestingly enough, religion played a federating role in this process as the frequency of intercommunal religious meetings has increased considerably over the past few years). This was notable among the younger generation, who had presumably lost the language in Saint-Georges but later proved to be almost monolingual parents. From a declining and fragile language continually losing importance in the face of French-based Creoles, Palikur has now become the main language allowing communication between the populations of Guyane and Brazil. Paradoxically enough, after a period of strong decline, and with Creoles losing ground, Palikur has become the only vehicular alternative for younger people from Guyane (speaking mainly French and Palikur) and those from Brazil (speaking mainly Brazilian Portuguese and Palikur). In addition, for political reasons and in view of claims relating to identity, people have become more interested in writing and knowledge transmission.

Before 2000, French Guianese Creole progressively replaced Palikur in daily exchanges and came to be spoken by the entire Palikur population, even in family contexts. It had a high social status and younger generations were strongly encouraged by their parents to use it. This corresponded with the role played at the time by Creole society in the villages containing Palikur settlements: speaking Creole used to be associated with social and professional success. During the early 2000s, however, Creole was increasingly replaced by French as a vehicular language, as a result of compulsory education in French

2 Intervenant en Langue Maternelle is a programme created in 1998, involving bilingual mediators supposed to help native children with learning difficulties in schools and to provide some exposure to native languages to native speakers within the educational system.

and the increasing presence of administrative apparatuses. In Palikur communities the Creole language continues to lose ground to Palikur in daily interactions. This is due to factors such as the changing status of Palikur and contacts—even marriages—generated by economically triggered Palikur migration between Brazil and Guyane.

If French was somewhat marginal before 2000, its use increased rapidly due to its compulsory status in schools and the administration. We have noticed that, at least in Espérance 2, younger people (between seven and 40) are more often than not more fluent in French than in Creole. It must also be noted that the Creole presence in villages like Régina and Saint-Georges has diminished dramatically while the number of people from metropolitan France has increased considerably.

Language preservation contexts in Guyane: Protestant and Catholic churches, anti-religious groupings and schooling

Alan Passes states that 'any rift among today's Pa'ikwené [Palikur] is less likely to do with country of residence than religion, in the form of antagonisms between Christians and non-Christians on the one hand, and, especially, converts to the different Protestant sects on the other' (1998, 19). Even though we cannot fully agree with Passes's statement (as linguistic situation cannot be so easily dissociated from the country of residence), it cannot be denied that today, language preservation or language loss depends heavily on religious factors.

Protestant churches

Three neo-Protestant churches[3] are present among the Palikur communities in Guyane: evangelical Pentecostalism (the Assembleía de Deus is omnipresent in communities in Brazil, and the most influential in Guyane), Adventism (in communities like Esperance 1) and Jehova's Witnesses (increasingly present in Guyane, at least in Saint-Georges). These three churches have different impacts on language and culture preservation.[4] The Assembleía de Deus is the most widespread and

3 For more on the relationship between the Palikur and religion, see Passes (1998).

4 All the information presented in this section comes from our field observations (2000–2014).

influential religious institution in the Palikur world, and has both a cultural and linguistic impact. Even though it denies traditional culture and rituals (traditional dances and music, shamanism and myths), it plays an important role in general language preservation and contact between the various communities in Guyane and Brazil. There are several major factors favouring language conservation. First, the religious service is performed in Palikur; second, the structure of the service—prayers accompanied by songs and dancing—makes it attractive for younger people who have become very involved in religious practice. Then there are several cross-border events each year: church thus becomes a place where people meet and an important factor in the creation of new Palikur couples. Finally, the most important written resource of Palikur—the translation of the Bible—is used by the Assembleía, thus encouraging reading and writing (by using the spelling system developed in Brazil). Consequently, as far as we could see, this church has played an important role in the revival of the language over the last few years.

The Adventist church is far less present in Palikur communities but seems to have had relatively dramatic effects on both language and culture as it banished all traditional knowledge (traditional medicine, music and dances, shamanic practices and culinary habits) and the services were held mainly in Portuguese. Also, it did not encourage community activities or conservation actions of any kind. The Jehova's Witnesses, finally, have only recently begun to interest Palikur people and the number of Palikur believers is too small for us too claim that this movement has had any influence at all on Palikur language and culture. However, it is worth noting that one of the most important elements in converting Palikur to this religion is that proselytizers make visible efforts to speak the language. This in itself clearly shows the new, high status of the language. Moreover, when a Palikur school was created in Esperance 2, the Jehova's Witnesses were among the first students eager to learn Palikur.

Catholic Church and anti-religious groups

Despite the Catholic Church's long history of violent conversion, in the Palikur context it is not exactly the most influential. It does not play a direct role in language conservation as the service is held in French and Creole. Yet, as it does not interfere with the traditional ways of life, it indirectly allows the preservation of a more specialized lexicon (for instance, the biolexicon and the lexicon concerning ritual practices since traditional medicine and rituals are not banned by this religion).

Even though it does not interfere with cultural heritage in the same way as other religions do, and grants a more visible conservation of non-linguistic traditions (rituals, dance, music), the Catholic Church nevertheless manages to alter traditional mythology and knowledge. Stories about the Palikur genesis featuring Adam, Eve and Noah,[5] but also the traditional hummingbird and heron, have been recorded with Catholic speakers in Trois Palétuviers, as have traditional feasts and dances for the Catholic Easter festival in Régina and Gabaret.

There are very few anti-religious Palikur. Some are in fact baptized in the Catholic religion but overtly mock religion and the Church. They actively try to preserve language and tradition and often complain that younger generations are not interested in transmission. They possess important cultural knowledge—of traditional rituals and techniques—as well as lexical knowledge, and they preserve the complexity of the language, including parts of the lexicon that are elsewhere subject to lexical erosion.

Schooling

The introduction of bilingual and cultural mediators in schools can be considered progress as far as the position of the French system regarding indigenous language conservation is concerned, and yet it is rather difficult to say that this measure has had any positive impact on the preservation of Palikur. Nevertheless, this form of presence of indigenous languages within the school system granted its speakers a place in society and consequently they began to declare themselves Palikur: something which had long been considered as shameful. Indeed, Palikur people unable to speak French or Creole would consider themselves inferior to others and think that their language and culture had a lesser value than the dominant ones (French and Creole). The system thus managed to contribute to the acquisition of a higher status for the language, which may eventually have a positive impact on conservation issues. It is too early to predict the effects of France's ratification of the European Charter of Regional Languages in January 2014, but it is possible that this may eventually lead to the production and diffusion of books in Palikur through the educational system.

The failure of the official education system led to parallel initiatives from Palikur speakers themselves. In Saint-Georges-de-l'Oyapock, the idea of a 'Palikur school' for people from outside the Palikur community

5 This kind of 'mythological pollution' also occurs with Protestant religions.

(in order to earn some money for an indigenous association, the Tinogbe association) has been circulating for several years now and the school was created in the summer of 2014 by the Tinogbe association in Espérance 2. More precisely, this association comes from the part of Espérance 2 that is also called 'Village Philogène' and which forms the core of language conservation efforts in Saint-Georges. Antonia Cristinoi, who was living in Village Philogène at the time, participated in the creation of the school and attended several classes. The set of students was quite unexpected and gave us some interesting insight into conservation issues. The attendees of the first classes were as might be expected: a Creole teacher, two Creole Jehova's Witnesses, a French/Creole-speaking Palikur from Espérance 1 and the linguist mentioned above, Antonia Cristinoi. This situation progressively changed during the classes which followed and in the end the classes were attended exclusively (except for the linguist) by Palikur-speaking people: either young people from the Gabaret community wanting to learn 'true Palikur', or older ones from the same village or from Village Philogène who wanted to learn 'how to write the language'. In the end it turned out that the main function of the school was to teach Palikur and Palikur spelling to native Palikur speakers. Ironic as it may be, this situation clearly shows how dramatically speakers' attitudes towards language transmission and conservation have changed in the last few years.

The speakers and the language

As shown above, during the last decade we witnessed the declining status of French Guianese Creole and the increasing use of Palikur. These changes were the result of both population migration and contact, and speakers' awareness of the advantages of claiming a Palikur identity—demanding the right to use specific territories for traditional activities, for example[6]—and thus their desire to present themselves as such.

Even though we can definitely see increasing interest in transmitting the language to the next generation, language competence is considered imperfect and incomplete by new generations in search of learning the 'true Palikur'. More complex, formal registers (such as *awnbukaki*, a

6 Indigenous people in Guyane have the right to claim so-called *Zones de droits d'usage* where they can freely exploit natural resources so as to preserve traditional activities.

formal language used by the ancestors that was not documented before 2014 and which we discovered during our lexicographical surveys) and *kyaptunka* (a ceremonial language used for inter-clan communication, first documented by Françoise Grenand in the 1980s) have almost or completely disappeared. This goes along with a growing interest in writing the language—as in the example of the Palikur school—and in documenting it, as in the active participation of the speakers in our dictionary-making process.

However, though these language dynamics are positive on the whole, different degrees of linguistic competence were recorded in Guyane depending on geographical position (ecology, isolation and contact with other populations), age and several other factors. This was shown in lexical erosion surveys that we conducted in 2014 in Saint-Georges, Macouria and Régina.

Lexical erosion (Cristinoi and Nemo 2013; Nemo and Cristinoi 2016) is a linguistic process of word or sense loss that affects a part of the lexicon closely related to specific cultural practices and to a particular lifestyle. It affects various semantic fields: fauna and flora, traditional activities, ritual practices, and formal and ceremonial language levels. The process can be fourfold: loss of a specific referent (object, ritual, etc.) and of the word used to designate it, loss of the referent but not of the word used to designate it (speakers know the word but not the object to which it refers), loss of the word but not of the referent (speakers know the referent, often an animal or plant, but not its name) and loss of specific senses of a word.

Our surveys revealed that lexical erosion affected different lexical spans depending on the age of the speakers (which is quite possible for any culture) but also on the environment the speakers evolve in; that is, the lexical competence of similar age groups varied according to eco-geographical factors and language contact.

In Macouria, linguistic competence regarding forest animals and plants was rather low while general daily vocabulary, even with quite subtle adjectives, was surprisingly high. For situations in which the referent was known but not the name, the Palikur name was replaced by a French one. One other surprising finding was that words concerning fishing techniques were better preserved in Régina than in Saint-Georges and better preserved in Brazil than in Guyane. If the loss of words concerning fishing techniques is explained by ecology in the second case (in Brazil, most Palikur live in marshlands and their main food source is fish, whereas in Saint-Georges the Oyapock River, too large and too dangerous, is not the Palikur's main source of fish), there is also an economic factor to be taken into account. Social aid allows Palikur in Guyane to buy food more easily, leading in turn to the loss of hunting and fishing techniques which are no longer necessary to provide food and thus of the loss of the words that go with them. However, if we go back to the first case, we can see that since access to shops in Régina is more difficult than in Saint-Georges, people tend to provide for themselves and hence preserve the part of the lexicon concerning this part of their life. Overall, and in all of the settlements covered by the survey, the lexical categories preserved are those concerning daily interactions: home, common activities, body parts, names of animals and plants with which speakers are in contact directly or use frequently.

It must also be added that cross-border interactions (occasional trips, marriages or permanent stays) play an important role in revitalizing linguistic competence in a given settlement. This was the case in the settlements near Macouria. Due to their proximity to the capital Cayenne, Palikur was almost completely replaced by Creole and French, but contacts with people from Brazil revitalized the language, since—as explained above—Palikur was the only possible vehicular language. The same goes for Palikur in the Village Favard settlement, which had almost disappeared.

Writing Palikur: still a challenge

Even though a written form of the language was proposed over 30 years ago, the spelling used in the key published works written in Palikur—the Bible translation, the Palikur-Portuguese dictionary (Green and Green, 2010), school books in Brazil, Launey's grammar (2003) and sets of traditional stories in Guyane—is failing to gain a foothold in the contemporary Palikur world. There is only one place to learn to write Palikur—school in Brazil—and, as the writing system is, on the one hand, adapted to Brazilian Portuguese spelling and, on the other, deprived of clear spelling rules, the Palikur in Guyane find it difficult to use and to understand. People capable of writing the language are thus highly considered and currently quite difficult to find.

Spelling is considered very complicated but Palikur people increasingly demand its standardization and tests performed in 2011 by François Nemo showed a strong heterography among the speakers. Some attempts to propose a new spelling system were made, and even though it is rather unusable, the current one has a symbolic value: it embodies the writing of the Bible, something which plays an important role in a world largely converted to evangelical Pentecostalism. Moreover, designing a new writing system adapted to a Francophone environment may create a new schism among Palikur people from Guyane and Brazil. Consequently, even though writing the language is becoming increasingly important for its speakers and has a crucial conservation value, the political stakes of changing or keeping the present writing system are not to be neglected and the situation is presently at something of an impasse.

There are major political issues at stake in writing the language on a global (French and Brazilian) basis. One of them is standardization and the creation, more or less artificial, of a linguistic norm in a context where major differences in terms of pronunciation and word forms are registered from one village to another. This is not to mention the differences generated by contact with French or Portuguese. To choose one form would be to favour one country or one settlement over another and would present the possibility of harmful repercussions.

However, there are some potential benefits to the unification of writing and language. These include the chance to create new written documents, to disseminate them through modern communication devices such as the internet and mobile phones, and the engagement of community members themselves in documentation work which would help preserve cultural specificities. Writing would also contribute to changing the status of the language among its speakers, by giving it more importance and a new sense of existence, and would alter the way the community is perceived at a wider regional or national scale (in this case, in Guyane). It would also give greater cohesion to the community and open the way for it to become more active politically. In particular, this could lead to requests for the right to use specific territories in Guyane, as is already the case in Brazil, and to a political recognition of the Palikur as part of the Guianese melting pot.

Conclusion

History, environment, contact, migration, religion and language have an important impact on how a specific population defines its identity. Throughout history, the Palikur identity has been constantly altered and redefined. Incessant movements between the two countries inhabited by the community, along with a certain exposure to religious, linguistic and cultural diversity, has contributed to preserving some of the Palikur's traditional values and to saving the language from certain extinction.

However, if we can presently see in Guyane the first generations of genuine 'French' Palikur, who do not identify as coming from Aukwa, the Palikur homeland, their existence would be impossible without the linguistic and cultural inflow from contact with the Brazilian side. The modern Palikur identity would be inconceivable without the constant exchanges between the two countries, which clearly shows that as far as the Palikur people are concerned, the location of Guyane transcends its current political borders.

Works cited

Aikhenvald, Alexandra Y., and Diana Green. 1998. 'Palikur and the typology of classifiers', *Anthropological Linguistics* 40.3: 429–480.

Alby Sophie, and Isabelle Léglise. 2006. 'L'enseignement en Guyane et les langues régionales, réflexions sociolinguistiques et didactiques', *Marges Linguistiques* 10: 245–261.

Cristinoi, Antonia. 2014. 'A la frontière entre morphologie et sémantique, les suffixes classificateurs en palikur', *Revue de Sémantique et Pragmatique* 35–36: 179–191.

Cristinoi Antonia, and François Nemo. 2013. 'Challenges in Endangered Language Lexicography', in *Lexicography and Dictionaries in the Information Age*, ed. Deny A. Kwary et al. Denpassar: Airlangga University Press, 126–132.

Green, Diana. 1994. 'Palikúr numerals', translated from 'O sistema numérico da língua Palikúr', *Boletim do Museu Paraense Emílio Goeldi, Belém-Pará* 10.2: 261–303.

Green, Diana, and Harold H. Green. 2010. *Yuwit kawihka dicionário Palikúr – Português*. Dallas: SIL International.

Grenand, Françoise, ed. 2009. *Encyclopédies palikur, wayana, wayãpi: langue, milieu et histoire, fascicule Encyclopédie des Amérindiens de Guyane*. Paris: PUO-CTHS.

Grenand, Pierre, and Françoise Grenand. 1987. 'La Côte d'Amapá, de la bouche de l'amazone a la baie d'Oiapoque, à travers la tradition orale Palikur', *Boletim do Museu Paraense Emílio Goeldi, Belém-Pará, n.s. Antropologia* 3.1: 1–77.

Leconte, Fabienne, and Claude Caitucoli. 2003. 'Contacts de langues en Guyane: une enquête à Saint-Georges de l'Oyapock', in *Contacts de langues Modèles, Typologies, Interventions*, ed. Jacqueline. Billiez. Paris: L'Harmattan, 37–60.

Launey, Michel. 2003. *Awna parikwaki: introduction à la langue palikur de Guyane et de l'Amapá*. Paris: IRD.

Launey, Michel. 2009. 'La Langue Palikur', in *Langues de Guyane*, ed. Odile Renault-Lescure and Laurence Goury. Cayenne: IRD, Vents d'ailleurs, 57–65.

Nimuendaju, Curt. 2009 [1925]. *Les Indiens Palikur et leurs voisins*. Orléans: Presses Universitaires d'Orléans/CTHS.

Nemo, François, and Antonia Cristinoi. 2016. 'Redefining priorities, methods and standards in endangered-language lexicography: From lexical erosion in Palikur to areal lexicography', in *Endangered Languages: Issues of Ecology, Policy and Documentation*, ed. Luna Filipović and Martin Pütz. Amsterdam/Philadelphia: IMPACT Studies in Language and Society.

Passes, Alan. 1998. *The Hearer, the Hunter and the Agouti Head: Aspects of Intercommunication and Conviviality among the Pa'ikené (Palikur) of French Guiana*. PhD dissertation, University of St Andrews.

CHAPTER NINE

Maroon Art in Guyane

New Forms, New Discourses[1]

Sally Price, www.richandsally.net

The organizers of the conference that gave birth to this volume asked (among other questions) whether Guyane is in some sense a 'margin of Europe'. Physically, of course, it's more like a margin of Suriname and Brazil. And culturally, at least from the perspective of my neighbours in Martinique, it seems like a very marginal extension of the Antilles. It could easily be argued that it's not really 'central' to anything, except perhaps outer space, because of the Ariane launch pad.

For the Suriname Maroons, Guyane was a decidedly marginal territory for most of the twentieth century. When Richard Price and I began our explorations of Maroon culture in the 1960s, our neighbours along the Upper Suriname River talked about Guyane as a faraway, decidedly mythical place. Many of the men from the village where we lived were working in 'Kuhu' (the Guyanais coastal town of Kourou), but they were not in any sense at home there. They stayed only long enough to earn the money they needed to buy supplies for life back in the interior of Suriname. And women, few of whom had ever ventured beyond Maroon territory, gave free reign to their imagination in the songs they composed

1 Some of the material in this essay appeared in Price (2007); the argument is further developed in 'An Anthropologist's Dilemma', to be published in *Maroon Cosmopolitics: Personhood, Creativity, and Incorporation*, edited by Olívia María Gomes da Cunha.

about Guyane on the basis of what they considered to be exotic tales brought back by returning kinsmen.

Around the time of Suriname's independence from the Netherlands, in 1975, all this began to change. The elders who had almost always said no when men asked permission to bring their wives with them to Guyane, started to acquiesce to their demands. And by the time of our own first entry into Guyane in 1986, we found whole families from our upriver village living in Kourou, adapting pretty well to their new life in the ramshackle Village Saramaka.

Since then, of course, the influx has mushroomed and fully 32% of Maroons are now living more or less permanently in Guyane (Price, 2013). Moving from a sleepy little neo-colony with a population in the tens of thousands mid-twentieth century to the booming home of the European space centre and a population fast approaching the 300,000 mark, Guyane has taken on an economically, politically and culturally new identity. In the process it has (or rather, France has) implemented a programme of *francisation* designed to bring Guyane into line in terms of French language, education, values and lifestyle. This assimilationist politics has had a profound impact on (among other things) the Maroon art of woodcarving, known in the various Maroon languages as *tembe*—or at least that considerable portion of *tembe* objects that pass through the new channels of distribution, from souvenir shops, cultural festivals and art exhibits to public commissions and government-supported cooperatives.

Local art enters the marketplace

One organizational instrument that has been moving Maroons into a more central position on the stage of Guyane's culture are the cooperatives that have been popping up with ever-increasing frequency. In the 1960s, 1970s and 1980s, the number of new *associations* mushroomed from 80 to 360 to 820 (Dourgnon, 1998). A quick introduction to the two most active Maroon cultural *associations*, Libi Na Wan and Mama Bobi, can illustrate the different kinds of activities they sponsor.

The Libi Na Wan *association* promotes Maroon artists, especially in connection with its goals of development and job training. Based in Kourou (home to the space centre that launches European Ariane rockets), it has close ties (in terms of both personnel and finance) to the company responsible for replacing the insalubrious shacks of the

Maroon section, built by Maroon men using detritus culled from the construction sites where they worked as labourers, with modern housing in this fast-expanding town where class and ethnicity correlate purposefully with the construction style of each separately designed neighbourhood. Libi Na Wan, in collaboration with the Architecture School of Grenoble, has authored a series of glossy books/catalogues on Maroon culture and art. It has received generous financial support from governmental agencies in Guyane, the European Community, the Architecture School of Grenoble and a number of other sources. The cabinetry workshop is especially active, but its creative design projects also include gift boxes, knife handles and beach chairs—all the combined product of European-inspired designs and decorative art by Maroon men and women. Members of Libi Na Wan have exhibited their art in a number of locations, including galleries in Paris.

The Mama Bobi cultural centre, based in the westernmost town of Saint-Laurent-du-Maroni with a second office upriver in the Aluku village of Apatou, was founded in 1990. Its vocal spokesman is Gérard Guillemot, a Frenchman who arrived in Guyane in the 1970s. Guillemot (universally known only as 'Gé') exerts tight control over the *association*'s activities, claiming political motivations related to an interest in decolonization and Guyane's independence movement. Mama Bobi supports programmes involving environmental concerns and alternative medicine, for example through ties to a drug rehabilitation centre and projects centred on the diffusion of knowledge about medicinal plants. In addition to art exhibitions and demonstrations of herbal remedies, the cooperative sells postcards, posters and t-shirts.

Redefining meaning

Associations concerned with Maroon art are in a privileged position to define, develop and promote not only the art itself, but also the discourse that explains its meaning. And as Maroons move into an ever more integrated role within the larger society, that means refitting both forms and discourses for a market economy—something that the European members of the *associations* are particularly well equipped to handle. In that context, certain ideas that have long dominated outsiders' imagination concerning Maroons have been called into service and refitted for promotional purposes. One of these centres on the assertion that the motifs used in Maroon art are heavily laden with symbolic meaning—the idea that men's woodcarving, *tembe*, constitutes a veritable language of symbols.

Each named motif, the argument goes, carries a specific meaning, and the various motifs on a given carving then work together to transmit a discursive message. As a non-Maroon forestry worker who compiled a dictionary of Maroon symbols put it,

> The motifs can be considered like words. ... By assigning the right meanings to these motifs and reading them correctly, just like letters and words, it is possible to bring out the maker's intent. Exactly the way a comma can change the sense of a sentence, the presence of a particular motif next to another one alters its meaning. (Muntslag, 1979, 31)

Where did outsiders come up with the idea that Maroon art was a symbolic language? Not from Maroons, who tend to express exasperation when outsiders demand a symbolic reading of a woodcarving. Reports in the literature of encounters in which visitors to Maroon villages were showing interest in a Maroon woodcarving, often with an eye to purchasing it, reveal a persistent tendency for them to insist on confirming preconceived notions about people they see largely as dark-skinned, barefoot, cicatrized natives. The stereotype includes a conviction that such people live in a world not only of superstition and magic, but also of pervasive (and predominantly erotic) symbolism. This same tendency has been amply documented by evidence from every corner of the non-Western world. Having devoted a whole book to the subject (Price, 1989), I won't belabour the point here, except to say that well-meaning visitors, enjoying the power of persuasion that comes from being on the privileged end of a financially unbalanced relationship, have more often than not been able to extract the interpretation that comforts their initial assumptions.

In the case of Maroon art, a second factor has reinforced the idea of pervasive symbolism in art. Men's woodcarving (the only medium to be taken seriously by outsiders, who have generally seemed only dimly aware that women also produce art) has traditionally served as an important instrument in the ongoing maintenance of sexual relationships; most carvings have been destined as gifts of affection for wives and lovers. In this sense they operate as messages of love, but messages of the same sort as a bouquet of roses, a diamond ring or a heart shape penned at the end of a letter in the Western world.

What then happens with the insistence on a symbolic language once Maroons start producing art in the new environment of twenty-first-century Guyane? Under the French assimilationist politics of recent decades, Maroons have been moving out of their villages in the interior, but they have not in any sense become mainstream Guyanais. Rather, they have shifted from a perceived status as Primitives into what has come to be known (see MacCannell, 1990) as 'ex-primitives'.

The role of residence status

But before I go further, there's an important caveat. Leaving Suriname behind in order to focus on the situation in Guyane, it would be disingenuous to talk about Maroons in general. Indeed, there's a significant disparity between those who are French citizens or legal residents and those many others who are maintaining a precarious existence as illegal immigrants in constant fear of deportation back to Suriname, where many of their villages were ravaged by the civil war of the 1980s and '90s. While Guyane's assimilationist efforts have brought new opportunities to Maroons who are citizens or legal residents, other Maroons in Guyane have been much less well-placed to reap the benefits.

Aluku artists (who are all French citizens, and have representation in the government) and those other Maroons who have been able to acquire residence papers (and in some cases even citizenship) have, quite logically, moved their time and energy away from the provision of traditional objects for their wives (who, in any case, have moved on to commercial replacements, from washing machines to rice-cookers) and into the more lucrative field of framed paintings and souvenir items that they can sell for cash. Some have also been able to land commissions for the decoration of public buildings such as schools and town halls. And exhibition opportunities have opened up, with cultural undertakings such as the massive Biennale du Marronnage in Matoury providing the venue for displays and sales to non-Maroon buyers. Articles on individual artists and Maroon art more generally appear with regularity in local publications and internet sites such as *Une Saison en Guyane*, *La Semaine Guyanaise* or *Blada*, giving their work welcome exposure to tourists and residents of Guyane alike. Some Maroon artists (but only those with residence papers) have had opportunities for travel (to places as far flung as France and China) that brings their work to the attention of an international clientele. And many have created their own websites or Facebook pages, which also attract new buyers for their art. In this paper, my comments refer principally to developments that affect those

Maroons who enjoy a legal status; the many Maroons who get by in Guyane through, for example, occasional off-the-books construction jobs or jerry-built roadside woodcarving stands, would call for a rather different commentary.

That said, let's look now at the kinds of development in Maroon art that have been nurtured by the proliferation of *associations*—first, changes in the forms produced, and second in the discourse used to promote those forms.

The tradition of innovation

One striking feature that has characterized Maroon art from its very beginnings in the nineteenth century is the extent to which it has depended on creative innovation. Maroon artists have always produced new forms, new designs and new techniques with impressive frequency. In the 1960s, for example, a Maroon woodcarver invented coffee tables for sale to tourists that had circular indentations designed to hold individual cocktail glasses. A later innovation involved the use of paint on calabashes. Or again, in the 1990s, when the AIDS prevention campaign was having trouble because the bananas they used to demonstrate condoms kept going soft, a Maroon woodcarver developed articulating dildos in wood for the purpose. Around the same time another Maroon artist began creating beautifully sculpted back seats for motorbikes. And Maroon women's arts are no less creative: recent examples range from openwork engravings on calabashes to painted designs on wrap skirts. In other words, the development of new forms has always been a fundamental part of the business of being a Maroon artist.

This focus on innovation—a kind of heightened appreciation of novelty—has fed productively into the new marketing economy for Maroon men's art, fuelling an important shift over the past several decades away from objects like canoes and door lintels, and towards a proliferation of novel forms, especially small paintings suitable for framing or large ones for installing on public buildings. The palette, too, has responded to the new clientele; while woodcarving by Eastern Maroons (that is, Alukus, Ndyukas and Pamakas) has since the early twentieth century included occasional painted accents, the new forms that are taking over the market are uniquely painted (that is, they include no carving). And the limited colour range of a generation ago, which rarely strayed from a muted red, white, and black, has given way to a vibrant palette of bright commercial paints.[2] In the process, two new terms have been added to the Guyanais vocabulary for Maroon art: *ferfi tembe* (painted *tembe*) and *art tembe* (presumably to clarify the product for Europeans, who might not be familiar with the term *tembe*).

The new dominance of brilliantly coloured art is not simply a matter of its aesthetic appeal. It also has its roots in the distinction that I mentioned between legal and illegal residents of Guyane, since Saamakas—the one group that has never used colour in its art—are heavily represented in the illegal portion of the Maroon population, and thus have less easy access to the new marketing outlets that have become available in Guyane. So the shift in the kinds of forms produced and the new focus on colour are hardly surprising developments. The shift in the explanatory discourse about Maroon art is a bit more complicated, and more interesting.

Promoting symbolism, inventing history

The first thing to note is that the idea of coded symbolic messages has become omnipresent in books, magazines, exhibit brochures, websites and media outlets such as radio and television. Just a couple of examples to illustrate the trend …

One of the many coffee-table books put out by the Libi Na Wan *association* asserts that:

> The symbolic figures … constitute a kind of lexicon that is transmitted from generation to generation. … Each sign is there both for the way its form contributes to the overall composition and for its meaning. The message can be romantic, moral, humorous, or even insolent … what we're dealing with here are actual messages, with the carved object generally serving as a 'gift' designed to illustrate the feelings of a man for a woman, and that not in any casual or devil-may-care fashion, but in such a way that the happy recipient can decipher, below the surface lines, a veritable discourse. Whether it's classic or provocative, humorous or austere, it always communicates something to someone. (Doat, Schneegens and Schneegens, 1999, 49, 122)

Or again, a lavishly illustrated coffee-table book on Maroon stools, written by a local politician, asserts that the designs constitute a 'language

2 For a large selection of full-colour images of Maroon art, see Price and Price (2005).

for use in relations between the sexes, a symbolic language that is intended to amuse and seduce the woman, ... it's a rebus that the man gives her to decipher' (Bruné, 1995, ix, 42–43, 32–33, 27). Claims of this sort had already become mainstream in the final decades of the twentieth century. Moving on to the twenty-first, we find some new twists in the discourse. My own introduction to them came when I discovered a colouring book for children called *Colorie tes Tableaux Tembe!* by an Aluku artist named Franky Amete. I had earlier attended the opening of an exhibition of Amete's work in a trendy upscale Cayenne bar, where glossy brochures provided by Libi Na Wan offered background information on Maroon art and I had been impressed by his unique contribution to the range of Maroon forms (for illustrations, see Price, 2007). His art was dominated by brightly colourful paintings in the Eastern Maroon style, but he also embodied the Maroon spirit of innovation by executing some of his characteristically Maroon designs in a subtle palette, using the warm-hued sands and soils of Guyane instead of commercial paint. His wife, a metropolitan French woman, had apparently told him about Navajo sandpaintings and he took it from there. These artworks were technically refined, quietly sophisticated and elegantly presented.

Amete's colouring book, however, which presumably also reflected his wife's influence, made no mention of sands and soils. Instead, it offered a discourse that foregrounded the role of colour, asserting that the motifs communicated symbolic meanings not only by their form but also by their colour. Each page carried a small diagram indicating which colour to use for each motif in order to make the design say, for example, 'Take care of yourself', 'You and me for eternity' or 'Marry me'. A page entitled 'A Secret Code' explained that *art tembe* can be studied like a language, with colours playing a part in the themes to be expressed. Red, it asserted, represents man and blood, white is woman and beauty, black is earth (soil), blue is the earth (planet) and so on.

But there's more. The colouring book also introduced a claim concerning the early history of Maroon art, declaring that:

> The art of *tembe* originated in the seventeenth century [when] it was used as a means of communication among plantation slaves, comparable to 'secret messages in code'. Rapidly, the slaves escaped their servitude and established themselves on the banks of the Maroni. ... [and] *tembe* became the written language of a community that had until then been based on an oral tradition. (Amete, 2004, 1)

Amete was a member of the Libi Na Wan cooperative when he wrote this text, but the Mama Bobi cooperative was also promoting the same version of the origins of *tembe*. A long, discursive hand-out composed for the 2004 Biennale du Marronnage entitled *Tembe: Repères essentiels* took readers back to the era of slavery with high drama:

> Knowledge of escape, charged with vigilance, calling each day on a new creativity. And at the beginning, communication. … Oral tradition tells us that everything began with a few lines furtively scratched in the soil. The mark of the Maroon in full power preparing his flight in complicity. Or already organizing that of others. The trace, the sign, the mark. … Coded messages, discreet, secret and ritualized. … From the gestures of a guerrilla, the *tembe* softened into gestures of tenderness. … Once peace came and freedom was won, there was leisure time, and the *tembe* was transformed into an artform. (Mama Bobi, 2004)

This depiction of *tembe*'s slave-era origins is a serious eyebrow-raiser, given the results of the decades-long multisite research that has clearly placed the beginnings of woodcarving in the early to mid-nineteenth century.

In 2013 I discovered another colouring book, *Mon Tembe-Magique* (self-published and undated) by an Aluku artist named Jean-Luc Maïs. Designed for children aged six to ten, it adds a novel pedagogical angle to the fun of art; the child answers a simple arithmetic exercise in order to discover the colour needed for each segment of a design; for example, '3+2' is marked 'red' in the key for the first design, telling the child to use red for parts of the design marked with a 5. Like Amete's colouring book, the one by Maïs includes both a page on colour symbolism and an introduction to the history of *tembe*. The lists of colours in the two books are essentially the same, but claims for their symbolic meanings do not match. In one, white is said to mean 'women and beauty while in the other it translates as power; in one, orange means sun, fire and gold and in the other it means the harvest; in one, grey means night and rain and in the other it means sadness. It is not completely clear how a child, or even an interested adult, might learn to read the colours and thus the message being transmitted when there are such divergent claims.

Maïs's book makes more ambitious claims regarding the early history of *tembe* than either Amete's or the text put out by Mama Bobi. Africans fresh off the boats from Africa (the 'beaux-sales'), we're told, invented a writing system for communication on the plantations that they then used to record the story of each slave's escape. This writing system also allowed them to record the genealogy of each family as well as information on 'customs, traditions, culture and other kinds of information that was indispensable for the transmission of their history and identity'. (With all this very detailed data preserved in *tembe*, one might wonder what need we have today for research in oral or archival history!)

Missing women

Leaving colouring books aside, there's a fundamental problem with the claim that *tembe* transmits messages from men to women. Here's the dilemma: if, indeed, the motifs carry meanings by which the man who makes the carving sends a message to the woman who receives it, one would hope that the woman could make out the message from her lover. That is, a system of communication works only if those who speak or write and those who listen or read agree on what the forms signify. Because almost all the descriptions of *tembe* in the literature come from male outsiders talking with male Maroons, the question of how much women can interpret the symbols has rarely come up. But when we do ask women about how they read *tembe* designs, the response is universally negative. I'll cite three kinds of evidence, all of which go in the same direction.

First, my own efforts over the past half-century to get women to 'read' trays, combs, stools and so forth have resulted in the identification of numerous names for motifs, but no symbolic meanings for them and no messages in the way they were combined. None whatsoever.

Secondly, a systematic survey was conducted over four or five months in 2008 by the CRABASI cooperative in Suriname involving a 72-item questionnaire to 54 Maroons (Saamakas, Pamakas and Alukus) (CRABASI 2008). As a supplement to the questionnaire, each person was shown ten *tembe* designs and asked to talk about what they meant. The great majority of the men said that they had no idea and the women said that they themslelves 'knew nothing about woodcarving'. The abstract idea of symbolic meaning was understood; several of the people interviewed excused their ignorance on the matter, suggesting that perhaps educational efforts could be made to teach Maroons about the symbols.

Third, I emailed Brazilian anthropologist Olivia da Cunha, who was conducting research with Ndyuka Maroon women in Suriname, sent her some sample *tembe* designs, and asked her to see what the women she was working with had to say about their symbolism. She kindly agreed and interviewed 12 women, aged 35 to 65, on the subject. Her reply:

'None of them know about Tembe or, even, have demonstrated interest on it. I think they thought somehow "funny" that I had addressed questions about Tembe to them! They always say there are other people that know (always men) but they don't'.

Thus, the abstract idea of motifs carrying meaning seems perfectly possible to Maroon women, but if such meanings exist, they say they do not have the key to them and could not read any messages the men might be trying to send them.

At some moments, even the most enthusiastic supporters of the new ideas concerning symbolism, such as the colour chart and the slave-era origins, recognize that they are dealing with an invented tradition. One Libi Na Wan publication, for example, asserts that 'The proper, unique meaning of an artwork belongs above all to the artist', and goes on to point out that older artists think of *tembe* in essentially aesthetic terms, in contrast to young artists who, 'motivated by economic and touristic considerations', attribute specific meanings to different colours (Barthelemy, 2009, 61, 74). As for the men, Eastern Maroons tend to be more open than Saamakas to the abstract idea of *tembe* symbolism, pointing most frequently to a motif called *geebi lobi* ('graveyard love') and explaining that it means 'eternal love'. But there's a big difference between such a one-to-one relationship between a motif and its meaning and the claim that full messages are being spelled out through grammatically structured combinations of motifs.

Take, for example, a painting by Antoine Lamoraille, one of the founders of the Mama Bobi cultural centre, presented in Mama Bobi's publication *Koti a Keti* (1998, 5). It's perfectly true that motifs like those in his art carry names such *motyo olo*, *amaka*, etc., and it might even be that they convey meanings. But putting them together to compose a message is another thing altogether. Lamoraille announces that it conveys the following message: 'You have been able to avoid the trap that caught your brothers. From now on, watch out when you see a tree that's bent over'. But there would seem to be a total disconnect between this message and the motifs that he identifies in the painting;[3] it's unclear how any

3 Lamoraille identifies the meanings of the painting's motifs as: whirlpool, self-control, prudence, the chain of friendship and solidarity, peace of the heart and soul, and hospitality. He provides the message it is intended to communicate in both Aluku and French: 'T rap u misi yu na nenge koonde Te i si bendi udu da mi mu fele. *Tu as su éviter le piège qui a pris tes frères; désormais méfie-toi de l'arbre qui penche*'.

woman would have even the foggiest idea of how to read it. It seems to me that this brings us into the realm of the famous Zen image that evokes the sound of one hand clapping—a language designed for communication between two people in which only one of them understands the words.

Cultural brokerage in Guyane and beyond

The fact remains, however, that in the context of a market economy there is much to recommend a discourse on *tembe* in which it incorporates symbolic meanings and has the power to transmit messages. Western expectations about 'exotic' peoples make the decision to adopt such a discourse a real no-brainer. Neither the metropolitan advisers who basically direct cooperatives like Mama Bobi and Libi Na Wan nor the artists who produce *tembe* in the context of present-day Guyane are unaware of the power of such a discourse for their clientele. And of course the more it is internalized as the truth of the matter, the more powerfully it can be put into play.

This phenomenon is hardly limited to Guyane. We find it everywhere in the world, from Australia and Africa to both North and South America. Sidney Kasfir, for example, has documented the way postcolonial cooperatives in Africa have succeeded in putting a new spin on the arts they promote, and the extent to which the new discourses are influenced by regional politics and national agendas. The hundreds of examples she presents demonstrate 'the emergence of new African art onto the world stage, beginning in the 1950s and 1960s, [as] a major act of cultural brokerage by a small number of mainly European supporters' (1999, 65). To cite just one example, the organizers of workshops in Namibia, acting in a 'protective' role towards Bushman artists lest they be exploited by unscrupulous outsiders, have ended up 'constructing and authenticating a Bushman culture for the benefit of the rest of the world, [linking] the workshop artists with a Bushman hunting and gathering past, even though none of the artists or their families has ever lived that way, because this gives their art a pedigree which spectators will recognize as authentic' (Kasfir, 1999, 63; see also Kasfir, 2007).

The new version of the history and meaning of *tembe* is established as fact not only in individual encounters, publications, exhibitions, media outlets and the like, but also, and very crucially, in school programmes, where the understandings of the next generation take root. The cooperatives in Guyane are taking full advantage of their access to classrooms, and young children are being instructed in the story they have chosen to tell.

To underscore the point, I would cite another case of claims for symbolic meaning, one that centres on quilts made by African-American women in the antebellum United States. A few years ago a large commemorative statue of the abolitionist Frederick Douglass was erected in Central Park at a cost of US$15.5 million. Next to the figure of Douglass was the granite representation of a quilt whose squares contained symbols that, according to an adjoining plaque, signalled 'the location of safe houses and escape routes' along the Underground Railroad, as well as other 'information vital to a slave's escape and survival'. But, as historians were quick to point out, the idea that quilts carried secret messages was, beyond the shadow of a doubt, historically inaccurate—nothing more than 'spurious history' that grew out of a book by two non-historians entitled *Hidden in Plain View* (Tobin and Dobard, 1999).

Nevertheless, the idea of quilts carrying messages that helped slaves escape to freedom was attractive enough that the historians' correction made no difference in the popular imagination. The book, which quickly sold several hundred thousand copies, was featured on the Oprah Winfrey Show and eagerly picked up by elementary school teachers, especially in districts with a heavy African-American population, who saw it as an inspirational pedagogical tool for the classroom. Even today, nearly a decade after historians pointed out the error, sales of *Hidden in Plain View* are up, amazon.com carries praise from people expressing gratitude to the authors for having opened up this inspirational contribution to African-American history and other children's books have promoted the same idea of quilts guiding slaves to freedom in the north. For example, *The Patchwork Path: A Quilt Map to Freedom* (Stroud, 2007) tells 'the story of two of the thousands who escaped a life of slavery and made the dangerous journey to freedom—a story of courage, determination, and hope' (and is commended in *School Library Journal* for 'working well as a lesson in African-American history').

The appeal that launched this 'secret code' claim, like that concerning *tembe* art, isn't hard to discern. As one op-ed columnist noted,

> Few aspects of the American past have inspired more colorful mythology than the Underground Railroad. It's probably fair to say that most Americans view it as a thrilling tapestry of midnight flights, hairsbreadth escapes, mysterious codes and strange hiding places. So it's not surprising that the intriguing (if only recently invented) tale of escape maps encoded in antebellum quilts ... should also seize the popular imagination. ...

> Eye-catching quilts and mysterious tunnels satisfy the human penchant for easily digestible history. Myths deliver us the heroes we crave, and submerge the horrific reality of slavery in a gilded haze of uplift. (Bordewich, 2007)

The parallel with the new discourse concerning the origins of *tembe* is striking. See, for example, the scenario concocted by a metropolitan member of the Libi Na Wan *association*:

> On the plantations, rumblings of anger and the perspective of a communal—and very real—force give courage to numerous men to take flight. The groups already in the forest have left messages showing them the route. But what is the best path signalled by all these interwoven bands? Only those concerned and initiated know how to read the code, and *Tembe* is born. (Barthelemy, 2009, 21)

It has been clear to anthropologists for at least several decades that a great many of the traditions long considered to be ancient in their origins were in fact invented comparatively recently (see Wagner, 1975; Hobsbawm and Ranger, 1983). Present-day Guyane, with the pressure it puts on assimilating segments of the population to adapt to new social, cultural and economic norms, would seem to provide a particularly fertile environment for Maroon culture to develop such 'invented traditions'. Given the active role of *associations* in the promotion of Maroon culture, it seems likely that the new discourse about *tembe*—its origins in slave rebellion, its power to transmit messages from men to women, and its dependence on the symbolic meaning of different colours—is very much here to stay.

Works cited

Amete, Franky. 2004. *Colorie tes Tableaux Tembe!* Cayenne: Editions Plume Verte.

Barthelemy, Karol. 2009. *Den taki foe a Tembe*. Kourou: Roger Le Guen.

Bordewich, Fergus M. 2007. 'History's tangled threads', *New York Times*, 2 February, A19.

Bruné, Paulin. 1995. *Sièges et sculptures chez les Noirs-Marrons des Guyanes*. Cayenne: Editions Equinoxe Communication.

CRABASI. 2008. *Surinam Maroon Tembe: A Means of Living* [booklet and CD]. Paramaribo: CRABASI Foundation.

Doat, Patrice, Daniel Schneegans and Guy Schneegans. 1999. *Guyane: l'art businengé*. Grenoble: CRATerre Editions.

Dourgnon, Paul, 1998. 'L'essor contrasté des associations guyanaises', *Antiane* 38: 22–25.

Hobsbawm, Eric, and Terence Ranger, eds. 1983. *The Invention of Tradition*. Cambridge: Cambridge University Press.

Kasfir, Sidney Littlefield. 1999. *Contemporary African Art*. London: Thames & Hudson.

Kasfir, Sidney Littlefield. 2007. *African Art and the Colonial Encounter: Inventing a Global Commodity*. Bloomington: Indiana University Press.

Maïs, Jean-Luc, undated. *Mon tembe magique (L'enfant du fleuve vol. 1)*. Guyane: self-published.

MacCannell, Dean. 1990. 'Cannibal tours', *Society for Visual Anthropology Review* 6.2: 14–24.

Mama Bobi, 1998. *Koti a Keti*. Saint-Laurent: Marwina Arts.

Mama Bobi, 2004. *Tembe: repères essentiels*. Manuscript.

Muntslag, F.H.J. 1979. *Paw a paw dindoe: Surinaamse houtsnijkunst*. Amsterdam: Prins Bernard Fonds.

Price, Richard. 2013. 'The Maroon population explosion: Suriname and Guyane', *New West Indian Guide* 87: 323–327.

Price, Sally. 1989. *Primitive Art in Civilized Places*. Chicago: University of Chicago Press.

Price, Sally. 2007. 'Into the mainstream: Shifting authenticities in art', *American Ethnologist* 34: 603–620.

Price, Sally, and Richard Price. 2005. *Les Arts des Marrons*. La Roque d'Anthéron: Vents d'ailleurs.

Stroud, Bettye. 2007. *The Patchwork Path: A Quilt Map to Freedom*. Somerville: Candlewick Press.

Tobin, Jacqueline L., and Raymond G. Dobard. 1999. *Hidden in Plain View: A Secret Story of Quilts and the Underground Railroad*. New York: Doubleday.

Wagner, Roy, 1975. *The Invention of Culture*. Chicago: University of Chicago Press.

CHAPTER TEN

Performing and Parading Gender in Guyane's Carnival

Catriona MacLeod,
University of London Institute in Paris

The carnival of Guyane holds an important place in both the cultural history and the current identity of this DOM. The celebration of carnival in the region was born of French colonial presence following the importation of the traditional festivities by European settlers, and as Guyane has moved from colonized territory to overseas *département*, carnival has remained part of its yearly calendar. Festivities begin at Epiphany (6 January) and consist of an extended period of street parades, performances and masked balls until Ash Wednesday, when the ritual burning of 'spirit of carnival' King Vaval's effigy closes the festival.[1]

In the twenty-first century, as one of the more broadcast elements of Guyanais life, the carnival brings some visibility to this DOM often ignored within metropolitan France, while its traditions and characters also underline the complexity of its hybrid Franco-Antillean existence. Within the territory, carnival acts both as a celebratory social ritual, bringing groups of people together for parades and balls, and as a performance of Guyanais cultural identity, the costumes worn and customs followed all shedding light on how contemporary Guyane is socially and culturally located by its own inhabitants. The evolution of carnival since its inception, and particularly over the latter half of the

1 For a detailed discussion of this figure see Contout (2000).

twentieth century, indicates certain notable changes in the expressions of identity presented via festival traditions and characters. The following chapter will consider this development in carnival performance and how it relates particularly to two carnival characters whose presence has become particularly popular since *départementalisation*—the *travesti* and the *touloulou*—asking what this reveals about gender relations in Guyanais society.

The changing carnival

Of the many developments undergone by Guyane's carnival, three twentieth-century evolutions are interesting to note here.[2] The first concerns the increasing importance of public space. Blodwenn Mauffret states that, although street parades existed in the early twentieth century, the Cayenne carnival of the 1940s and '50s (records prior to this period proving elusive) 'est spécifiquement celui des bals … au détriment de la création d'autres manifestations culturelles et du carnaval de rue' (2005, 89–90).[3] The modern carnival, however, is shared between the 'open' space of the dominical street parades and the 'closed' space of the weekend dance halls. This popularization of the street parade is linked to the late 1970s phenomenon that saw the cultural 'claiming' of carnival by the *petite bourgeoisie créole guyanaise* (Stephenson, 2010, 34). Where, previously, parading was eschewed by the latter and considered 'l'affaire du bas peuple, des "petites gens" et de quelques jeunes-gens'[4] (Stephenson, 2010, 34), from the end of the 1970s this element of carnival was adopted by the dominant social classes aiming to demarcate the carnival as a key feature and depiction of their cultural identity and, thus, it took on a new importance.[5]

Alongside the street parade's increased visibility came a notable progression in its organization: the procession of individuals incarnating specific carnival characters waned in popularity as the tendency to

2 For studies of other aspects of the carnival's evolution, see Stephenson (2010), Hidair (2005) and Mauffret (2005).

3 'was specifically concerned with balls … to the detriment of the street carnival and the creation of other cultural expressions'. All translations in this chapter are my own.

4 'something for the hoi-polloi, the "little people" and some youngsters'.

5 See Stephenson (2010, 34) and Mauffret (2005, 103–104) for further analysis of the *créolisation* of the Guyane carnival.

parade in groups took significantly greater hold. These groups sometimes represented a certain carnival theme or, testifying to the increasing diversification of Guyanais society in the latter half of the twentieth century, displayed the traditions of a certain nationality to spectators, as indicated by Mauffret: 'Les Chinois défilent en Chinois: parapluies de papier, chignon, robe en soi, musique, … les Saint-Luciens en Saint-Luciens. Les Haitiens en Haitiens' (2005, 95).[6] Since 1990, a further evolution has become evident within the group tradition, particularly in Cayenne, with a distinguishable difference visible between the older groups, conceived from the 1970s onwards, and newly formed groups. The latter tend to consist of younger carnival-goers who engage less with the disguise and dressing-up elements of the parade important to the longer-established bands of participants. Often these groups represent a neighbourhood, rather than a carnival theme (Hidair, 2005, 23).

Linked to the development of parade groups is the third change important to note here: the disappearance of the mask. As the newer group style becomes a more popular part of the Sunday parade, in addition to the regular appearance of influences from other national carnival customs (notably Brazilian), traditional Guyane carnival characters are beginning to disappear. The costumes of these characters, such as the *Jé farin* and the *gorille*,[7] typically included masks. In the modern-day carnival, however, the mask as carnival parade accoutrement has progressively disappeared, ceding its place to make-up and decorations that adorn the face but do not hide the identity of the wearer from the watching crowd (Stephenson, 2010, 35).

These three interrelated changes to the Guyane carnival—the development of the street parade alongside the increase of carnival groups and the disappearance of masks—suggest a growing shift in the manner of using the carnival to express Guyanais identity. Where previously

6 'The Chinese parade as Chinese: paper umbrellas, chignons, silk dresses, music … the Saint Lucians as Saint Lucians. The Haitians as Haitians'. For further discussion of immigration into Guyane after departmentalization, see Mam Lam Fouck (2002, 77–84).

7 The *Jé farin*, a figure dressed all in white and wearing a pointed white hat, is a carnival character that represents the hope of future agricultural abundance. Traditionally, the *Jé farin* threw flour at spectators (mostly children) (Hidair, 2005, 32), with this carnivalistic inversion (the waste of foodstuffs) intended to invite agricultural prosperity. The *gorille* character charges at the watching public and pretends to kidnap young women. This figure symbolizes masculine virility (Hidair, 2005, 38).

concealment of 'real-world' identity was key, both via the dominance of the masked ball and the regular wearing of masks in the less-frequented street parade, the modern carnival allows increasing scope for the visible retention of the participant's identity during festivities. The progressive disappearance of characters representing traditional carnival symbols (in addition to those directly linked to Guyane's history of slavery)[8] in favour of delineated groups often divided on the basis of geographical provenance or residence, suggests an increasing focus on establishing 'oppositional' identities by underlining via carnival activities the differences between certain groups of Guyane's inhabitants (see also Hidair, 2005, 55–61). Thus, this carnival appears no longer to be a festivity, as Bakhtin suggested of the carnivalistic, of dualism, representing 'both poles of change and crisis, birth and death, blessing and curse' (1998, 253) or of inversion of the status quo, one in which the normal hierarchical nature of modern life is suspended (251),[9] but rather of difference, emphasizing and underlining schisms in Guyanais society, whether of age, neighbourhood or country of origin. Hidair notes in *Anthropologie du carnaval cayennais* that these expressions of difference can be confrontational rather than celebratory and have the potential to end in violence (2005, 55).

Le travesti

The societal differences highlighted via the developing modern practices of the Guyane carnival also include sex and gender, seen most clearly in the two figures of the *travesti* (also referred to by some scholars as the *travesti grotesque*), incarnated by men, and the *touloulou*, incarnated by women.[10] Male-to-female transvestism is a practice found throughout Latin American and Caribbean carnivals and, among the festivities in French territories, has been most documented within the Martinique

8 The *coupeuse de cannes* figure is one example of this.

9 For a critical discussion of Bakhtin's theory of carnival see Stallybrass and White (1986).

10 The word *touloulou* may be used to describe any disguised carnival-goer (hence the use of the term *touloulou sale* to describe a certain category of male character); however, it is most commonly used to describe a specific, female-incarnated carnival figure which will be discussed fully in the second part of this chapter (also sometimes referred to as a *fem'touloulou* (see, for example, Mauffret, 2010, 140). For an explanation of the etymology of the word *touloulou*, see Marshall (2009, 254).

carnival.[11] In Guyane, this phenomenon is generally found in two carnivalistic instances: during the Sunday street parades and during the *mariages burlesques* of *lundi gras*. Female-to-male transvestism is much less common and tends to be restricted to the *mariages burlesques* when women are in the company of men also disguised as the opposite sex (Bruneteaux and Rochais, 2010, 114).

Mauffret cites two principal instances of male-to-female cross-dressing in the street parades of Guyane—drag queens (either 'Créole' or 'Brazilian' in style), who 'prennent soin de leur habillement et de la représentation au "féminin" qu'ils mettent en place au sein des défilés dominicaux, entretenant ainsi une certaine ambiguïté quant à leur véritable sexualité'[12] (2010, 137), and *travestis grotesques*, whose ostensible goal is to make spectators laugh by means of exaggerated gestures and costumes.[13] As the latter category is largely specific to carnival—while instances of the former are less time- (and place-) dependent—it will be discussed in what follows. Definitive information regarding the introduction and evolution of the *travesti* phenomenon in Guyane is difficult to obtain. In addition to the less-than-abundant nature of the records kept regarding carnival prior to departmentalization, this may also be due to the fact that male transvestism in general is, and has been, ignored by the local press and has remained absent from promotional materials concerning the carnival in favour of less 'vulgar' imagery (Hidair, 2005, 50).[14] In their study of carnival transvestism in Martinique, however, Bruneteaux and Rochais state that the *travesti* character's status as a common element of the carnival

11 See King (2004) and Murray (1998).

12 'pay attention to the feminine countenance and style of dress they don during the Sunday parades, thus provoking a certain ambiguity as to their real sexuality'.

13 Mauffret also cites the presence of a third possible category of transvestite: the *touloulou* (2010, 140–141). However, as the *touloulou* (a figure which will be discussed fully below) is principally incarnated by women and due to the fact that instances of men taking on this role can only be hypothesized (as the *touloulou* costume covers any trace of identity), it will not be discussed here.

14 This is also, according to Rosamund King, true of male transvestism in the Trinidadian carnival, despite the fact that the Dame Lorraine transvestite character is accepted as a traditional part of the festivities (2004, 29). King also states that scholars are guilty of omitting references to, and studies of, male transvestism in favour of more 'acceptable' carnival practices, thus 'perhaps unconsciously continuing the nineteenth century European project of sanitizing carnival by either ignoring, dismissing, or remaining unaware of more "vulgar" characters' (2004, 35).

does not pre-date the Second World War (2010, 122). As, prior to 1945, the Guyane carnival placed less emphasis on the street parade element of festivities in which the *travestis* now take part, it seems likely that the post-war popularization of this phenomenon is also true of Guyane.[15]

Greater variation is possible within the costume of the *travesti* than in other more traditional figures such as the *Jé farin*; however, a common feature of sexualized exaggeration may be noted among participants. Men wear make-up, wigs and dresses padded out with oversized 'breasts' and 'buttocks', often contrasting with signs of biological maleness, such as beards and chest hair, which are left visible to the spectator.[16] The carnival behaviour of the *travesti* ranges from 'flirting' with male spectators as they walk in the parade to miming sex acts in pairs or simulating childbirth.[17]

Several theories may be proffered as to the carnivalistic function of this relatively modern addition to the festivities. Hidair suggests that the mimed copulation and childbirth performed by some *travestis* 'rappelle que l'un des rites essentiels du carnaval est celui de la fécondité' (2005, 50).[18] However, the fact that these actions are not performed consistently by these *travesti* characters indicates that other explanations for their presence are necessary. That a key carnivalistic notion is 'inversion' (the *Jé farin*'s wasting of flour to promote abundance is one traditional Guyanais example of this) suggests that the male *travesti* may be a comical incarnation of this notion: a member of one sex masquerading as another, thus inverting traditional sexual identity.[19] In his study of male transvestism in the Martinique carnival, Murray investigates this

15 It should be remembered, however, that transvestism in carnival was also present in representations of the traditional carnival characters—the figure of the *Balayeuse*, for example (an old woman in a dress who sweeps dirt onto the feet of carnival spectators) tended originally to be played by men (in the modern carnival, women have also played this role) (Hidair 2005, 38).

16 This contrasts to the costume of the 'Créole drag queen' character, who habitually wears a Venetian mask (Mauffret 2010, 137), in part to obscure such signs of masculinity from the watching crowd.

17 The behaviour and costume of the *travesti (grotesque)* correspond to the Bakhtinian notion of 'grotesque realism' described by Stallybrass and White (1986, 9) thus: 'Grotesque realism images the human body as multiple, bulging, over- or under-sized, protuberant and incomplete. The openings and orifices of this carnival body are emphasized, not its closure and finish'.

18 'refers back to fertility as one of the essential rites of carnival'.

19 The term 'sexual identity' here relates to the notion of identity as belonging to one or other (or both) sexes, not identity as it relates to sexual orientation.

possibility, stating that the phenomenon of carnivalistic sex/gender inversion would be 'curious' due to the promotion of the highly masculine, heterosexual ethic that is 'a feature of many Caribbean societies' (1998, 345). However, in Guyane as in Martinique, the relative lack of reciprocity (women dressing as men) in addition to the visible mix of male physical features and exaggerated female features that is ubiquitous in these carnival *travestis* suggests that an inversion, and thus transgression of 'normalized' sexual identities, is not the goal of this figure. Rather, the *travesti* predominantly consists of two key elements: the prominent display of corporeal masculinity, attesting to male power and dominance over the female body it purports to represent and, second, the mocking of a comically grotesque incarnation of 'womanhood', which represents the female as a collection of sexualized body parts. Hidair suggests that acting as a *touloulou sale*,[20] of which the *travesti* is a principal category, may be a rite of passage which initiates young men into male society as it underlines and emphasizes differences between the sexes (2005, 49). Murray contends in relation to the presence of the *travesti* in the Martinique carnival that one dominant function of this figure is to 'further perpetuate the dominance of an ideology of normative male heterosexuality articulated in daily Antillean discourse' (1998, 349), suggesting that the prominent display of male physiological markers, such as beards and chest hair, combined with exaggerated female attributes mocks both women and the perceived 'femininity' of homosexuality. He also suggests another reading of the Martiniquan *travesti* which may be applicable to their Guyanais equivalents. Noting the historical tendency to express the colonial relationship via the idiom of gender, Murray contends that the *travesti*'s comedic mix of a dominant male body with an exaggerated depiction of femininity may be a carnivalistic mocking of the historically feminized metropolitan French view of Martinique and 'a sarcastic commentary of ongoing French control of the political and economic institutions of Martinique' (1998, 348). In his work, Murray refers specifically to this gendered phenomenon as a feature of the metropolitan France-Martinique relationship; however, the feminization of the colonized territory being a trope common to colonialism more generally,[21]

20 A *touloulou sale* is a a male carnival-goer whose costume is intentionally provocative and often of poor quality, who frequently sings crude or satirical songs whilst parading (see Mauffret 2010, 139).

21 This is a fact attested in multiple scholarly works. See, for example, Kuntsman (2009) and Roy (2005).

this interpretation of the Guyanais *travesti* may also prove applicable to studies of this territory's carnival. While this reading of the *travesti*'s function in the Guyane carnival remains possible, the lack of specific features linking the figure to the French/Guyanais (post)colonial dynamic, and the fact, noted above, that other characters linked to the territory's colonial history are becoming a less visible part of the modern street parade, indicates that this interpretation is less viable than the others available. Rather, the clear opposition of strong masculinity to exaggerated femininity, in addition to the tendency of the contemporary carnival to highlight differences within Guyanais society, suggests that this character mocks not the feminization of the territory but femaleness within the territory. This mocking reduction of the female by the male to a collection of exaggerated body parts may, in fact, reflect a certain, very sexualized, view of women in modern Guyane which is borne out by certain illuminating statistics. Studies of the birth rate in the territory by the Institut national de la statistique et des études économiques (INSEE, n.d.) reveal that Guyane continually has the highest birth rate of all the French *départements*, including other DOMs such as Martinique and Guadeloupe, in addition to exhibiting a significantly higher birth rate in recent years than the national averages of its nearest geographical neighbours, Brazil and Suriname.[22] Women are more likely to be young mothers in Guyane than in metropolitan France: INSEE studies for both 1999 and 2009 show that women in Guyane are most likely to have their first child at 20 years of age, compared to 30 for their metropolitan counterparts (INSEE: Antilles-Guyane, 2013) and the Ligue des droits de l'Homme stated in 2014 that rates of teenage pregnancies are some 40 times higher in Guyane than in the Metropole ('Les Violences faites aux femmes en Guyane', 2014).[23] The Ligue has also noted that the incidence of sexual violence against women is particularly high in Guyane: its 2014 report states that the territory showed the highest record of reported rape in France, its numbers rising far above those of the other DOMs.

22 The Guyanais birth rate, 26.2 per 1,000 inhabitants in 2015 was more than twice that in Guadeloupe and Martinique (11.9 and 10.5 respectively). The average for metropolitan France in 2014 was 11.8 (L'Institut national de la statistique et des études économiques, n.d.). According to data (calculated in whole numbers only) provided by the World Bank, the Brazilian birth rate in 2015 was 14 per 1,000 inhabitants and that of Suriname was 18 (World Bank, n.d.).

23 The same report notes that in 2010 the percentage of under-16s giving birth in the hospital of Saint-Laurent in Guyane was 80 times higher than the European average for the same year.

These figures, in addition to the lack of employment among Guyanaise women—a *France-Guyane* report from 2014 states that only a third of women of working age in Guyane were *actives* (Fayet, 2014)[24]—indicate that the principal role of women in Guyanais society is corporeal, whether as sexual partner or mother. This primacy accorded to the sexual and reproductive function of women is a key feature of the *travesti grotesque*'s costume and behaviour, as its representation of 'women' is reduced to the display of exaggeratedly prominent sexualized body parts (notably 'breasts' and 'buttocks') with the miming of copulation or childbirth sometimes part of the act. Whether the parodying of the female body is interpreted merely as carnival humour or as mocking disparagement, that 'woman' is depicted by her sexual function, her body dominated by a male corporeal presence, is indisputable. The male *travesti* physically wears the sexualization of women in Guyane, underlining the 'difference' between men and women alongside the parading of other societal schisms.

The *touloulou*

The most well-known carnival figure of Guyane's yearly festivities is the *touloulou*. The *touloulou* is a character incarnated by female carnival-goers and, although sometimes visible during the Sunday street parades as part of the dwindling category of solo paraders, is predominantly associated with balls held in dance halls (also known as *universités*) on Saturday nights throughout the carnival period.[25] Dressing as a *touloulou* requires the complete concealment of the wearer's identity. The woman in question wears a dress in addition to tights, gloves, a hood covering the head and neck, a mask and sometimes a wig. Anonymity during the *touloulou* balls is strictly respected: women ensure that their costume reveals nothing of their skin and hair colour as their body shape is concealed by the voluminous dress (sometimes padded in strategic places to alter the wearer's figure) and voices are disguised by adopting an unusually high or low pitch when speech is

24 According to the report, 'sur les 75,000 Guyanaises en âge de travailler, seulement 27,000 sont actives' ('of the 75,000 Guyanais women of working age, only 27,000 are employed') (Fayet, 2014).

25 In and around Cayenne, two nightclubs are most commonly associated with carnival *bals touloulous*—Soleil Levant (nicknamed 'Nana' and linked to the early popularization of the *touloulou* phenomenon) and Polina. See Mauffret (2005, 127–130) for a detailed discussion of these dance *universités*.

necessary. During a *touloulou* ball, only the disguised *touloulous* may invite a partner to dance. Attending men must wait to be chosen and tradition dictates that they are not allowed to refuse. Following a dance, if a *touloulou* indicates that she would like a drink, the male partner is obliged to pay for it.

The masked ball has for centuries been a part of the European carnival. Belfort-Chanol states that the Guyanais variation, the *bal paré-masqué*, was an evolution of the more traditional masked ball first associated with white colonizers (2013, 48). However, Ndagano theorizes that the *bal paré-masqué* may trace its origins to a practice dating to the plantation era, which he terms 'le samedi-nègre', when 'Les maitres autorisaient leurs esclaves à se défouler loin des habitations, entre deux semaines de labeur. Au petit matin, ils revenaient vers les habitations en dansant, au rythme du tambour' (2010, 60).[26] Although there is no consensus on the precise origins of Guyane's costume ball,[27] the *touloulou* character, unlike the more widespread *travesti*, seems to have been born of Guyane, the practice of entirely disguising one's body, rather than merely the face as is the more common custom of the masked ball, apparently developing in Cayenne from the last years of the nineteenth century.[28]

26 'masters allowed their slaves to blow off steam away from the plantations between two weeks of labour. At daybreak, they danced back to the plantations to the beat of a drum'. See Mauffret (2005, 47–51) for an interesting discussion of the ambiguous connection between slavery in Guyane and the practice of dancing—encouraged both on the part of the colonizer in order to increase productivity in the plantations and performed by plantation labourers as an act of revolt against slavery.

27 Serge Mam Lam Fouck's discussion of the provenance of dances performed at the *touloulou* balls reveals some of the political considerations at play when determining the origins of certain carnival practices in Guyane: 'Les adeptes de l'assimilation culturelle veulent voir dans les danses traditionnelles créoles avant tout des "analogies avec les anciennes danses des provinces françaises"; et les défenseurs des valeurs de la négritude, des danses venues directement d'Afrique' ('Those interested in cultural assimilation principally see "links with the old French regional dances" in the traditional Creole dances, whilst for those focused on Négritude values, the dances come directly from Africa') qtd in Hidair, 2005, 73.

28 Some uncertainty as to when the *bal pare-masqué* first began in Guyane appears across published studies on the subject. Belfort-Chanol indicates that it developed progressively following the opening of new carnival *soirée* venues in 1896 (2013, 51), while Mauffret suggests that the practice began later, in the 1920s (2005, 124). Both agree that the *touloulou* tradition is emblematic of the Guyane

In its original incarnation, the *bal paré-masqué* invited both men and women to disguise themselves, with the sole gender-based restriction that women alone were permitted to invite non-disguised male revellers to dance (Belfort-Chanol, 2013, 52). During the 1950s, *bal paré-masqué* practice evolved to allow only women to disguise themselves and to choose a dance partner of the opposite, un-costumed sex. The arrival of the male equivalent, the *soirée tololo* (during which only men dress up and invite undisguised women to dance), did not appear until the close of the twentieth century.

Varied hypotheses have been suggested to explain the gender-based post-war reorganization of the carnival costume ball that saw the restriction of the *touloulou* to the female carnival-goer. Excepting Belfort-Chanol's proposition that this feminization of the *touloulou* during the 1950s was intended to 'empecher l'homosexualité' (Belfort-Chanol qtd. in Mauffret, 2005, 124),[29] such hypotheses generally fall into two categories: those that look towards a shift in the gender demographic of post-war urban Guyane following army conscription, emigration and geographical displacements due to gold mining, and those that emphasize the changing social and economic status of women in the post-war period, influenced in part by the growing metropolitan feminist movements (Mauffret, 2005, 124). The latter hypotheses concerning the evolution of the *bal paré-masqué*, paired with the apparent inversion of traditional gender behaviour represented by the *touloulou*'s power to choose her dance partner (while male attendees cannot refuse and must remain ignorant of the *touloulous*' identity), have contributed to a popular understanding in the modern-day carnival of the *touloulou*

carnival, an opinion supported by the movement begun in 2014 to have the carnival and, specifically, its *touloulou* figure recognized by UNESCO as an expression of 'intangible cultural heritage' (Lama, 2015). However, it should be noted that since the 1970s the *touloulou* has also been incorporated into the Martinique carnival (Virassamy, 2013).

29 'to prevent homosexuality'. The proposed link between the *touloulou* character and homosexuality in Guyane is an interesting and complex issue, but one that does not belong in the current study. It is interesting to note, however, that despite the restriction of the *touloulou* phenomenon to women from the 1950s onwards and the creation of *tololos* from 1990, a *France-Guyane* article published in 2012 affirmed that the complete anonymity of the *fem'touloulou* has, on occasion, permitted this character to be secretly incarnated by men and that this practice, although restricted to a small minority of partygoers, is a regular carnival rumour (Virassamy, 2012).

character as a symbol of female power and liberation. Belfort-Chanol, for example, identifies the *touloulou* as a 'signe de libération. La femme au bal paré-masqué est le témoignage vivant du changement de la condition féminine dans la société guyanaise' (2013, 52).[30] However, although the *touloulou* has become, since the 1950s, a highly publicized and celebrated carnival character (unlike the *travesti* which, as noted above, remains largely ignored by the media and official carnival organizers) and is often referred to as the 'reine de la carnaval guyanaise', the interpretation of the *touloulou* as a feminist carnival symbol is problematic. Hidair's analysis of the *touloulou* phenomenon runs counter to this popular understanding of the figure, for example, suggesting that the modern *bals paré-masqués* are, in fact, devoted to men (2005, 75). Although women are in control of their choice of dance partner, Hidair contends that this choice is often based on criteria which correspond to 'la description de l'homme idéal du point de vue de la société créole cayennaise' (2005, 75);[31] that is, to be chosen, a man should have a good reputation in the local community, a good job, a certain level of wealth (in order to pay for the *touloulou*'s drinks for the evening) and should be a good dancer. According to this theory, the rules of the *touloulou* ball serve to valorize the social hierarchy of the male community in Guyane and to teach younger male dancers the rules of this hierarchy (Hidair, 2005, 76), rather than to empower female attendees. A further, if indirect, refutation of the understanding of the *touloulou* as a 'signe de libération' comes from Ndagano, whose analysis of the practicalities of the *bal paré-masqué* suggests that one of the reasons for the habitual ending of these festivities at five o'clock in the morning is that 'Le *touloulou* est avant tout épouse et mere. Elle se doit donc d'être chez elle avant le lever de la maisonnée car d'autres responsabilités l'attendent: le ménage, le marché et même la messe du dimanche matin' (2010, 76).[32]

In addition to these analyses, several other features of the *touloulou* phenomenon also suggest that the function of the character is not to represent increasing female independence over the twentieth century. These features indicate, rather, that this carnival figure acts much as the

30 'sign of liberation. The women of the masked costume ball are living proof of the change in women's place in Guyanais society'.

31 'the description of the ideal man from the point of view of Cayenne's Creole community'.

32 'the *touloulou* is, above all, a wife and mother. She must therefore be back home before her family wakes up as other responsibilities await her: the housework, the shopping and even the Sunday morning mass'.

travesti does—to emphasize the difference between men and women in Guyane and to reflect the bodily, sexual role of women in the territory. The first concerns the status of this 'emancipatory' figure as a carnival character. The understanding that the performance of the *touloulou* role belongs, like the *Jé farin* or the *gorille*, solely to the carnival period suggests that the social power attributed to the *touloulou* women during the weekend balls is an exceptional, carnival-dependent inversion. The creation and continued existence of this inversion thus seemingly confirms the lack of power attributed to women during the non-carnival majority of the year. It is also interesting to note that, despite this time-specific inversion, one particular aspect of the *touloulou* ritual—the male partner's purchasing of drinks for the *touloulou* should she request it, without expectation of reciprocation—appears un-inverted, clearly recalling traditionally gendered social behaviour. This feature of the *bal paré-masqué* suggests that the public performance of economic power is one element of gendered behaviour in Guyane which cannot, even temporarily, be inverted.[33] From the restricted enactment of female 'liberation' associated with the *touloulou*, then, a certain picture of the female role in Guyane outside of carnival period can be viewed.

The second notable feature concerns the *touloulou* costume. Entirely covering the wearer from head to toe, the disguise strips the wearer of her identity and individuality, presenting her to other ball attendees simply as 'woman' (and, thus, 'not man'). While other carnival characters have progressively shed their masks in recent years, allowing their personal identity to become part of their costume, the *touloulou* figure has retained her full-body disguise, this fact emphasizing the importance of her anonymization to the incarnation of the character's carnival meaning. The simplified symbolism of 'woman' expressed by the *touloulou* not only combines with the division of behaviour between men and women within the dance *universités* to underline a strict separation of the sexes

33 In support of this assertion, it is also interesting to note that during the much more recently conceived *tololo* masked balls (which began in the early 1990s), at which it is men who disguise themselves and have the power to ask un-costumed women to dance, the swapping of carnival practice between men and women entailed by this 'inverted inversion' does not extend to the economic division accompanying the *touloulou* balls. Rather, participants pay a set amount of money on entry to the *tololo* dance hall, which entitles them to refreshments during the evening and, thus, the male display of wealth to women associated with the *touloulou* phenomenon is never inverted. For more information on the *tololo* character and its origins, see Ndagano (2010, 78–82).

Figure 11: Touloulous and partners dancing during the Cayenne carnival (photograph by Charles Outters).

and of their respective social roles, it also emphasizes and contains female bodily 'difference'. The costume, while allowing the outline of the female form to be visible, covers up its many bodily specificities—skin and hair colour, arrangement of facial features—in order to present a unified visual expression of 'woman'. Recognizable differences between *touloulous* are thus generally restricted to the exterior of their costumes (the pattern, colour or shape of the mask). One aspect which *has* evolved over time, according to Belfort-Chanol, is the attention dedicated to rendering the *touloulou* disguise aesthetically pleasing, in line with modern standards of idealized femininity: 'De plus en plus, ces héroïnes du samedi soir se rapprochent des canons de beauté des magazines en mettant en évidence des silhouettes de mannequin dans des robes de princesse, en utilisant à profusion le strass, les accessoires brillants, les parures clinquantes' (2010, 173).[34] The symbolism of *touloulou* as 'woman' is, then, progres-

34 'these Saturday night heroines are taking more and more inspiration from beautiful magazine cover stars by emphasizing model figures in princess dresses using lots of glitter, shiny accessories and flashy jewellery'.

sively being linked to popular understandings of female beauty, meaning that the eradication of individual female bodily difference implied by the costume is replaced by a socially imposed understanding of the physically ideal woman. Where the *travesti*, incarnated by male carnival-goers, emphasizes female bodily difference via extravagant visual exaggerations, the *touloulou* character, performed by women, underlines this physical difference by symbolizing 'woman' as an increasingly 'beautified', but covered and, thus, contained figure.

Linked to the above is the final feature of the *touloulou* phenomenon that must be considered in the current analysis: the nature of the movements performed at the *bals paré-masqués*, which include dances that, according to Ndagano, 'miment l'acte sexuel au son d'une musique assourdissante' (2010, 62).[35] Marie-José Jolivet agrees, even stating that 'Selon les critères occidentaux, indéniablement, la danse est obscène' (1994, 538).[36] The combination of the symbolism of the *touloulou*—woman—and the sexualized movements this particular carnival figure performs with her chosen partner once again links the carnivalistic representation of the female to a sexual and reproductive role. Although achieved in a different way to the *travesti*, who draws attention to this role via comic displays of 'breasts' and 'buttocks' and a pretence of performing sexual acts, the effect of the *touloulou*'s combination of costume and movement is similar: the primacy of woman's body is underlined.

Conclusion

Guyane's carnival has, since the late twentieth century, increasingly become a festival of difference. The figures of the *travesti* and the *touloulou* contrast in several ways—the *travesti* parades openly in the street, displaying exaggerated body parts and revealing his identity while the *touloulou* generally restricts herself to the dance hall and fully covers her body and identifying features—but both exist to symbolize the same thing: the difference between women and men and the importance of women's corporeal roles. Murray states of carnival that these 'spectacles cannot be isolated from the ongoing practices of

35 'mime the sexual act to deafening music'. For a discussion of the music played at today's *bals touloulous* see Belfort-Chanol (2013, 59–69).

36 'according to Western criteria, the dance is undeniably obscene'.

everyday life … Rather, these spectacles are part of a ritual of intensification, in which forces that govern ordinary life are expressed with salience and clarity' (1998, 345) and, indeed, the symbolism of these characters appears to reflect a certain sexualized role attributed to women in the region, as discussed above. The wider study of Guyane's carnival reveals further information about this DOM: the competing origins claimed for various carnival features, for example, illustrates the negotiation between European and African cultural legacies, and the increasing tendency of the carnival throughout the latter half of the twentieth century to underline oppositional identities and draw attention to different community groups may highlight the tensions of an increasingly diverse and populated society. Analysis of *travesti* and *touloulou*, however, shows that the performance of the sexualized role of women is undertaken by both male and female carnival-goers, indicating an unusual unity in this particular depiction of difference. This fact is revelatory of the pervasive nature of the characters' shared symbolism regarding women and of the continued belief in this symbolism after the burning of King Vaval, in 'non-carnival' Guyanais life.

Works cited

Bakhtin, Mikhail. 1998. 'Carnival and the carnivalesque', in *Cultural Theory and Popular Culture: A Reader*, ed. John Storey. Harlow: Prentice Hall, 250–259.

Belfort-Chanol, Aline. 2013. *Du touloulou au tololo. Le bal paré-masqué, son évolution*. Matoury: Ibis Rouge Editions.

Belfort-Chanol, Aline. 2010. 'Le Mythe du Touloulou dans le carnaval guyanais', in *Penser le carnaval. Variations, discours et représentations*, ed. Biringanine Ndagano. Paris: Editions Karthala, 165–174.

Bruneteaux, Patrick, and Véronique Rochais. 2010. 'Le Carnaval des travesti grotesques makoumè à la Martinique. Quelques propositions sur le sens de l'inversion sexuelle', in *Penser le carnaval. Variations, discours et représentations*, ed. Biringanine Ndagano. Paris: Editions Karthala, 113–136.

Contout, Auxence. 2000. *Vaval: l'histoire du carnaval de la Guyane française*. Matoury: Ibis Rouge Editions.

Fayet, Rosane. 2014. 'La Femme guyanaise à la loupe', *France-Guyane*, 8 March. http://www.franceguyane.fr/actualite/societe-social-emploi/la-femme-guyanaise-a-la-loupe-190239.php (accessed 1 November 2016).

Hidair, Isabelle. 2005. *Anthropologie du carnaval cayennais. Une représentation en réduction de la société créole cayennaise.* Paris: Editions Publibook.

INSEE. n.d. *Natalité en 2015: comparaisons régionales et départementales.* http://www.insee.fr/fr/themes/tableau.asp?reg_id=99&ref_id=TCRD_053 (accessed 10 August 2016).

INSEE: Antilles-Guyane. 2013. 'La Fécondité est le premier moteur de la croissance démographique en Guyane.' *Institut national de la statistique et des études économiques.* 14 January 2013. https://www.insee.fr/fr/statistiques/1290957 (accessed 4 June 2016).

Jolivet, Marie-José. 1994. 'Créolisation et intégration dans le carnaval de Guyane', *Cahiers des Sciences Humaines* 3.3: 531–549.

King, Rosamund S. 2004. 'Dressing down: Male transvestism in two Caribbean carnivals', *Sargasso* Special Issue: 25–36.

Kuntsman, Adi. 2009. *Figurations of Violence and Belonging: Queerness, Migranthood and Nationalism in Cyberspace and Beyond.* Oxford: Peter Lang.

Lama, Catherine. 2015. 'Le Carnaval de Guyane bientôt inscrit au patrimoine immatériel de l'Unesco', *Franceinfo*, 7 July. http://la1ere.francetvinfo.fr/guyane/2015/07/05/le-carnaval-de-de-guyane-bientot-inscrit-au-patrimoine-immateriel-de-l-unesco-269278.html (accessed 12 August 2016).

Mam-Lam-Fouck, Serge. 2002. *Histoire générale de la Guyane Francaise: des débuts de la colonisation à la fin du XXe siècle: les grands problèmes guyanais.* Guyane: Ibis rouge.

Marshall, Bill. 2009. *The French Atlantic: Travels in Culture and History.* Liverpool: Liverpool University Press.

Mauffret, Blodwenn. 2005. *Le Carnaval de Cayenne. Le jeu carnavalesque: une esthétique de proximité.* Matoury: Ibis Rouge.

Mauffret, Blodwen. 2010. 'Les Différentes modalités du travestissement de l'homme en femme dans le carnaval de Cayenne', in *Penser le carnaval. Variations, discours et représentations*, ed. Biringanine Ndagano. Paris: Editions Karthala, 137–153.

Murray, David A.B. 1998. 'Defiance or defilement? Undressing cross-dressing in Martinique's carnival', *Sexualities* 1.3: 343–354.

Ndagano, Biringanine. 2010. 'Rituel d'un bal paré-masqué. Bal-touloulou et bal-tololo', in *Penser le carnaval. Variations, discours et représentations*, ed. Biringanine Ndagano. Paris: Editions Karthala, 59–92.

Roy, Anumpama. 2005. *Gendered Citizenship: Historical and Conceptual Explorations.* New Delhi: Orient Longman.

Stallybrass, Peter, and Allon White. 1986. *The Politics and Poetics of Transgression.* New York: Cornell University Press.

Stephenson, Elie. 2010. 'Le Carnaval guyanais. Evolution ou substitution?', in *Penser le carnaval. Variations, discours et représentations*, ed. Biringanine Ndagano. Paris : Editions Karthala, 33–42.

'Les Violences faites aux femmes en Guyane', *Ligue des droits de l'Homme*, 4 April 2014. http://www.ldh-france.org/Les-violences-faites-aux-femmes-en/ (accessed 21 June 2016).

Virassamy, Audrey. 2012. 'Le Carnaval permet de vivre ses fantasmes', *France-Guyane*, 31 January. http://www.franceguyane.fr/actualite/culture-et-patrimoine/le-carnaval-permet-de-vivre-ses-fantasmes-115435.php (accessed 17 October 2016).

Virassamy, Audrey. 2013. 'Touloulou: un etre venu de Martinique ou de Guyane', *France-Guyane*, 23 January. http://www.franceguyane.fr/actualite/culture-et-patrimoine/touloulou-un-etre-venu-de-martinique-ou-de-guyane-150521.php?archive=1 (accessed 20 October 2016).

World Bank. n.d. *Birth rate, crude (per 1,000 people)*. http://data.worldbank.org/indicator/SP.DYN.CBRT.IN (accessed 1 February 2018).

CHAPTER ELEVEN

Equality and Difference

Queering Guyane?

Bill Marshall, University of Stirling

On 29 January 2013, Christiane Taubira, then French Minister of Justice and *garde des sceaux*, former deputy for Guyane, ended her impassioned speech in the National Assembly in favour of gay marriage (*le mariage pour tous*) with a quotation from Léon-Gontran Damas: the action the government would accomplish was 'beau comme une rose / dont la tour Eiffel assiégée à l'aube / voit s'épanouir enfin les pétales / … Il est grand comme un besoin de changer d'air …, fort comme l'accent aigu d'un appel / dans la nuit longue' (Damas, 1964, 11).[1] On 5 February 2013, she did the same with Damas's 'Nous les gueux' from the 1956 collection *Black-Label*: 'Nous les gueux / nous les peu / Nous les riens / nous les chiens / nous les maigres / nous les nègres / Qu'attendons-nous / … pour jouer aux fous / pisser un coup / tout à l'envi / contre la vie / stupide et bête / qui nous est faite' (1956, 50).[2]

The fact that the argument for same-sex marriage, which exposed many fissures in contemporary French society, was momentarily cast

1 'beautiful as a rose / whose petals open at last / in the gaze of the besieged Eiffel Tower … tall as a need for a change of scene … , strong as the acute accent of a call / in the long night'. Thanks to Christine Pagnoulle for help with these translations from Damas. All other translations, unless indicated, are my own.

2 'We the beggars / we the littl'uns / we the slurs / we the curs/ we the scrawny / we the Niggers / what are we waiting for … to make a mess/ for once to piss/ just as we like / against the life / stupid and dull / we have to live'.

as an affair between Guyanais speaking authoritatively is perhaps not accidental. First, the rhetorical procedure of Taubira, a black woman citing Damas in order to draw homologies between racial and other inequalities and oppressions, is one which is well-established within recent French anti-homophobic thought, notably through Didier Eribon, whose *Réflexions sur la question gay* (1999) articulated with some originality the relevance of Pierre Bourdieu's class-determined notions of social devaluation, inferiorization, shame and insult to homophobia and the formation of gay subjectivity. In *Une morale du minoritaire: variations sur un thème de Jean Genet*, Eribon is more explicit in linking these ideas to colonial subjectivities, adopting Patrick Chamoiseau's vocabulary from *Ecrire en pays dominé* (1997) of 'la "sentimenthèque" que les individus se constituent pour échapper à la colonisation de leur esprit'; 'il s'agit de "désagréger la domination", cette domination "qui germe et se développe à l'intérieur de ce que l'on est"' (Eribon, 2001, 38).[3] Ever with its ear to the ground of political gossip, the weekly *Le Nouvel Observateur* signalled Taubira's attendance in February 2015 at the stage adaptation of Eribon's 2009 memoir *Retour à Reims* accompanied by dissident ex-ministers as a prelude to herself leaving the Manuel Valls government, and this indeed came to pass in January 2016 ('Taubira', 2015).

Second, of the three founders of Négritude, there is no doubt that Damas lends himself particularly to these lateral connections. He was close to André Gide, and to gay African-American poets and writers such as Langston Hughes (on whom he wrote an unfinished biography, and who translated three of Damas's poems) and Alain Leroy Locke, joining them and other figures from the Harlem Renaissance in the 1920s in a weekly salon hosted by Pauline Nardal in a suburb of Paris. Kathleen Gyssels has argued for the greater gender fluidity of Damas's persona and work, witness his self-fashioning as a dandy, and his adoption of a female voice in the poems 'Douleur de femme' and 'La Maîtresse servante' (Gyssels, 2008; see also her contribution to this volume).

Third, Taubira's citation of Damas in the 2013 parliamentary debates speaks to significant points of tension in specifically French arrangements concerning equality and difference, and these in turn are illuminated by

3 'the "library of feeling" that individuals create for themselves in order to escape the colonization of their mind'; 'it's about "breaking up the structures of domination", the domination "that grows and develops inside what we are"'.

debates in gay/queer politics around sexual identities and their potential dissolutions. Taubira was in fact responding to the following statement by the conservative opposition UMP spokesman Hervé Mariton:

> Dois-je rappeler à Mme la garde des sceaux, qui cite Léon-Gontran Damas dans son discours introductif—vous avez de bonnes lectures, chère madame—, que ce poète a très souvent exprimé, dans son œuvre, l'idée que les différences entre les personnes ne devaient pas être niées, mais assumées, acceptées et promues? Bref, qu'il considérait que la différenciation était préférable à l'identification.
> Vous qui citez un poète prônant que, face à des situations différentes, l'on refuse une assimilation ne correspondant pas à la réalité des choses—ce qui n'attente en rien à la dignité des personnes—, pourquoi cautionnez-vous cette construction extravagante qu'est l'article-balai?[4]

This exchange, and Taubira's retort—that 'jamais la différence n'est un prétexte justifiant l'inégalité des droits'[5] and that Mariton's argument represented a striking *détournement* of Damas's work—encapsulates the strength of French republicanism and her robust adherence to it (*le mariage pour tous* and not *le mariage gay*, a cleverly universalist rather than minoritarian formulation shaping a universal republicanism that means it. Her subsequent resignation from government was over the proposal to strip dual nationals convicted of terrorist activity of their French nationality). However, Mariton's wilful misreading paradoxically points to a fundamental deficiency in many other versions of French republicanism.

Queerness and difference

Writing in 1982 on the Spanish conquest of the Americas, Tzvetan Todorov argued that Columbus and Cortés inaugurate in the modern

4 http://www.assemblee-nationale.fr/14/cri/2012-2013/20130135.asp#P433_73595. 'Must I remind the Minister, who quotes Léon-Gontran Damas in her introductory speech—you have good taste in reading, dear lady—that this poet often expressed in his work the idea that differences between people should not be denied, but accepted and promoted? In short, that he considered that differentiation was preferable to identification. Since you quote a poet who advocated, faced with different situations, the refusal of an assimilation that does not correspond to reality—a refusal that in no way threatens people's dignity—why are you giving support to this extravagant measure?'

5 'Difference is never an excuse for justifying the inequality of rights'.

era 'les deux figures élémentaires de l'altérité' (1982, 28):[6] a consideration of the indigenous peoples as equal *and therefore* as the same or identical, *égalité-identité* ('equality-identity'), the logic of assimilation; or a view that sees them as different *and therefore* as unequal or inferior, *différence-inégalité* ('difference-inequality'), the logic of slavery and massacre. These are the classic figures of French republican colonialism, and notably it is against the assimilationist pull of *égalité-identité* that Damas and other anti-colonialists attempted to place themselves, a pull well established in late nineteenth-century Guyane among middle-class Creoles. The quest might therefore be for that elusive, non-narcissistic *égalité-différence* ('equality-difference'). But how might these distinctions inform debates about gay marriage, the meaning of 'queer', and the specificity of the space of Guyane in relation to the French Republic and non-heteronormative desire?

In France, including the overseas *départements* created in 1946, gay politics has included this egalitarian republican-constitutional strand, of which the equalization of the age of consent in 1982 and *le mariage pour tous* are two examples, bringing lesbians, gay men and same-sex couples into a framework of recognition previously denied them both before and after the demise of the *ancien régime* in 1789–1792 (analogous, then, with the emancipation of slaves and women's suffrage). At the same time, elements in civil society have accompanied and often impelled these transformations, in fighting against homophobia, or militating in the context of the AIDS/HIV emergency of the 1980s and after (AIDES, ACT-UP Paris; the *association* Le Refuge, which supports young people who are victims of homophobia and transphobia, and which held its first meeting in Guyane at Matoury in April 2016). At one level, much of this activity may be said to correspond to what Eve Kosofsky Sedgwick called a 'minoritizing view' of 'homo/heterosexual definition', seen 'as an issue of active importance primarily for a small, distinct, relatively fixed homosexual minority' (1990, 1). The outcome of this view may not necessarily be assimilationist: *le mariage pour tous* may be seen as a manifestation of *égalité-identité*, but urgent questions of recognition and survival in relation to healthcare, pharmaceutical companies, prevention and discrimination in the context of AIDS/HIV have often taken more provocative forms. Indeed, it is possible to argue that one of the issues in the delays and inadequacies of the French state in getting safe-sex messages out to gay men in the 1980s was the

6 'the two elementary figures of the experience of alterity' (Todorov, 1992, 42).

absence in the universalist French republican tradition of interpellating 'minorities' as such.

Sedgwick's second formulation concerning homo/hetero definition is what she calls a 'universalizing' one, where it is seen 'as an issue of continuing determinative importance in the lives of people across the spectrum of sexualities' (1990, 1). Among the possibilities that arise here are more disruptive challenges to heterosexual norms, gender binaries and family arrangements that concern everyone. Indeed, where the modern gay rights movement in the United States after the Stonewall riots of 1969 emerged on to a terrain largely, but not completely, defined by the civil rights movement ('minoritizing'), in France it emerged in 1971 onto a post-1968 landscape in which a comprehensive *gauchiste* critique of capitalism and the French state held sway ('universalizing': the role of the FHAR—Front homosexuel d'action révolutionnaire). It is here that we may usefully invoke the term 'queer': while some of its recent usage is as shorthand for the identity coalitions of LGBTQ, its purpose in the 1990s was defiant and provocative appropriation of the abject and the insult ('Nous les gueux' indeed) and a rejection of strategies of minoritized acceptance, tolerance and petitioning for rights. Seeking to destabilize binaries, it refers to 'the open mesh of possibilities, gaps, overlaps, dissonances and resonances, lapses and excesses of meaning when the constituent elements of anyone's gender, of anyone's sexuality, are made (or *can't be* made) to signify monolithically' (Sedgwick, 1994, 8). Moreover, the tension between identity and non-identity, minoritarian and universalist (whose sexuality ever signifies monolithically?) implied in 'queer' may in fact contain certain eloquent lessons about identity itself, speaking to political identities both posited and deconstructed, called into being and then called into question.

It is noteworthy that Christiane Taubira's *Murmures à la jeunesse* is marked both by her characteristically robust French republicanism and by an interest in the non-identitarian, indeed rhizomatic intellectual traditions of Gilles Deleuze, Félix Guattari and Edouard Glissant (2016, 78). For her, these thinkers seem to work as correctives to the risk, which repeats itself in French history, of ethnicizing (as white) and hetero-sexualizing the Republic. Let us extend these debates to the territory of Guyane itself: how might this mobilizing of challenges to heterosexual norms and even (sexual) identity itself inform our understanding of the way in which same-sex desire and non-heteronormative sex have been imagined and represented in a territory whose historical and present reality is a unique, anomalous, creative and tragic cocktail of indigenous peoples, slavery, colonialism and racism, uneven Creole assimilation, penal colony and abjection, space programme and exaltation, immigration and a nationalism that can neither attain plenitude nor cease to exist? In the rest of this chapter, I shall briefly examine three instances in which queer sexuality/ies is/are problematically present: the penal colony, anti-colonial culture and recent fiction.

Penal colony

One source for understanding fantasies of Guyane in the colonial period is a work by 'Dr Jacobus X', first published in Paris in 1893 under the title *L'Amour aux colonies, singularités physiologiques et passionnelles observées durant trente années de séjour dans les colonies, Cochinchine, Tonkin et Cambodge, Guyane et Martinique, Sénégal et Rivières du sud, Nouvelle-Calédonie, Nouvelles-Hébrides et Tahiti*. Republished in 1927 and 1931 as *L'Art d'aimer aux colonies*, the work identifies itself as that of a naval doctor who served in the colonies, including three years in Guyane, where the author observes that same-sex activity—'la pédérastie et la Sodomie, ces deux vices si communs en Extrême-Orient'[7]—is almost unknown to the black and mixed-race Creoles. The only two cases he records are a young mulatto who had been sodomized, whom he treated for anal gonorrhoea, and a 15-year-old black boy—'un négrillon'—who had accepted 'les offres impudiques d'un Arabe libéré'[8] who had plied him with drink. The boy had told his mother that a goat's horn did it, but the doctor, on seeing the well-worn anus, forced out the truth: 'sur ma menace de ne pas le soigner s'il ne disait pas la vérité, il finit par avouer tout' (Jacobus X, 1927, 156);[9] the slippage from a previous description of these 'mœurs inavouables' ('unconfessable practices') to the demand for confession shows the author's and the book's prurience barely disguised by the occasional moral pronouncement. The Indian *coolies* and the North Africans are a different matter, however. Among the former, from the *paria* caste and willing to do anything for money, 'Le jeune garçon de quinze à vingt ans se livre à la pédérastie, dont les amateurs se trouvent

7 'Pederasty and Sodomy, the two such common vices in the Far East'.

8 'the lewd advances of a released Arab'.

9 'At my threat of withholding care if he didn't tell the truth, he eventually confessed everything'.

chez les Arabes et Européens libérés du bagne'[10] (163). As for the latter, 'L'Arabe est un pédéraste invétéré' (167),[11] always active in anal sex. The penal colony has no doubt exacerbated 'le vice pédérastique' in Guyane, but the good doctor does not attribute this to the all-male environment: rather, the cause is 'une dépravation héréditaire. C'est une loi d'atavisme, et une véritable maladie mentale, comme la science médicale le démontre maintenant. Dans toutes les réunions d'individualités humaines, les semblables s'attirent, et il se forme des associations particulières entre gens ayant les mêmes goûts et les mêmes mœurs' (166).[12]

The historian Robert Aldrich uses this text as one starting point for his examination of the relationship between homosexuality and the second French overseas empire, 'modern' discursive and social manifestations of the former coinciding with the establishment of the latter. Needless to say, his description of the work as 'specious anthropology and sexology, punctuated with racist views and personal prejudices, voyeuristic soft-porn masquerading as science' (Aldrich, 2001, 205; see also Aldrich, 2008) is accurate. However, I wish to follow his procedure here and suggest that these perceptions and fantasies of same-sex activity, however filtered, not only proclaim its existence and even abundant presence, but point the way to discussion of the ways in which discourses on (homo)sexuality were then and subsequently have been constructed, in the case of Guyane and more generally, namely the imbrication with race, and the 'situational' homosexuality created by the all-male environment of the *bagne*.

Dr Jacobus X notes that black Creole women never have sex with convicts or *relégués* (those who had to remain in Guyane for the equivalent period of their sentence once released, under the system of *doublage*), referring to such a person as 'un esclave du Gouvernement' ('a slave of the government', 166). If the visible degradation of white people has been a recurring element in Guyane's history since the Kourou expedition of 1763, then the penal colony might be seen as a manifestation of, in Peter Redfield's words, 'A civilizing mission at home

10 'The young fifteen- to twenty-year-old boy commits pederasty, *aficionados* of which are to be found among the Arab and Europeans released from the penal colony'.

11 'The Arab is an inveterate pederast'.

12 'a hereditary depravity. It's one of the laws of atavism, and a real mental illness, as medical science now demonstrates. Whenever human individualities gather, like attracts like, and particular associations are formed between people with the same tastes and mores'.

and a civilizing mission abroad [which] meet in a specter of degradation, the potential downward path from modern to primitive' (2000, 91). The penal colony might then be understood as that collapse of gender and racial categories, as same-sex activities became the norm, and the colonized were now the free and often in charge. The authorities frequently used North Africans (who represented approximately 25% of convicts), who were relatively isolated among the European prisoners, more vulnerable and potentially more trustworthy, as *porte-clefs* who were responsible for locking and unlocking the cells and searching the inmates. In turn, what was for the convicts a collapse of master Eurocentric identities could be integrated into an identity narrative for the Creole bourgeoisie which they composed in complex ways with different categories of white people according to status.

Testimonies and representations, in both literary and popular culture, are of course frequent of same-sex activity in the penal colony. There is the anonymous song 'Jean Fagot', dated to 1912 and appearing in Antoine Mesclon's *Comment j'ai subi quinze ans de bagne*, first published in 1924: 'Ah! Quel tableau! / Comme tout l'monde est célibataire, / On cherche la peau / D'un gars qui bientôt s'abandonne / A volupté. / C'est pour un mâle qu'il se passionne / Le transporté'.[13] Mesclon is keen to point out, however, that according to his observations during his sentence, 5% of prisoners were 'homosexuels constants' and 10% 'occasionnels', and that these proportions, 'bien qu'élevées', 'ne cadrent sûrement pas avec l'idée que l'on s'en fait en France' (1931, 243–244).[14] Other memoirs broach the subject, such as those of Auguste Liard-Courtois: 'L'Algérie apporte aussi son contingent. Les transportés arabes sont presque tous actifs ... Au nombre de ces condamnés militaires comptait un dégénéré qu'on appelait simplement la Fille et qui répondait en tout point à son sobriquet' (1903, 289–290).[15]

Jean Genet's unfinished play *Le Bagne*, which he worked on between 1958 and 1964, reconstituted via different manuscripts and published in 1994, is the most complex and sustained literary reflection on the Guyane penal colony. In Genet, however, the *bagne* is a self-consciously

13 'Ah! What a picture! / As everyone is single / You seek the skin / Of a guy who soon loses himself / To fleshly pleasure / It's for a male that he feels passionate / The deportee'.

14 'although high, certainly don't fit with the idea we have of it in France'.

15 'Algeria has its contingent too. The Arab convicts are nearly all active ... Among the sentenced military men there was a degenerate known simply as "the Girl" and who fitted his nickname to a tee'.

constructed myth (from convict memoirs and the sensationalist paper *Détective*), as he writes in *Journal du voleur* (1949), the institution having been abolished: 'J'aspire à la Guyane. Non plus à ce lieu géographique, émasculé—mais au voisinage, à la promiscuité enfin, non dans l'espace mais dans la conscience, des modèles sublimes, des grands archétypes du malheur' (1982, 289).[16] One of his earliest works, the poem 'Le Condamné à mort', written in Fresnes prison in 1942, is the first to mobilize this poetry of power, death, confinement, abjection, as well as beauty, consolation and redemption: 'Ô mon vieux Maroni, ô Cayenne la douce! / je vois les corps penchés de quinze à vingt fagots / Autour du mino blond qui fume les mégots / Crachés par les gardiens dans les fleurs et la mousse' (1999, 19).[17] *Le Bagne* creates a mythical drama of same-sex love when a glamorous, prestigious and defiant new arrival sets in motion jealousies and power plays among convicts and administrators, juxtaposing violence, ugliness and transcendence.

If Genet's myth of the penal colony seems as sealed off from the 'reality' of Guyane as the extraordinary stage set within which it takes place, his work nonetheless sheds light on two key problematics which need to be aired before looking at Guyanais cultural production. The first is that of the all-male environment and its relationship with race; the second concerns the appropriateness of applying the term 'queer' to Genet's art over and beyond its preoccupation with same-sex contact. In a reforming rather than either moralizing or prurient mode (and therefore eschewing the theories of 'atavism' we saw with Dr Jacobus X), Dr Louis Rousseau blamed 30% of same-sex activity in the penal colony on the 'groupement humain d'où la femme est exclue': 'Le mâle riche en gamètes tend à s'en débarrasser. ... S'en indigner ne sert de rien. Il vaut mieux rechercher les causes de l'homo-sexualité que de la reprocher à ses adeptes' (1930, 208).[18] Rousseau's categorizations according to age, sexual role, interest, experience or non-experience

16 'I aspire to Guiana. No longer to that geographical place now depopulated and emasculated, but to the proximity, the promiscuity, not in space but in consciousness, of the sublime models, of the great archetypes of misfortune' (Genet, 1965, 227).

17 'Oh my old Maroni, oh Cayenne the sweet! / I see the bent-over bodies / of fifteen to twenty convicts / gathered around the blond pretty-boy / smoking butts spat by the guards / into the flowers and the moss' (Genet, 2010, 16).

18 'human grouping from which woman is excluded'; 'The male rich in gametes tends to rid himself of them ... It is useless to be outraged by this. Better to find the causes of homosexuality than to criticize its enthusiasts'.

of prison life (208–220)—'Il est des homo-sexuels de toutes sortes'[19]—speak largely to a situational homosexuality which for him would not exist without the institution of the *bagne*. Recent work by American scholars, however, has emphasized the inextricability of racial and sexual categories. In distant echoes of Dr Jacobus X, Jane Ward writes of 'the ways that whiteness continues to function … as a stand-in for "normal" sexuality', so that 'white privilege' enables straight white men 'to circumvent homophobic stigma and assign heterosexual meaning to homosexual activity' (2015, 21). Reformist attitudes in France, following Albert Londres's exposé, *Au bagne* (1923), could partake of this desire to stabilize the meanings associated with the homo/hetero boundary in the penal colony.[20]

It is the role of 'queer' precisely to destabilize these boundaries. In Genet, a self-conscious exploration of the roles and power relations associated with whiteness—rendered visible and 'other' as opposed to invisible and 'normal'—is of course present in his 1958 play *Les Nègres*, and the black soldiers acting as chorus in *Le Bagne* do the same *vis-à-vis* the white protagonists. While the paradox of associating Genet's often phallic and virile world with femininity has been the subject of lively debate (see for example Hanrahan, 1999 on the Cixous/Genet relationship), we might ask of a 'queer' Genet that he introduces instability and mobility into gender and sexual binary arrangements. *Le Bagne*, while replete with gender binary images—sun/moon, dry/moist, hard/soft—mingles them oxymoronically so that masculinity is both asserted and feminized. To take one example, the 'feminine' *veuve* ('widow'), the guillotine which dispenses monthly executions and which presides over the scene, is looked after by the 50-year-old convict Ferrand: 'Comme une femme, une fois par mois je lâche les écluses: le sang inonde des linges. Une fois par mois je suis intouchable. Je dispose de la mort … Et c'est par là que je suis femelle!' (Genet, 1999, 39).[21]

19 'There are homosexuals of all kinds'.

20 A recent *bande dessinée* (comic) album, *Paco: les mains rouges*, has its *instituteur* sent to Guyane in the 1920s for murder, where he both endures sexual violence (a gang rape) and a loving physical relationship with a fellow convict. A whole page is devoted to seven panels in which the narrator's *récitatif* struggles to come to terms with their sexual congress (Vehlman and Sagot, 2014, 35). In a Guyane largely absent of black faces, the album seems to convey a rather contemporary form of 'heteroflexibility' which it is difficult to disentangle from white privilege.

21 'Like a woman, once a month I open the floodgates: blood inundates the

Fictions: anticolonialism and heteronormativity

In Guyane, homosexuality in the penal colony may indeed have been seen as situational and therefore reformable by some writers in its later period of existence, or as a source of poetic and political contestation and renewal by Genet, but the response of some Guyanais and Caribbean thinkers was a reassertion of heterosexual masculinity. The profound sense of lack displayed in Léon Gontran-Damas's poem 'Je suis né' may metonymically, in its tour of the Cayenne region, refer to the penal colony, located at Buzaré in the north of the town, 'dont l'ombre rafraîchit / et les rochers depuis toujours supportent / plus d'une amour ardente et chaude' (1956, 61–63).[22] Bertène Juminer's novel *Les Bâtards* (1961) portrays a group of Guyanais students in Montpellier, France in the early 1950s. Their identity problems, faced with the assimilationism of the French education system—a white girlfriend asserts, 'Tu n'es pas un colonisé. La France t'a adopté' (1961, 19)[23]—find a key term in 'bastard': 'Ce qui le troublait surtout, c'était de se sentir un déséquilibré, un bâtard que guettait l'aliénation tout court' (36).[24] This lack is seen in gendered and sexual terms in a colonial version of the family romance. The dentist, Cambier, is haunted in France by the fear of impotence. His colleague Ségaye cries 'Vive la Guyane!' after sex with a white woman, a possible take on Fanon's anecdotal diagnostic example of the 'Vive Schoelcher!' shouted by a black man at orgasm in a similar coupling (Fanon, 1952, 51). The doctor, Chambord, at the end sees himself as a 'bâtard intégral' ('out-and-out bastard'), as his own 'mother', here Guyane, 'le reniait' ('was disowning him') (Juminer, 1961, 196; 1989, 226). Aimé Césaire in his preface presents the novel's portrayal of Guyanais society as 'le spectacle de la médiocrité dévirilisant, lentement mais sûrement, un peuple',[25] adding that, just as Octavio Paz's *El laberinto de la soledad* presents Mexico as torn between a Spanish father (Cortés) and Amerindian mother (la Malinche), here the father is Europe and the mother Africa, the West Indian being the bastard child,

sheets. Once a month I am untouchable. I have the power of death ... And that's why I am female!'

22 'In the cool of Buzaré's shadow / where rocks have for ever harboured / more than one hot and fiery embrace'.

23 'You're not colonised. France adopted you' (Juminer, 1989, 8).

24 'What was most troubling was the feeling of being off balance, of being a bastard, easy prey to alienation' (Juminer, 1989, 30).

25 'The spectacle of mediocrity de-virilizing, slowly but surely, a whole people'.

'partagé entre ce père qui le renie, et cette mère qu'il a reniée' (Césaire in Juminer, 1961, 8).[26]

The family romance of *Les Bâtards* can be read in terms of an abandonment neurosis (by France then, possibly, Guyane), and of disavowal (of Africanness), at the level of the ego. Juminer's *Les Bâtards* is a colonial-Oedipal text as it constantly posits a lack—of purity, of a fullness of identity—in hetero-masculinist terms that are dependent in turn on the impossibility of identifying with, or of eliminating, a parental figure. The debate on whether there is a 'black Oedipus' crystallizes around Fanon's rather far-fetched notion that, as 'repression' and 'neurosis' do not exist in Caribbean societies, nor can an—at least *unresolved*—Oedipus complex. Notoriously, Frantz Fanon (1952, 146) denied the existence of homosexuality in the Caribbean, in these terms:

> Mentionnons rapidement qu'il ne nous a pas été donné de constater la présence manifeste de pédérastie en Martinique. Il faut y voir la conséquence de l'absence de l'Œdipe aux Antilles. On connaît en effet le schéma de l'homosexualité. Rappelons toutefois l'existence de ce qu'on appelle là-bas 'des hommes habillés en dames' ou 'Ma Commère'. Ils ont la plupart du temps une veste et une jupe. Mais nous restons persuadé qu'ils ont une vie sexuelle normale. Ils prennent le punch comme n'importe quel gaillard et ne sont pas insensibles aux charmes des femmes,—marchandes de poissons, de légumes. Par contre en Europe nous avons trouvé quelques camarades qui sont devenus pédérastes, toujours passifs. Mais ce n'était point là homosexualité névrotique, c'était pour eux un expédient comme pour d'autres celui de Souteneur.[27]

On the one hand, the disavowals in this passage might be seen to reverse what was noted earlier about situational homosexuality

26 'Torn between the father who is disowning him, and the mother whom he has disowned'.

27 'Let me observe at once that I had no opportunity to establish the overt presence of homosexuality in Martinique. This must be viewed as the result of the absence of the Oedipus complex in the Antilles. The schema of homosexuality is well enough known. We should not overlook, however, the existence of what are called there "men dressed like women" or "godmothers". Generally they wear shirts and skirts. But I am convinced that they lead normal sex lives. They can take a punch like any "he-man" and they are not impervious to the allures of women—fish and vegetable merchants. In Europe, on the other hand, I have known several Martinicans who became homosexuals, always passive. But this was by no means a neurotic homosexuality: For them it was a means to a livelihood, as pimping is for others' (Fanon, 1986, 139).

and whiteness: by attempting to reinvest blackness with something approaching 'privilege', or at the very least, prestige, same-sex 'lapses' are put to use in bolstering black heterosexual masculinity. On the other hand, what Fanon might understand here as 'pédérastie'—perhaps what he observed in educated, bourgeois circles in metropolitan France—need not, it is true, be mapped in some kind of master sexually dissident identity on sexual landscapes elsewhere. If, as Celia Britton (2002) has argued, Fanon's psychoanalytic tussles in *Peau noire, masques blancs* are more often a question of the ego than the unconscious, then at the very least we might be invited here to leave Oedipal accounts behind and look for a process of 'queering' not bound to such (modern, western gay) identifications.

The history of Guyanais sexual arrangements is complex. The *Code noir* stipulated (articles 10 and 11) that slaves could not marry without the permission of their masters, and that children born of such unions became the property of the mother's master, not the father's if they were different (article 12). In the case of unions between free blacks and slaves, it was the mother's status which decided that of the children (article 13). Although the 'slow abolition' of slavery instigated under Louis-Philippe attempted to regulate slaves' sex lives by promoting marriage, in reality sexual survival practices often continued: multiple sexual partners, assertions of virility by black males who did not always recognize their offspring, a tendency therefore to matrifocal families and the importance of *marrain/parrain* figures and grandparents (see Cherubini, 1988, chapter three). Blodwenn Mauffret locates the origin of Guyanais and West Indian heterosexual machismo in the plantations, where male physicality (and often sexual prowess in the reproduction of the slave population) was valorized, female sexuality mistrusted because of the possibility of liaisons with masters and overseers, and there was a reluctance to add parental responsibilities to the burden of slavery (2005, 85–86). These traditions form the context of the empowering of women at the *touloulou* balls at carnival time, and the simultaneous regulation of gender and sexual roles that accompanies this masking and disguising of women from head to foot when they take the initiative in asking men to dance, an invitation that cannot be refused. Subject and not object of the desiring gaze, for one night at carnival time the *touloulou* undoes this Oedipal and patriarchal logic in the context of contemporary Caribbean heterosexual machismo. 'Veiled' but not passive, she also avoids the feminization of Guyane in the colonial-scopic regime.

Fictions: queerings of the self

In recent Guyanais novels, the country's natural landscape, as much as its culture, seems to promise transformations and even dissolutions of the self. Micheline Hermine's *Les Iguanes du temps* (1988) has a Basque militant hiding out in a beach hut near Cayenne, an isolation, coupled with dialogues with young or immigrant Guyanais neighbours, which begins to trigger a process of becoming-other: 'Je devenais autre, j'étais en train de renaître. J'étais un serpent de l'ombre qui abandonnait sa vieille peau dans la boue' (1988, 9); 'ma matière s'est perdue, celui que j'étais s'est dissous dans ces terres aquatiques' (18); 'Je suis un être hybride, entre la vie et la mort. J'ai l'âme métisse, je suis de tous les mondes, en deçà et au-delà de toutes les limites' (131).[28] He even becomes an intermediary in the passionate and perhaps physical friendship between two teenage girls, with one putting him forward as the other's partner in order to maintain that intimacy, but the end of the novel is marked by the teleological resolution of consummated heterosexual sex ('J'étais un zombie, je suis redevenu un homme') (165).[29]

A more convincing example of becoming-other to the point of queering is found in Valérie Rodrigue's *Fanta, fleur et martyre* (2006), in which the not particularly attractive heroine, a scientist in her late thirties, unmarried, with various family difficulties and a fantasy life online, tries to find her way through her identity issues at the *touloulou* ball. There she flirts with a Cuban striptease artist with whom she has previously had sex. Preparations for the ball had evoked the identity transformations, and this 'becoming-other' is confirmed at the dance hall: 'Dans le miroir face à la fresque, l'espace d'un instant, Fanta ne se reconnut pas ... Drôle de bal, celui qui faisait douter de sa propre identité' (Rodrigue, 2006, 240).[30] And in the car park afterwards as he lies down drunk, Drago the Cuban is the object of a carnivalesque inversion, and indeed, a *queering*:

> Elle l'allongea, puis s'installa de son côté, se défit de plusieurs de ses

28 'I was becoming-other, I was being reborn. I was a snake in the shade shedding its old skin in the mud'; 'the matter that made me up was gone, who I was dissolved in these watery lands'; 'I am a hybrid being, between life and death. My soul is mixed blood, I am of every world, within and beyond all limits'.

29 'I was a zombie, I have become a man again'.

30 'In the mirror opposite the fresco, for an instant, Fanta failed to recognize herself ... What a strange [queer?] ball it was that made her doubt her own identity'.

> jupons bariolés pour l'en recouvrir, pauvre homme tremblant de froid malgré la chaleur moite. Dans ces couleurs en excès, disposées sur lui et autour de sa tête, la perruche, la marionnette, c'était lui! Finies, les moqueries! Drago Nelson, soudain, fut démuni, devant les caprices du corps, lui qui se donnait un mal fou pour tout maîtriser. (262)[31]

Here we might invoke Judith Butler's work on drag, performance and performativity, and combine it with Deleuze and Guattari's idea of the *mot d'ordre*, applying it to gender and sexual norms. In a sense, Fanta goes further than any *touloulou*. The 'command' that is gender (the sign 'girl' in 'It's a girl') is here not only suspended in terms of its content (the sexual assertiveness, and, sometimes, in dress) and the dodging through disguise of unattainable heterosexual gender ideals. Drago the *dragueur*'s attempt at 'mastery', at 'being in charge' of the codes of gender turns into an imposition of 'drag' by the female spectator that is Fanta. This is poles apart from the sexual performance—the publicly revealed penis—of his striptease act. On one level, we here get what the hyperbole of drag at its best achieves, 'the understated, taken-for-granted quality of heterosexual performativity', in which gender norms are taken 'not as commands to be obeyed, but as imperatives to be 'cited', twisted, queered, brought into relief as heterosexual imperatives' (Butler, 1993, 237).

However, as Butler also argues, the jury is out on whether those norms are therefore inevitably subverted. In the Guyanais context, they cannot be disentwined from colonial and racial history. The *coup de théâtre* at the end of the novel, in which Fanta has Drago, and herself, devoured by one of the carnivorous plants she collects, displaces Guyanais identity from the city to the forest, and the urban realist novel into South American magical realism. Over and beyond poor Fanta's emotional disarray, this performance is a vortex, a *mise en scène*, a revision and revenge of memory:

> Les yeux de vermine jaugèrent la femme qui ne cilla pas. Pas question de perdre une miette de ce théâtre baroque dont elle allait devenir un rouage essentiel ... Nourrir de sa propre substance une plante de combat, qui

31 'She laid him down, then got down beside him, took off some of her multicoloured petticoats and covered him with them, poor man, shivering with cold despite the humid heat. In these lavish colours, arranged over him and around his head, *he* was now the exotic bird, the marionette! The mockery was over! The fickleness of his body had suddenly left Drago Nelson bereft, he who strained always to be in charge'.

> guiderait toute son armée de molosses dans la domination du végétal sur l'humain, orchestrant la revanche des petites gens et des descendants d'esclaves, c'était une juste cause, servir le dessein de l'univers, rien de moins. (Rodrigue, 2006, 329)[32]

We can understand that this is the ultimate carnivalesque moment for Fanta, for all her identity issues are not only suspended but transcended: she is the object of a gaze that is non-human, which both enables a hyperbolization of the self and its dissolution, its becoming-imperceptible, along with all notions of identity, subjectivity and gender, in the digestive tracts of the plant and the boundless extensiveness of nature and the universe.

Conclusion

Following the burkini bans on certain beaches in the summer of 2016, in which an official French embrace of *égalité-différence* was exposed as lacking, it may be instructive to track the concept's peregrinations—absences, detours and artistic propositions—in contexts located elsewhere in space and time. The question of 'homo/hetero-sexual definition' in this light speaks to various historical fault lines in French and Guyanais history structured by an outward metropolitan gaze as well as an inward, Creole one. It touches the defining elements of Guyanais society: the legacy of slavery, the abjection and racial politics of the penal colony, the composition of Creoles with the reality of French republican rule and departmentalization, the temptations of nationalism and Afrocentrism, the fluidities and minoritizations of the contemporary era (in which less than 40% of the population of Guyane are Creoles born there, compared with 70% in 1946) ('Guyane française'). Moreover, the issues bound up with 'queer' reveal important and creative possibilities for cultural and political identities in general, calling potential subjects into being through a movement of dissensus and simultaneously propelling a questioning of that being. Queer*ing*

32 'The vermin eyes sized up the woman, who did not blink. No way was she going to miss one jot of this baroque theatre, of which she herself was going to be an essential piece ... To nourish with her own substance a fighting plant, which would guide its whole army of monsters in the domination of the vegetable over the human, orchestrating the revenge of the humble and the descendants of slaves, this was a just cause, in the service of the universe's plan, nothing less'.

therefore has the potential to actively energize attention not only to specific groups within colonial and postcolonial societies, but moreover to the ways in which symbolic formations such as nations, diasporas and even *départements* are marked by hierarchical (hetero)sexual binaries whose normativities can be disrupted and undone.

Works cited

Aldrich, Robert. 2001. 'Homosexuality in the French colonies', *Journal of Homosexuality* 41.3–4: 201–218.
Aldrich, Robert. 2008. *Colonialism and Homosexuality*. London: Routledge.
Britton, Celia. 2002. *Race and the Unconscious: Freudianism in French Caribbean Thought*. Oxford: Legenda.
Butler, Judith. 1993. *Bodies that Matter*. London: Routledge.
Chamoiseau, Patrick. 1997. *Ecrire en pays dominé*. Paris: Gallimard.
Cherubini, Bernard. 1988. *Cayenne ville créole et polyethnique: essai d'anthropologie urbaine*. Paris: Karthala.
Damas, Léon Gontran. 1964. *Névralgies*. Paris: Présence africaine.
Damas, Léon Gontran. 1956. *Black-Label*. Paris: Gallimard.
Eribon, Didier. 1999. *Réflexions sur la question gay*. Paris: Fayard.
Eribon, Didier. 2001. *Une morale du minoritaire: variations sur un thème de Jean Genet*. Paris: Fayard.
Fanon, Frantz. 1952. *Peau noire, masques blancs*. Paris: Seuil.
Fanon, Frantz. 1986. *Black Skin White Masks*, trans. Charles Lam Markmann. London: Pluto Press.
Genet, Jean. 1965. *The Thief's Journal*, trans. Bernard Frechtman. London: Anthony Blond.
Genet, Jean. 1982. *Journal du voleur*. Paris: Gallimard-Folio.
Genet, Jean. 1999. *Le Condamné à mort et autres poèmes*. Paris: Gallimard.
Genet, Jean. 2010. *The Genet Translations: Poetry and Posthumous Plays*, trans. Mark Spitzer. Toad Suck, AK: Polemic Press.
'Guyane française (2) composition territoriale', http://www.axl.cefan.ulaval.ca/amsudant/guyanefr2.htm (accessed 28 August 2016).
Gyssels, Kathleen. 2008. '"Scandale": queer avant la lettre', in *Queer: écritures de la différence? I. Autres temps, autres lieux*, ed. Pierre Zoberman. Paris: L'Harmattan, 219–241.
Hanrahan, Mairéad. 1999. 'Genet and Cixous: The intersext author(s)', *The French Review* 72.4: 719–729.
Hermine, Micheline. 1988. *Les Iguanes du temps*. Paris: Editions caribéennes.
Jacobus X, Dr. 1927. *L'Art d'aimer aux colonies*. Paris: Georges-Anquetil.
Juminer, Bertène. 1961. *Les Bâtards*. Paris: Présence africaine, 1961.

Juminer, Bertène. 1989. *The Bastards*, trans. Keith Q. Warner. Charlottesville: University of Virginia Press.

Liard-Courtois, Auguste. 1903. *Souvenirs du bagne*. Paris: Fasquelle.

Londres, Albert. 1923. *Au bagne*. Paris: Albin Michel.

Mauffret, Blodwenn. 2005. *Le Carnaval de Cayenne. Le jeu carnavalesque: une esthétique de proximité*. Matoury: Ibis rouge.

Mesclon, Antoine. 1931 [1924]. *Comment j'ai subi quinze ans de bagne*. Paris: Mesclon.

'Ouverture du mariage aux couples de personnes de même sexe', http://www.assemblee-nationale.fr/14/cri/2012-2013/20130135.asp#P433_73595 (accessed 2 March 2018).

Redfield, Peter. 2000. *Space in the Tropics: From Convicts to Rockets in French Guiana*. Berkeley: University of California Press.

Rodrigue, Valérie. 2006. *Fanta, fleur et martyre*. Paris: Ramsay.

Rousseau, Louis. 1930. *Un Médecin au bagne*. Paris: A. Fleury.

Sedgwick, Eve Kosofsky. 1990. *Epistemology of the Closet*. Berkeley: University of California Press.

Sedgwick, Eve Kosofsky. 1994. *Tendencies*. London: Routledge.

'Taubira, Filippetti et Montebourg s'affichent au théâtre', *Le Nouvel Observateur*, 4 February 2015. http://tempsreel.nouvelobs.com/politique/20150204.OBS1700/info-obs-taubira-filipetti-et-montebourg-s-affichent-au-theatre.html (accessed 2 March 2018).

Taubira, Christiane. 2016. *Murmures à la jeunesse*. Paris: Philippe Rey.

Todorov, Tzvetan. 1982. *La Conquête de l'Amérique: la question de l'autre*. Paris: Seuil.

Todorov, Tzvetan. 1992. *The Conquest of America: The Question of the Other*, trans. R. Howard. New York: Harper Perennial.

Vehlman, Fabien and Sagot, Eric. 2013. *Paco les mains rouges, Tome 1: La grande terre*. Paris: Dargaud.

Ward, Jane. 2015. *Not Gay: Sex between Straight White Men*. New York, NY: New York University Press.

Conclusion

Remaking Guyane?

Sarah Wood and Catriona MacLeod

In 2016, as former president Nicolas Sarkozy began campaigning in an attempt to return to the Élysée, newspapers reported the revelation of remarks he had allegedly made about Guyane while president between 2007 and 2012. Sarkozy, it seems, had claimed in derogatory terms that half of Guyane's population was illiterate[1] and complained (presumably having never been to the lively Crique district nor to carnival) that there was nothing to do of an evening. The presidential contender thus articulated personal distaste for—and cultural distance from—this particular part of 'Overseas France'. But his statements also confirm the impression, conveyed by many contributors to this volume, that Guyane has as a matter of course been misunderstood and misconstrued at the heart of French government, notwithstanding attempts made by its own *ressortissants*, as discussed in the chapters by Wood and Marshall, to shape Guyane and France together in the image of a truly universal Republic. Given the prevalence of the negative tropes used by journalists and authors, as described by Evanson, Richard Price and Marshall, the

1 In 2013, 6% of Guyane's population was classified as *analphabète* (unable to read and write, having not been to school) by the INSEE (the national average for France is 1%). See Bayart et al. (2013). The rate of *illettrisme*—that is, having 'great difficulty' reading and writing—was estimated at around 40% for the population as a whole and 20% for people aged 16–65 who had been schooled in the French system.

endurance of ignorance alone might be unsurprising. But in Guyane, the contempt implicit in Sarkozy's remarks meant that they were met with an indignant response on the part of local politicians, at least one of whom mentioned 'independence'.[2] Thus the controversy briefly revived a faint and long-buried spectre: the possibility that this extra-Hexagonal component of France might be severed from the metropole. If central and local politicians could agree that Guyane was not quite France, because they harboured certain historical and cultural (mis)apprehensions about the place and its people, or because they wished to dissociate themselves from a Sarkozian conception of French identity (in which 'dès que vous devenez Français, vos ancêtres sont les Gaulois' [*Le Monde*, 2016]), then they might also agree to give up on the idea that the Guyane's Frenchness was necessary or mutually useful.

The endeavour of *Locating Guyane* is an important one in that it enhances our understanding of the multifaceted relationship between (former) colony and (former) imperial metropole, at a time when the future of this bond is in question. The chapters in this book reveal this endeavour to be already underway: it is being pursued actively from both within and without the region, not only by academics but also by politicians, local historians, carnival participants and other cultural actors. Certain questions—for example, about the impact of migrants and migration—merit much fuller consideration, and are slowly beginning to attract it (as in the cases of Marjo de Theije, Frédéric Piantoni and Clémence Léobal, whose work is mentioned in the Introduction). Our work contributes to these discussions by emphasising Guyane to be a place of permeable borders in terms of cultural and 'ethnic' links—to Brazil (Cristinoi and Nemo), Suriname (Maurice), Martinique (MacLeod) and African *francophonie* (Gyssels).

Another development in the ongoing evolution of the region as multipositional space, and meriting further consideration, is the construction of a bridge over the Oyapock River between France and Brazil. Initiated in 1997 by the countries' erstwhile presidents, Jacques Chirac and Henrique Cardoso respectively, the bridge was completed in 2011. However, it remained closed to traffic until March 2017, ostensibly because of delays in putting together a road infrastructure and regulatory framework appropriate to the bridging of the Franco-Brazilian border (Boudoux d'Hautefeuille, 2010). The bridge is a physical reminder of the likelihood that, as Bishop et al. suggest (2016, 6), Guyane will become increasingly

2 See 'Le Parti socialiste' (2016).

characterized by its relationship to Brazil—an ever-more powerful cultural, political and economic force in the region. Hitherto, Guyane has been excluded from French free-movement treaties such as the Schengen agreement, and as of 2017, Brazilians still face many restrictions on their circulation in Guyane and need visas to stay officially in the territory for more than 90 days. Yet the bridge over the Oyapock represents the potential for sanctioned free movement and trade between Brazil and France/the European Union. Thus, Guyane has been used as a bargaining chip in the negotiation of economic deals between France and the South American powerhouse with which it shares a border. These governmental negotiations belie the fact that the border is crossed informally many times every day by river transport. The present and future nature of Guyane's links to its regional neighbours will, it seems, complicate—and perhaps reinforce—Guyane's location relative to the French metropole. This positioning is described here by Richard Price as 'profoundly colonial', and indeed it may be insofar as a government assumes the power to do what it will with a place and its people. However, as the links between Guyane and its neighbours take on additional importance in terms of French relations with Brazil and 'Latin America', it remains to be seen whether, and in what ways, the 'colonial' elements of Guyane's ties to France will be enhanced, dismantled or otherwise remade.

What we hope this volume does make clear is that ascribed categories and relationships, including colonial ones, are and have been subject to change. Yarrington's concept of 'use-value' shows the apparently contradictory ways in which Guyane was located in relation to the metropole prior to departmentalization: first as sugar plantation 'suitably close' to the metropole, then as a penal colony appropriately far from it. The location of the region shifted both physically and ideologically with regard to how the land could be exploited. Contemporary developments suggest that this process continues today. Many other 'use-values' not covered in this book have situated Guyane in particular ways throughout the twentieth and twenty-first centuries. Among these are the space centre (on which Redfield's 2000 work has not been bettered nor yet updated), gold (see Heemskerk and de Theije, 2009) and, potentially, petroleum and other marine-related resources (Hecquet, 2005; Roth, 2007). From this, we might conclude—as did Gaston Monnerville and Léon-Gontran Damas—that it would be a surprising move on the part of a French government to cut Guyane adrift, given its apparent potential to be economically and geopolitically 'beneficial' to France. However, to draw such a conclusion would be to reproduce, rather than to historicize, the discourse of use-value that has consistently characterized Guyane's relationship to central government.

Scholarly critiques of state development discourses based on rationalization and use-value are well-established: James Ferguson (1994), James C. Scott (1998) and David Scott (2005) are among those who have identified and explored the coloniality of power and the limits of state knowledge, planning and efficiency. The present collection of essays allows us to extrapolate further how statecraft strategies based on 'use-value' are punctured by two further, related variables: on the one hand, the unpredictability of the future, and on the other, the human agency of individuals and groups. French state 'visions' and knowledge have overlooked, among others, Maroons, 'Amerindians' and others with complex backgrounds who have been affected by histories of colonialism but are not fully defined by them. As the chapters of *Locating Guyane* make clear, such people may challenge and even instigate the alteration or undoing of state systems in ways that the latter cannot predict. Governmental understandings of value, so often based on capitalist assumptions with roots in colonial history, may not remain relevant in a future that is unpredictable, complex and 'super-diverse' (to quote Vertovec, 2007). It is also the case that interpretations of the past and its meanings, as Wood suggests in her chapter, have changed and will continue to do so as Guyane's social make-up changes; a majority-migrant culture, for instance, is likely to create new 'sites of memory' and new perspectives on French and on regional history. The agency of the Guyanais—as much as, or more than, that of French politicians, transnational corporations or other governmental actors—will ultimately determine the course of Guyane's future. Yet Guyane's cosmopolitan population—and in particular, its youth—requires access to tools which can enable them to understand their situation (without having to travel to Paris to do so fully) and, from it, to realize their immense and unique potential.

The chapters in this book offer an introduction to how Guyane is located from within, but there remains potential for more work. A recent series of actions suggests a desire to formalize and localize Guyanais culture and identity as distinct, in new ways. In 2014, for instance, a group of academics and volunteers in Guyane set up an 'Observatoire régional du carnaval de Guyane' with the aim of having the Guyane carnival and particularly the *touloulou* recognized by UNESCO as an element of the world's 'intangible cultural heritage' (Lama, 2014). This would constitute the first UNESCO heritage site for Guyane, and is a particularly interesting development since the Observatoire looks for the first time beyond France and to the international framework for cultural validation and protection. In the same year, university workers in Guyane declared their independence: not from France but from the University of the Antilles and Guyane (UAG). This move followed months of increasing tension between university 'poles' in Martinique and Guyane, during which teachers and administrators in Cayenne raised grievances including a lack of communication and financial and managerial commitment from their Antillais counterparts, and led strikes in Cayenne. The separation process was finally triggered in October 2013 after a private email was leaked in which Raphaël Confiant—theorist of Créolité and co-author, with Jean Bernabé and Patrick Chamoiseau, of the famous *Eloge de la Créolité* (1993)—who was also a member of UAG staff in Martinique, referred in disparaging terms to university members in Guyane and implied that they practised anti-Antillais and anti-African 'racism' (*France-Guyane*, 2013). In response, Guyane's university unions released a document entitled 'Nous avons marronné! Université marronne versus Université bananière', announcing that they were 'marooning' themselves in response to UAG's alleged banana republic-style management. The statement recuperated for the strikers the historical actions of the Maroons and connected them to 'creolization according to Glissant', respect for which (it claimed) was 'unscathed' in Guyane. The document located (Guyanais) *marronage* and creolization in opposition to the (Antillais) *créolité* of Confiant et al. The latter, it asserted in a florid French that was far from the direct Kreyol of Confiant's email, was an ephemeral fabrication on the part of 'a handful of overpriced intellectuals and mandarins' and nothing but 'varnish soluble in Guyanais *marronage*'.[3] It was in a context of indignation and political and cultural conflict, then, that the University of Guyane came into being the following year, 70 years after the territory's first *lycée* was opened in Cayenne. The future of Guyane's new university remains uncertain: will the change lead to independence and opportunity for Guyane's intellectuals, or to Balkanization and limitation?

Alongside such processes, which encompass (or claim to encompass) Guyane in its entirety, there have been developments in which separate groups within the department have sought to construct 'oppositional

3 'la créolisation selon Edouard Glissant est intacte; mais la créolité, quant à elle, n'était que le vernis soluble dans le marronnage guyanais de l'arrogance d'une poignée d'intellectuels et mandarins surcotés' (quoted in Intersyndicale du Pôle Universitaire Guyanais, 2013).

identities'—as MacLeod outlines in her chapter on carnival—or to reconnect with declining specific linguistic or cultural heritages (as in Cristinoi and Nemo's chapter on the Palikur language). Such actors have sometimes sought specific forms of change to educational systems—as Maurice describes in his chapter on the Boni—or to established cultural practices. From within, then, Guyane is located in complex and multidirectional ways; its inhabitants act on the cultural landscape and—as Sally Price's chapter on Maroon artistic discourses makes clear—make and remake narratives in ways which, although they more often than not reflect uneven power structures, nevertheless defy generalization.

In contrast to long-held, external narratives about Guyane as a colonial 'outpost' of France, the articles in this book reveal a constant flux—whether in the present, due to transnational flows, regarding the past via the questioning of historiography, or in the reimagining and reinventing of traditions. In conclusion, we do not claim exceptionality for Guyane. Rather, we offer our interpretation of this place—for which Glissant's concept of Creolization does indeed seem apt (see Cottias, 2011)—as an invitation: first, to continue to reinterpret this and other localities perceived as bounded or limited; and, second, to recognize the potential of marginalized groups and individuals to creatively remake the world.

Works cited

Bayart, Pierre-Adrien, Philippe Dorelon and Benoit Hurpeau. 2013. 'Lire, écrire, compter: des savoirs fragiles en Guyane', *INSEE: Premiers resultats* 97. https://documentation.outre-mer.gouv.fr/i-Record.htm?idlist=1&record=19125693124919438759 (accessed 31 October 2016).

Bernabé, Jean, Patrick Chamoiseau and Raphaël Confiant. 1993. *Éloge de la Créolité*. Paris: Gallimard.

Bishop, Matthew Louis, Peter Clegg and Rosemarijn Hoefte. 2017. 'Hemispheric reconfigurations in Northern Amazonia: The "Three Guianas" amid regional change and Brazilian hegemony', *Third World Quarterly* 38.2: 356–378.

Boudoux d'Hautefeuille, Madeleine. 2010. 'La Frontière et ses échelles: les enjeux d'un pont transfrontalier entre la Guyane française et le Brésil', *Cybergeo: European Journal of Geography*, document 514. http://cybergeo.revues.org/23405.

Cottias, Myriam. 2011. 'Édouard Glissant, de la créolisation au Tout-Monde', *Nuevo Mundo Mundos Nuevos*. https://nuevomundo.revues.org/61823 (accessed 31 October 2016).

Ferguson, James. 1994. *The Anti-Politics Machine: 'Development', Depoliticisation, and Bureaucratic Power in Lesotho*. London: University of Minnesota Press.

Hecquet, Vincent. 2005. 'L'espace des Caraïbes: structures et enjeux économiques au début des années 2000', *INSEE: Les cahiers Antilles-Guyane*. http://www.insee.fr/fr/insee_regions/guyane/themes/cahiers/espaceCaraibe/CAG_caraibe.pdf (accessed 31 October 2016).

Heemskerk, Marieke and de Theije, Marjo. 2009. 'Moving Frontiers in the Amazon: Brazilian Small-Scale Gold Miners in Suriname', *European Review of Latin American and Caribbean Studies* 87: 5–25.

Intersyndicale du Pôle Universitaire Guyanais. 2013. 'Nous avons marronné! Université marronne versus Université bananière', *Blada*, 26 October. https://www.blada.com/data/File/2013pdf/lettreouvuag25102013.pdf (accessed 28 October 2013).

Lama, Catherine. 2014. 'Un observatoire régional du carnaval guyanais pour mieux le préserver', *Franceinfo: Guyane 1ère*, 19 February. http://la1ere.francetvinfo.fr/guyane/2014/02/19/un-observatoire-regional-du-carnaval-guyanais-pour-mieux-le-preserver-123469.html (accessed 17 August 2016).

'Le Parti socialiste guyanais piqué au vif par Nicolas Sarkozy', *France-Guyane*, 21 September 2016. http://www.franceguyane.fr/actualite/politique/le-parti-socialiste-guyanais-pique-au-vif-par-nicolas-sarkozy-314114.php.

'Pour Nicolas Sarkozy, nos ancêtres étaient les Gaulois mais aussi « les tirailleurs musulmans »', *Le Monde*, 24 September 2016. http://www.lemonde.fr/election-presidentielle-2017/article/2016/09/24/pour-nicolas-sarkozy-nos-ancetres-etaient-les-gaulois-mais-aussi-les-tirailleurs-musulmans_5002989_4854003.html (accessed 12 January 2017).

Redfield, Peter. 2000. *Space in the Tropics: From Convicts to Rockets in French Guiana*. London: University of California Press.

Roth, Patrice. 2007. 'Espaces maritimes: multiples contentieux de basse intensité', *Atlas Caraïbe*. http://atlas-caraibe.certic.unicaen.fr/fr/page-122.html (accessed 12 September 2016).

Scott, David. 2005. 'Colonial governmentality', in *Anthropologies of Modernity: Foucault, Governmentality, and Life Politics*, ed. Jonathan Xavier Inda. Oxford: Blackwell, 23–49.

Scott, James C. 1998. *Seeing Like a State: How Certain Schemes to Improve the Human Condition Have Failed*. London: Yale University Press.

'Université: polémique autour d'une lettre de Raphaël Confiant', *France-Guyane*, 14 October 2013. http://www.franceguyane.fr/actualite/education-sante-environnement/universite-polemique-autour-d-une-lettre-de-raphael-confiant-175321.php (accessed 31 October 2016).

Vertovec, Steven. 2007. 'Super-diversity and its implications', *Ethnic and Racial Studies* 30.6: 1024–1054.

Index